AF477079

Drawing **Perspective**
Methods for Artists

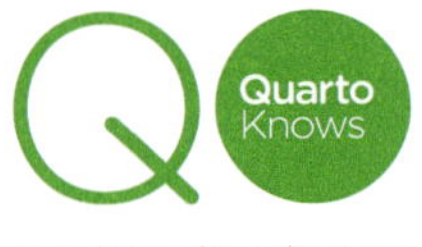

Brimming with creative inspiration, how-to projects, and useful information to enrich your everyday life, Quarto Knows is a favorite destination for those pursuing their interests and passions. Visit our site and dig deeper with our books into your area of interest: Quarto Creates, Quarto Cooks, Quarto Homes, Quarto Lives, Quarto Drives, Quarto Explores, Quarto Gifts, or Quarto Kids.

Peter Boerboom and Tim Proetel

Drawing
Perspective
Methods for Artists

85 Methods for Creating Spatial Illusion in Art

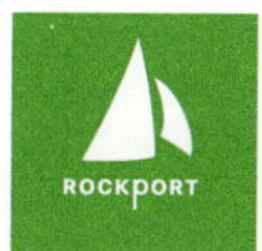

Contents

The Spatial Illusion

It is as mundane as it is intriguing: Correctly placed, a few lines on a piece of paper can create spatiality—to be more exact, the illusion of space. The interest to draw space might come first and foremost from the purpose of wanting to depict the visible reality. But it has a more basic meaning: to create depth is a primary aspiration of every artistic design, whether for illustrations or architectural outlines, posters, Roman mosaics, or graffiti.

Spatiality fascinates the viewer; it independently draws him or her into the picture, whether it is objective or abstract. This book teaches methods of artistically depicting space: big and small, overlap, folds and waves, one-point perspective, shaping, fade, light, and shadow.

Big and small objects placed next to each other lead us to assume that the smaller one is farther back. An object partially covered by another in front of it allows us to see an overlap. Tracks that meet in the distance are moving toward a vanishing point, which is called one-point perspective. A circle turns into a ball when the object is shaped with light and shadow. Mountain ranges in the distance are paler than the boulder that is closer to us. Blurry shapes give us an inkling of vastness, while proximity is precisely represented. The features of three dimensionalities are based on the methods introduced here. When working on the exercises, the methods can be varied, combined, and refined, and they can be applied in both representational and new image creations.

1. Big and Small

Sucessively reducing the size of objects and things creates the impression that they are positioned behind each other. On the other hand, children (similar to artists in the Middle Ages) draw the sizes of objects depending on importance, not distance. The top of the picture represents the back to them.

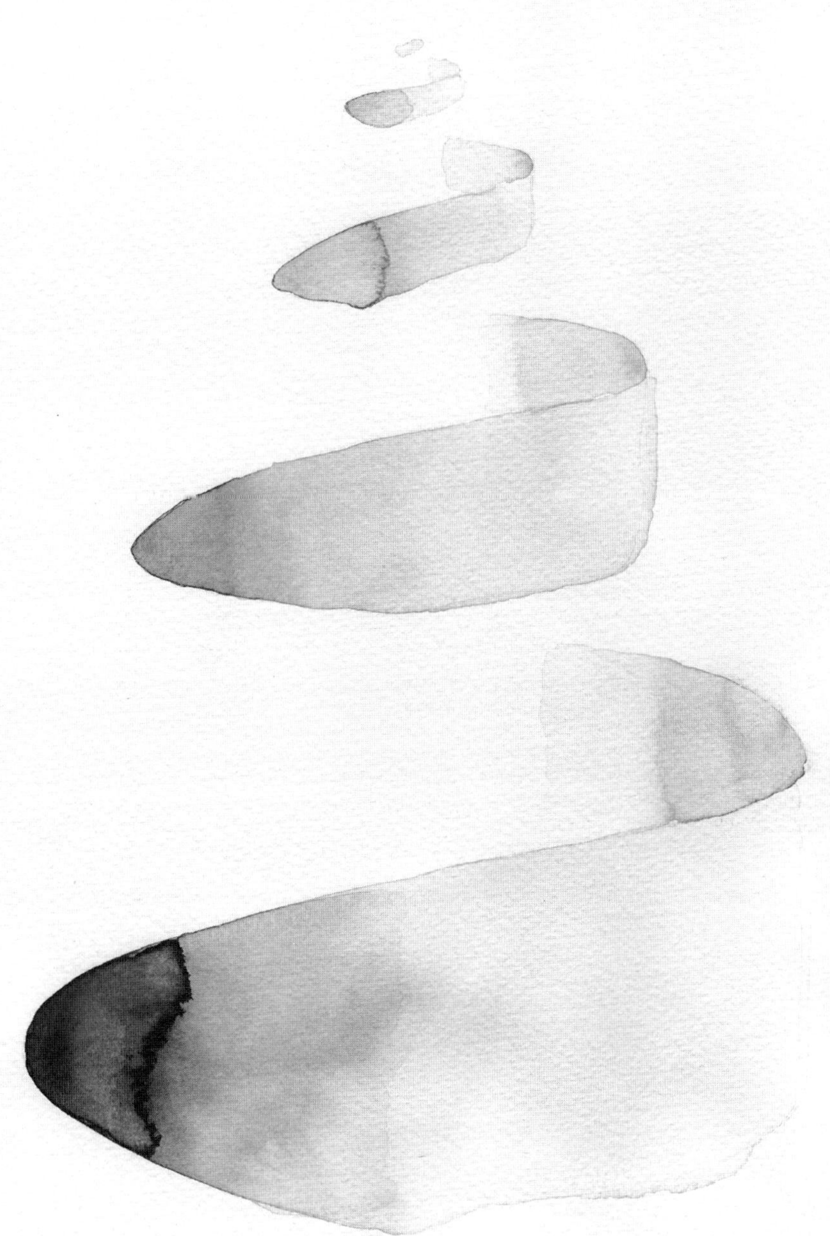

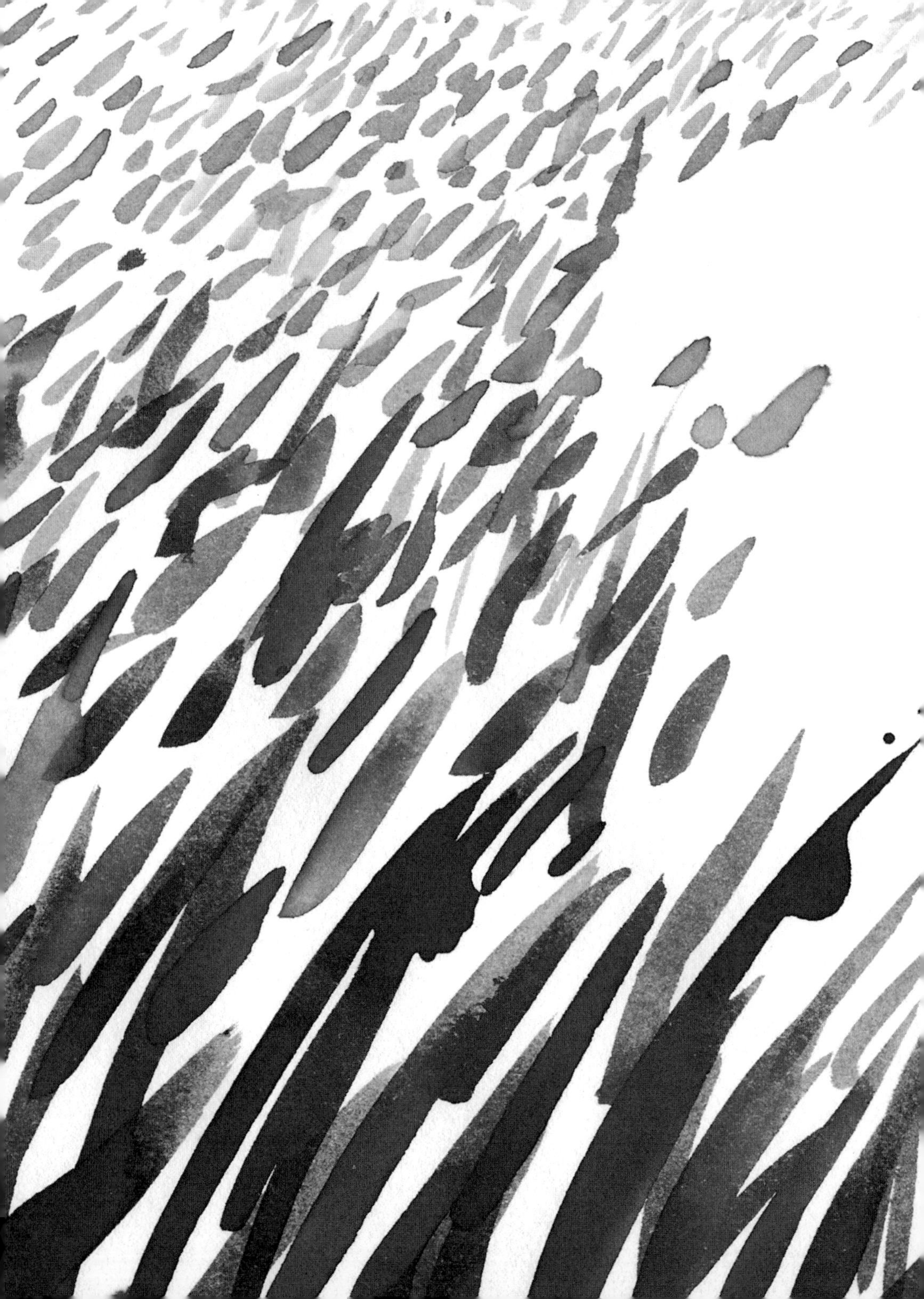

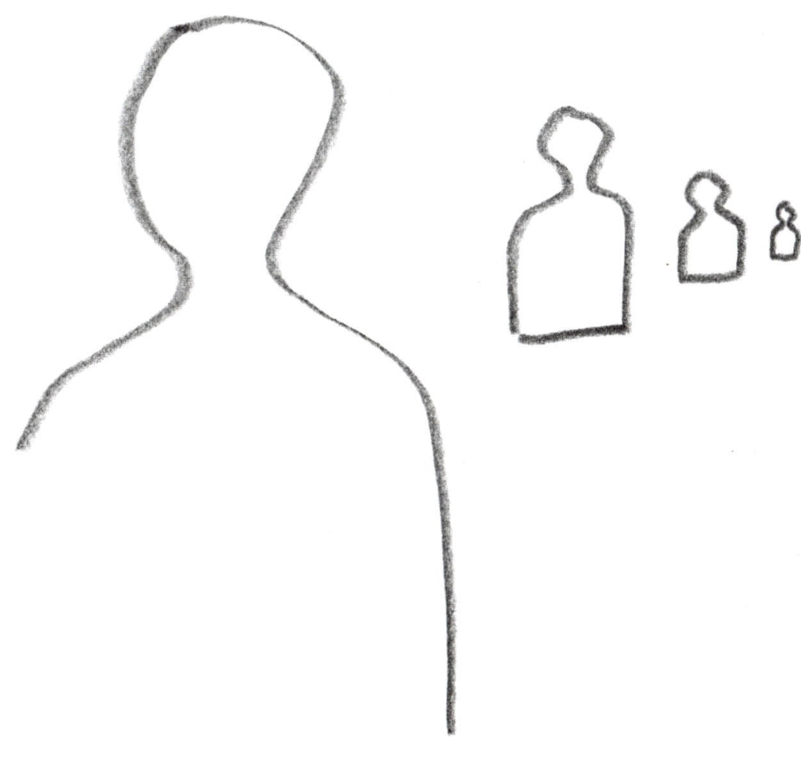

With objects of identical shape, the smaller ones
appear to sit farther back.

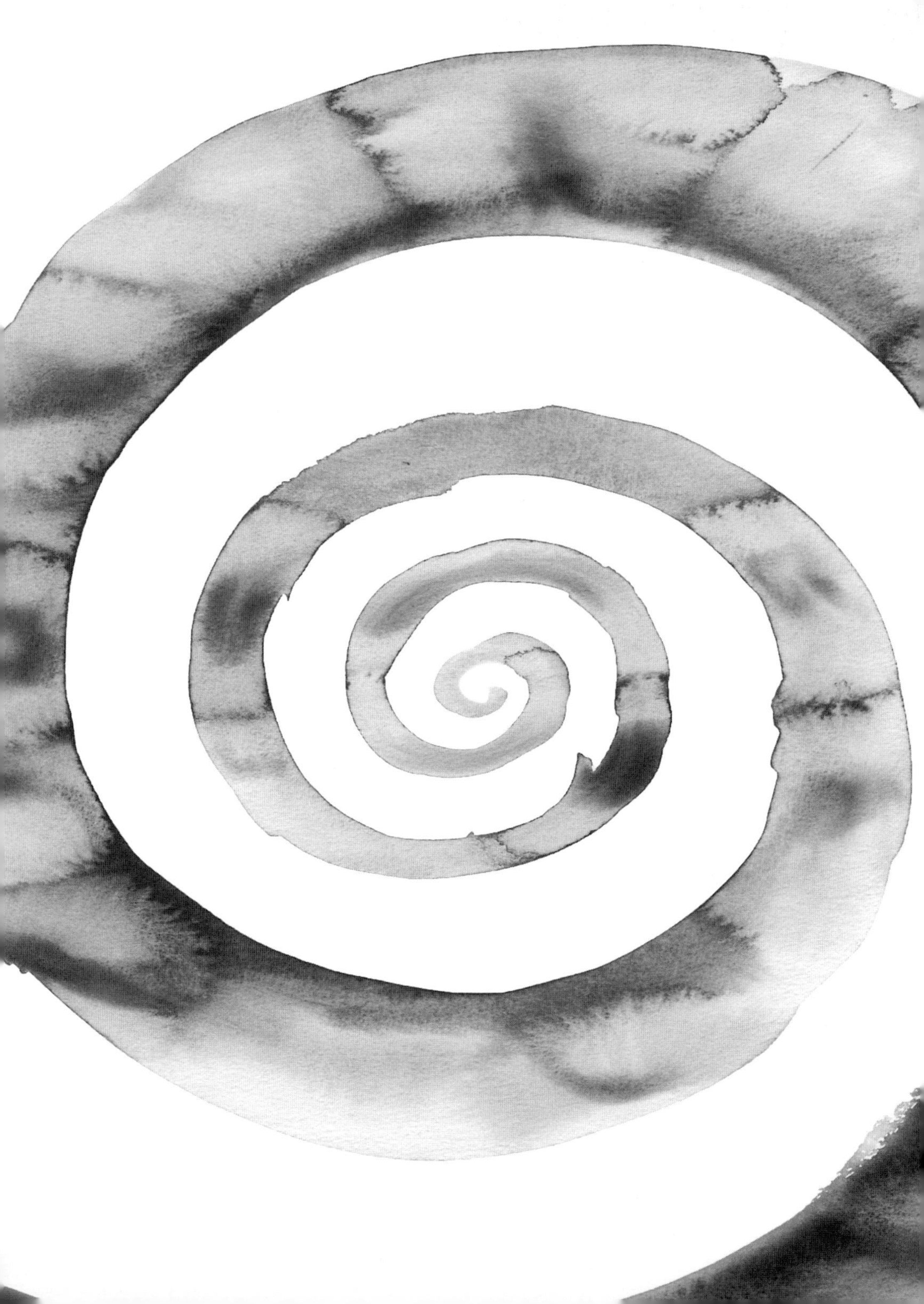

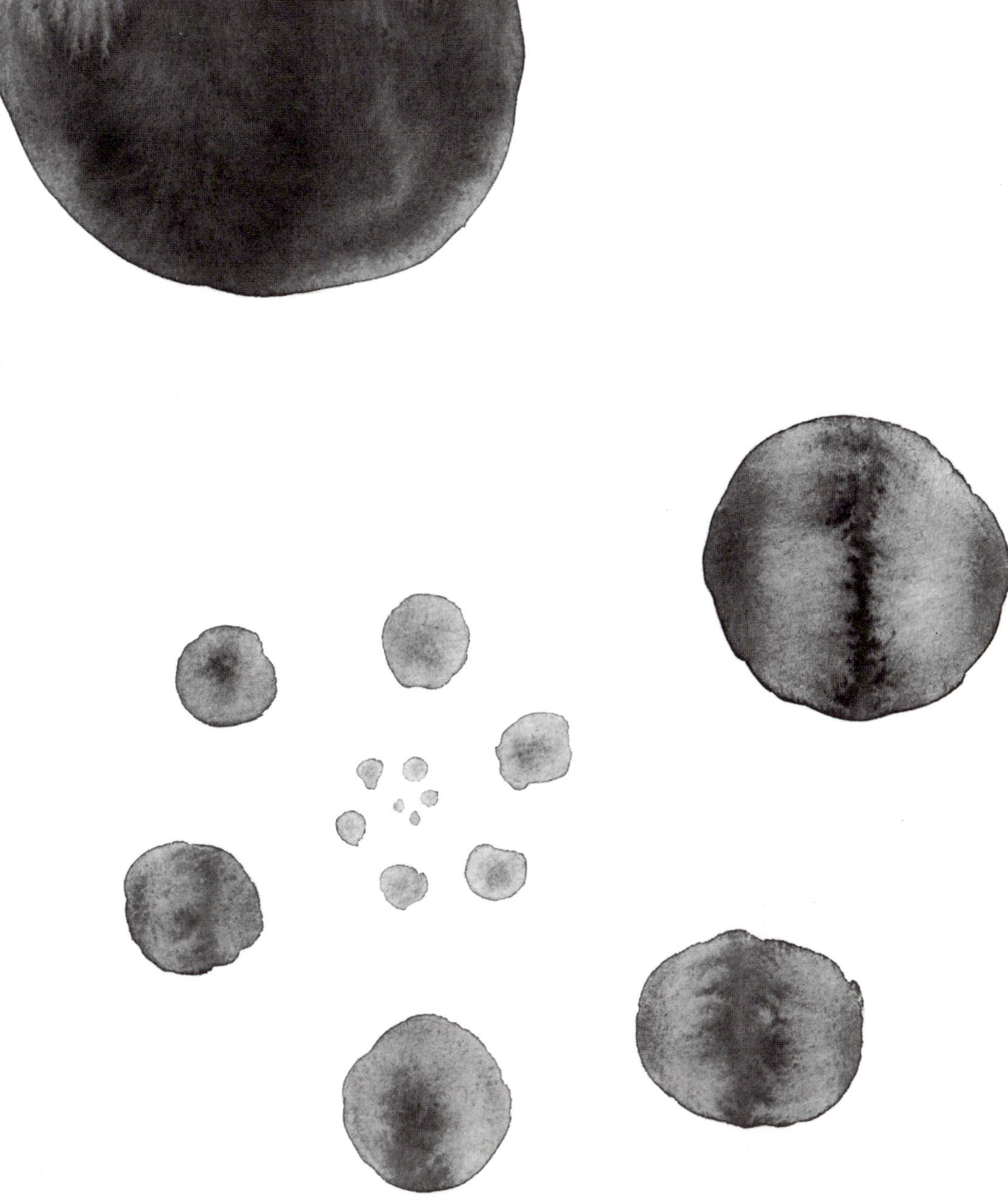

Not only do shapes become smaller, the distance between them becomes shorter the farther back they are.

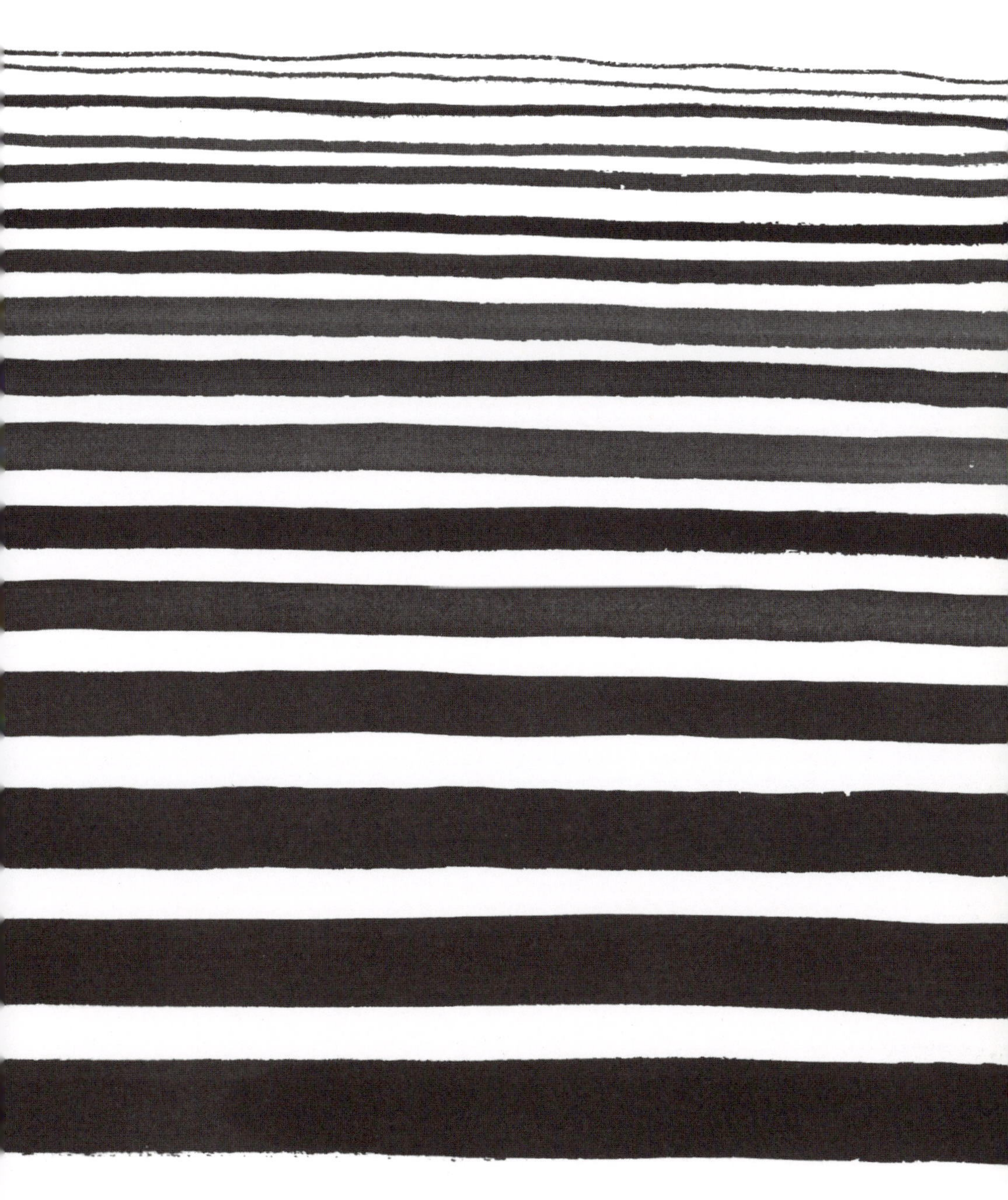

Wide lines become thinner the more distant they are. The impression of regular repetition is important for depth perception.

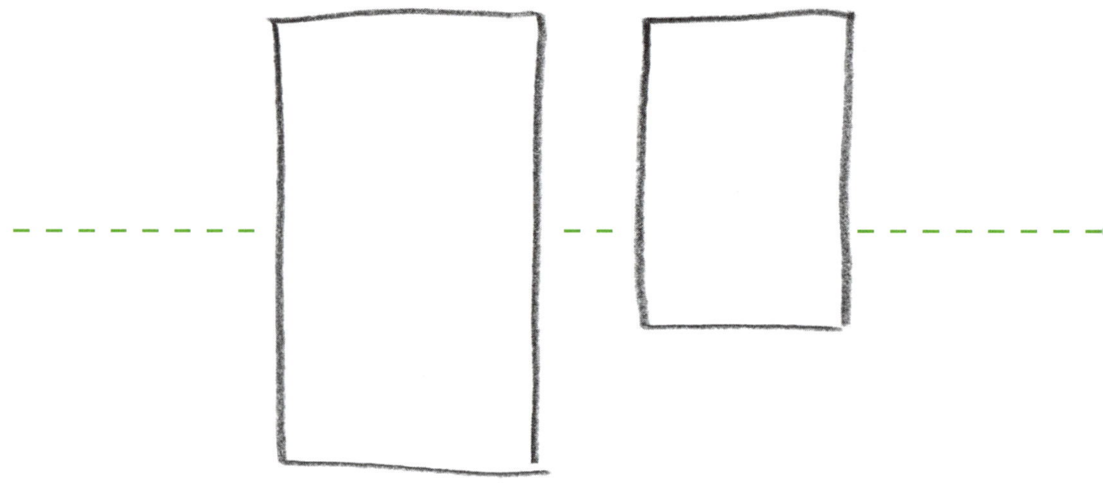

The imagined horizon line staggers the areas in space.

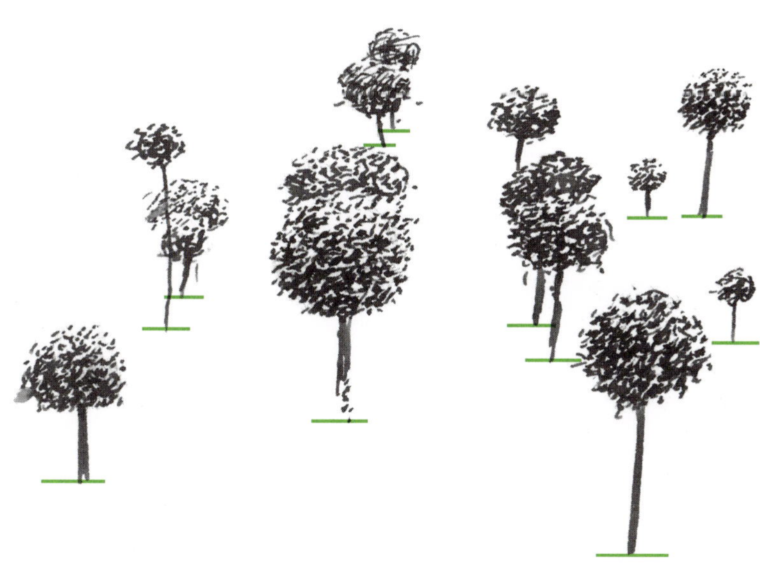

Below is in front; above is in back—
no matter how big the trees are.

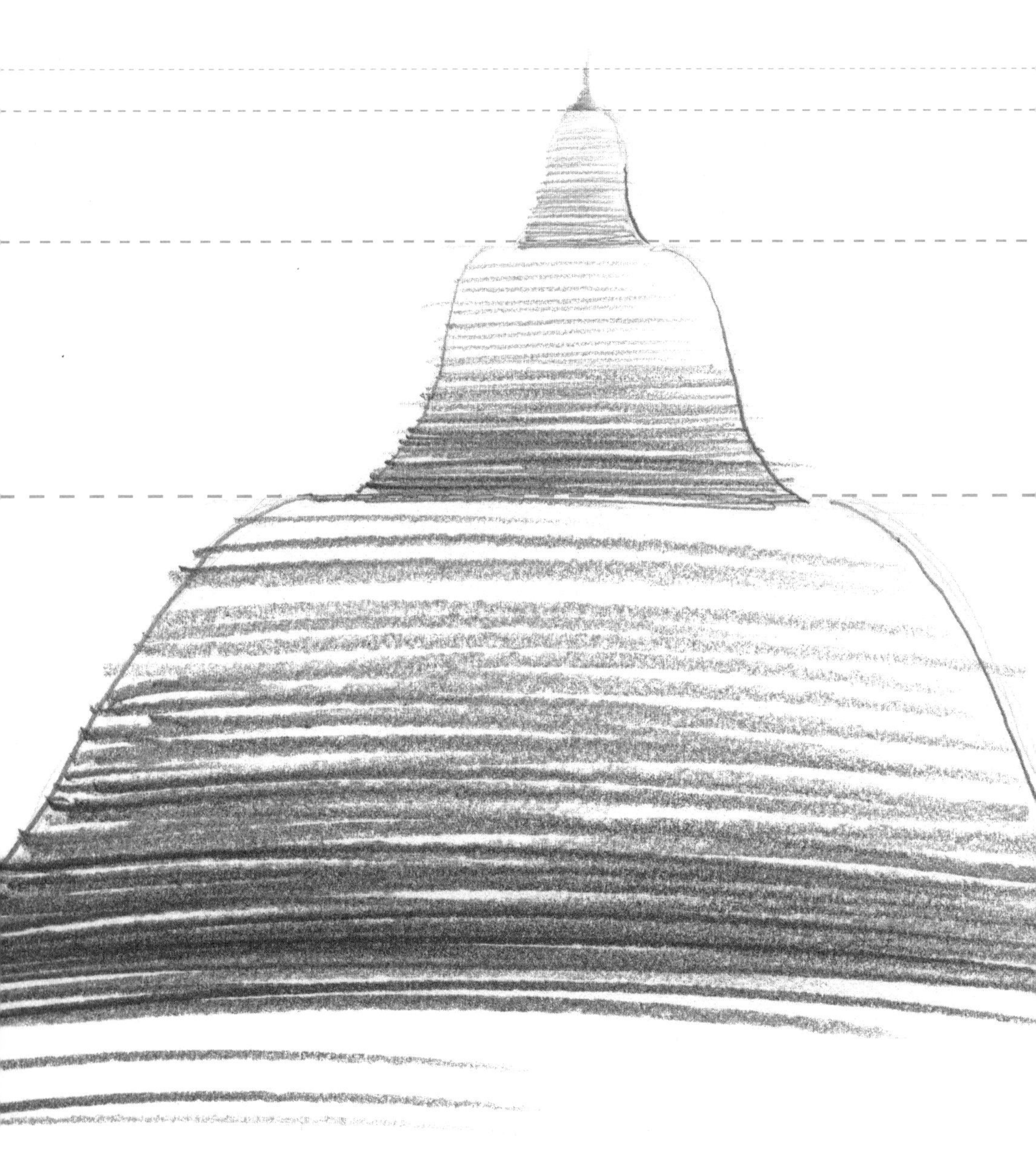

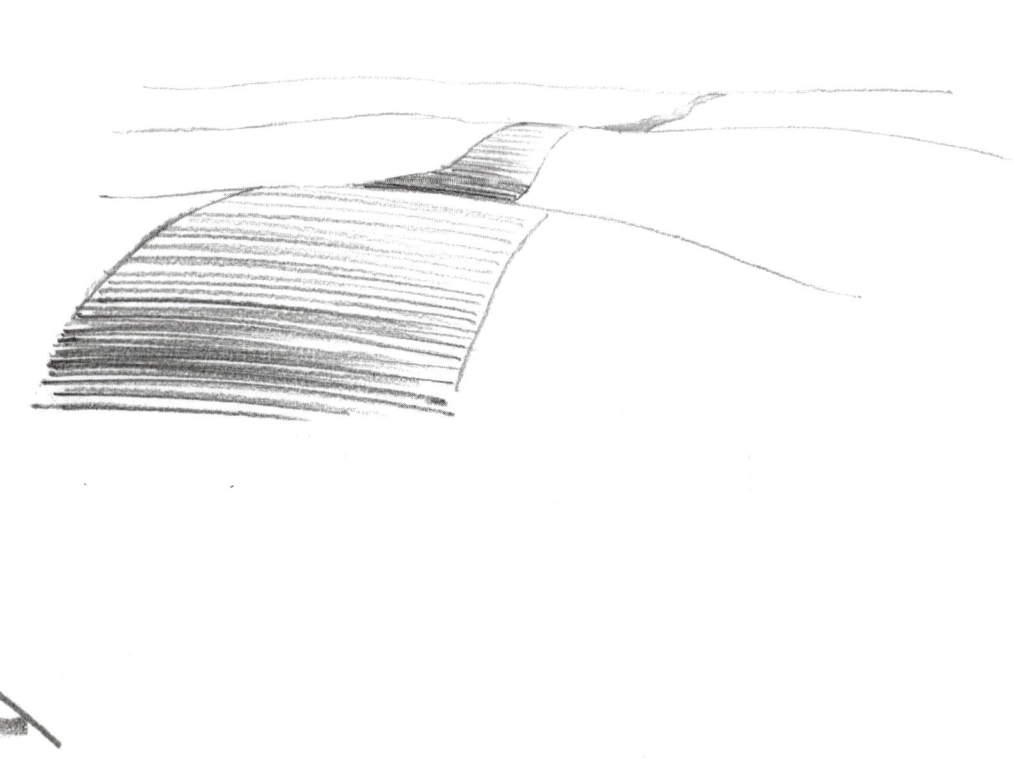

The street edge defines the terrain. That's why the gradually receding street disappears behind the hills, its smooth course broken up.

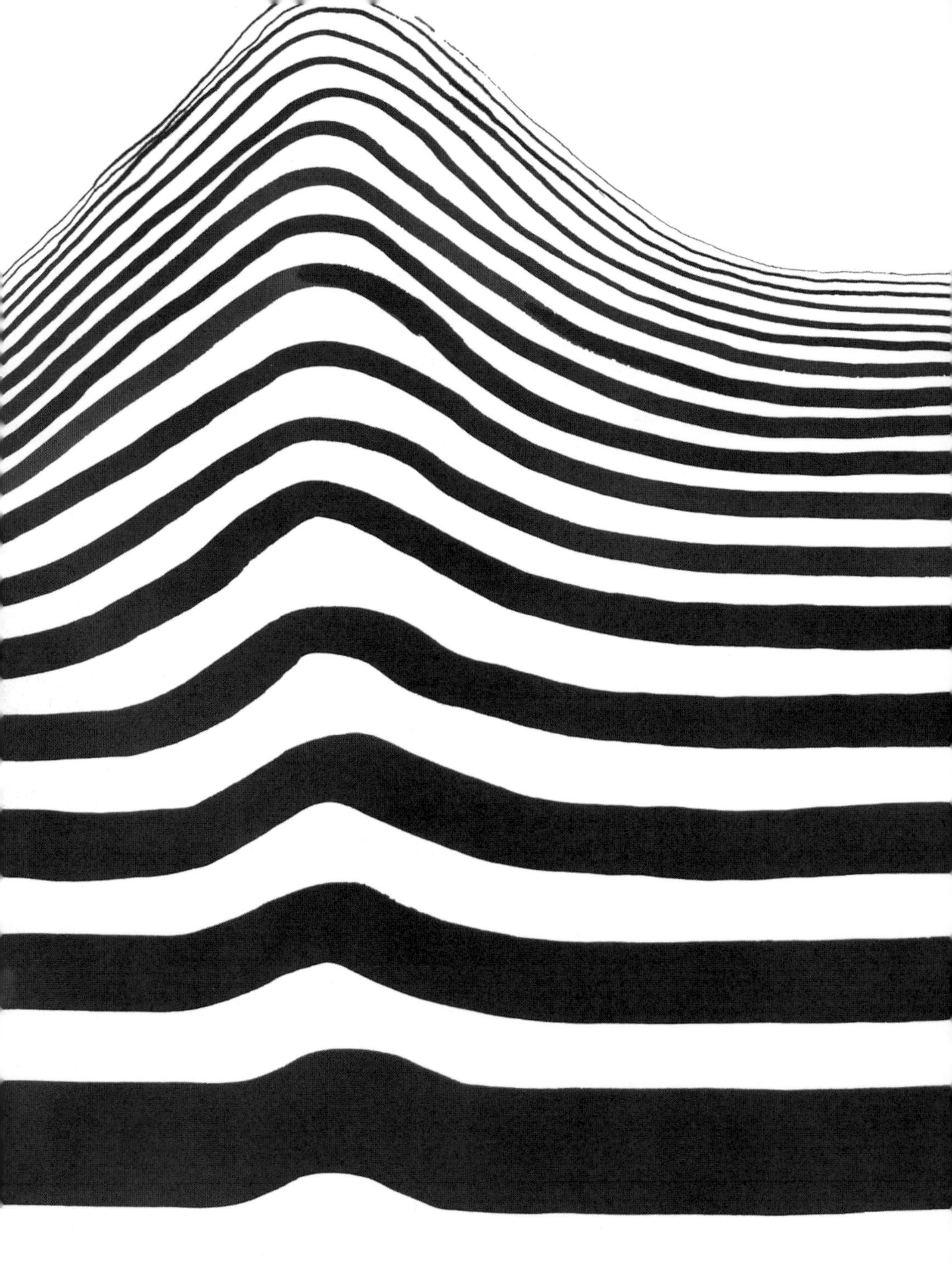

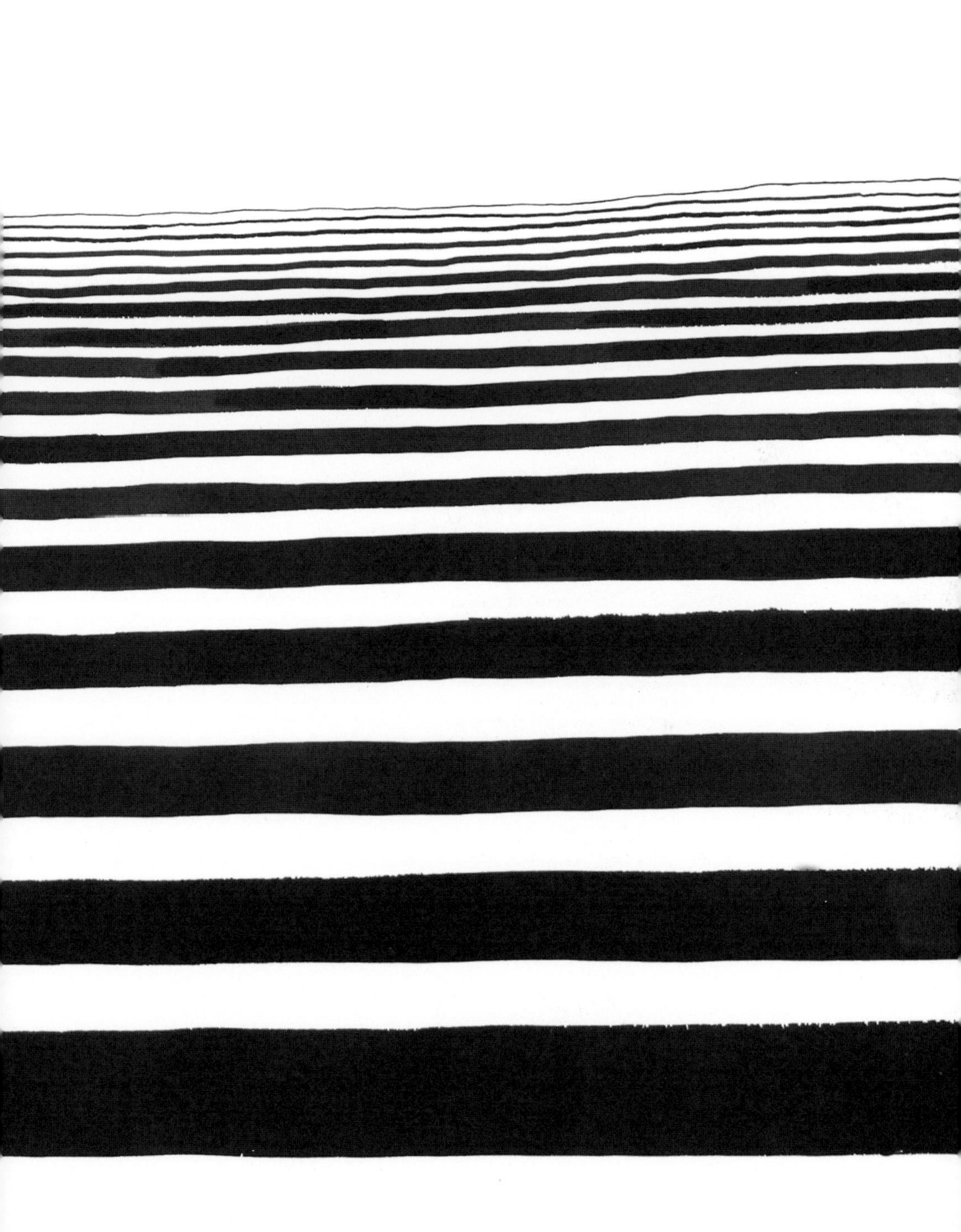

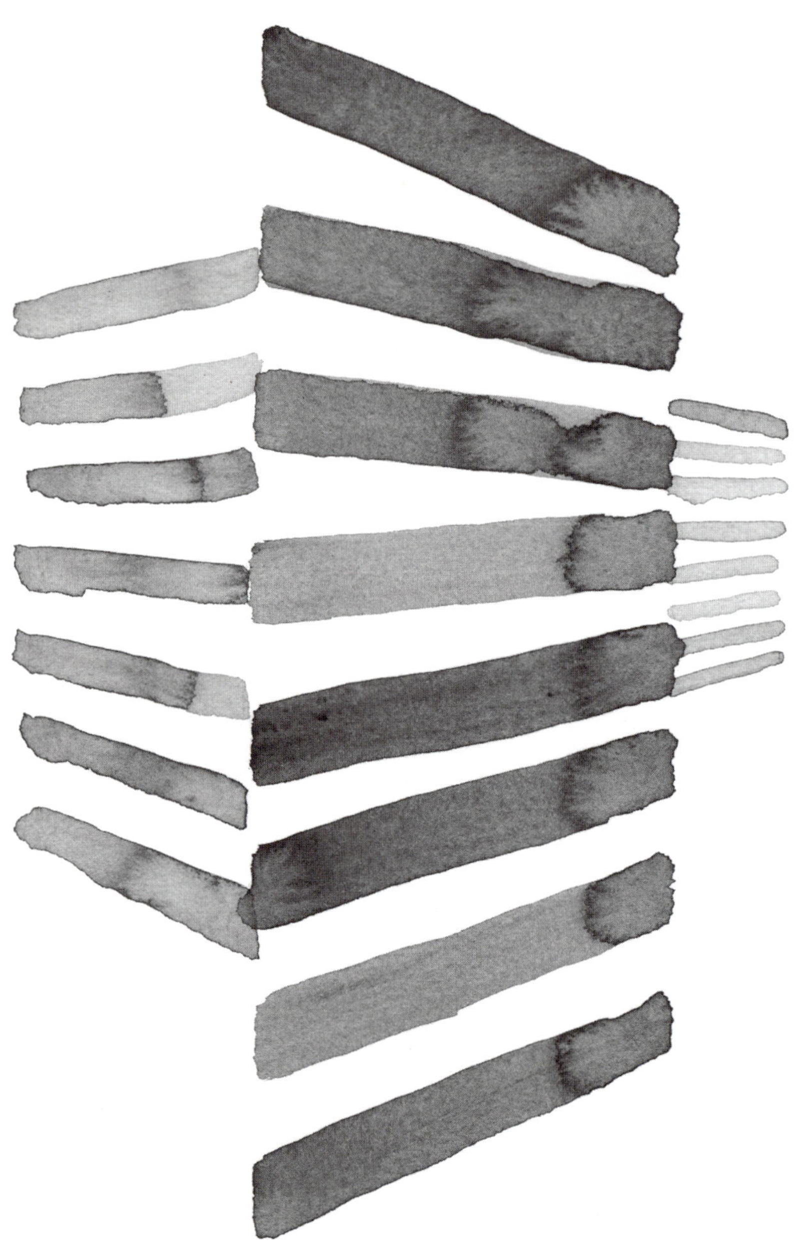

The various line widths show the
spatial order of the three walls.

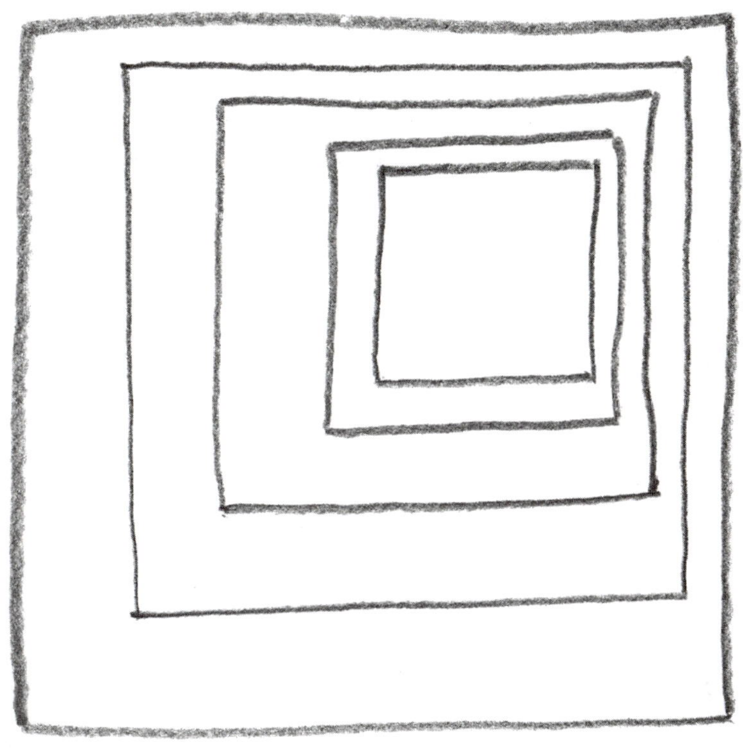

When clear overlaps are missing, it is not always obvious
whether the small shapes are farther back than the bigger ones.

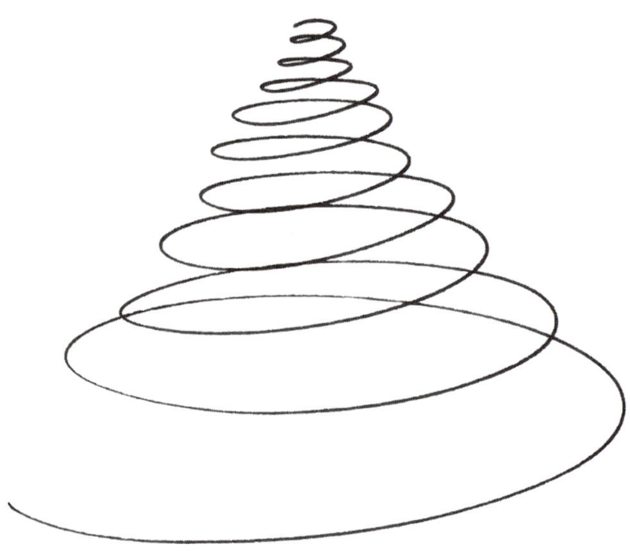

Depicted here are sounds swinging in space: quiet and loud.

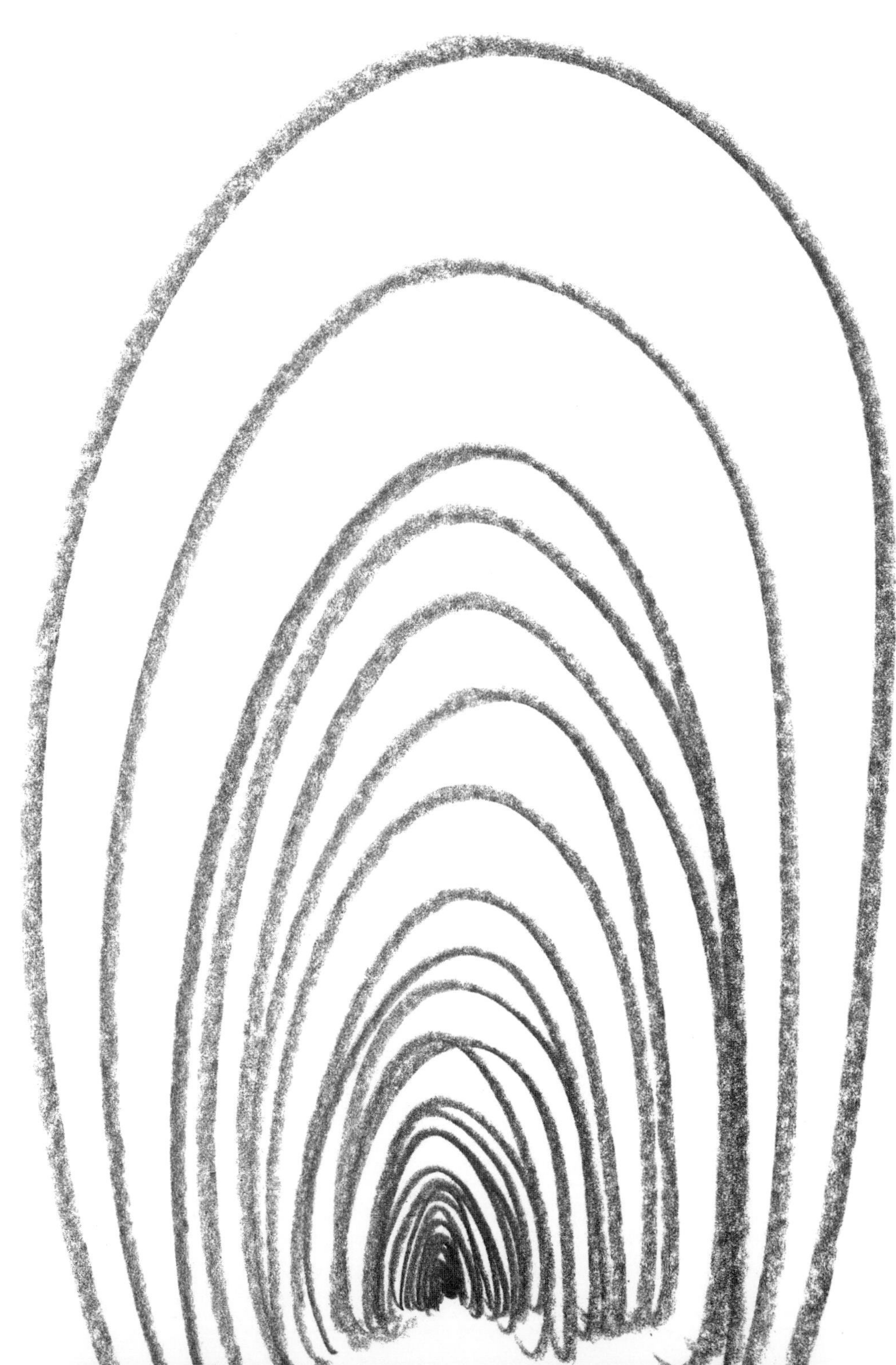

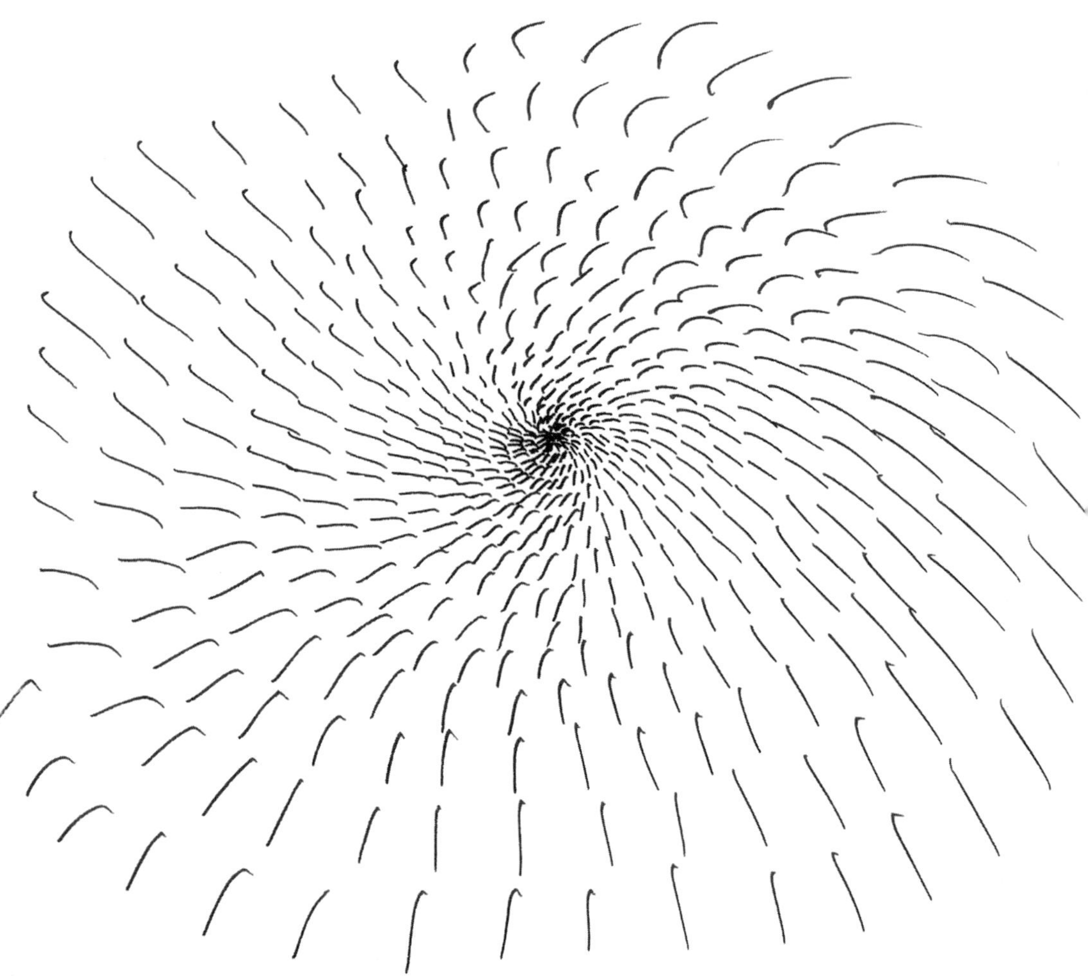

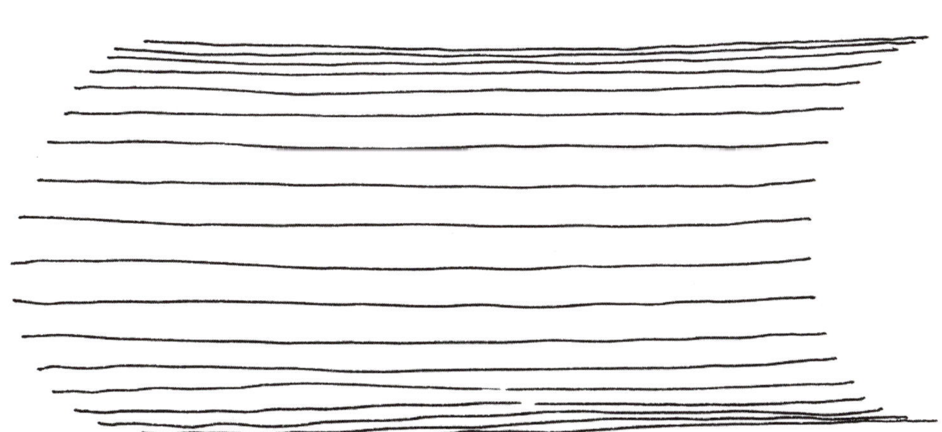

Condensing generates depth. The space pulls
together at compressed areas because the
distance between the lines is smaller there.

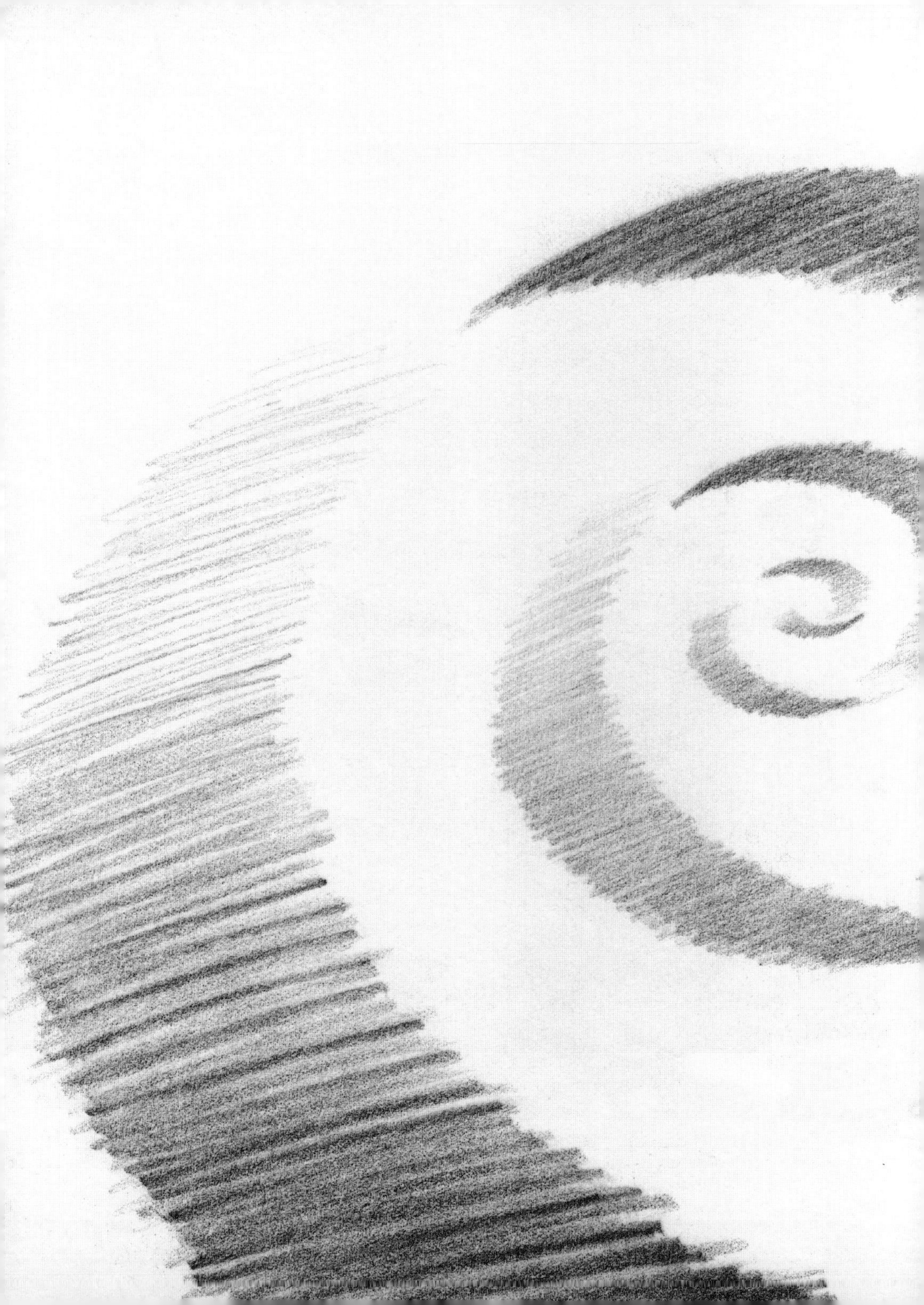

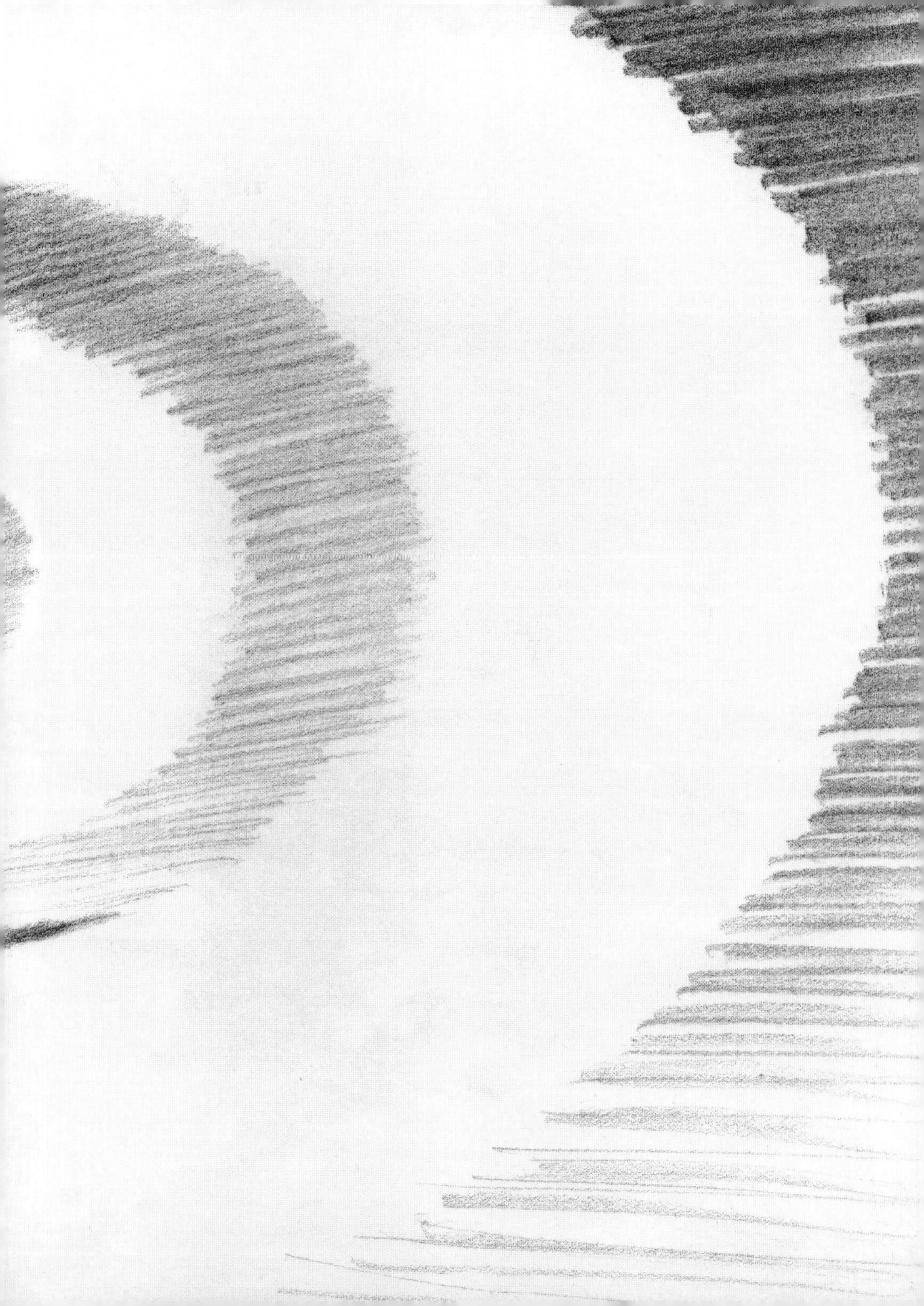

2. Overlap

The visible reality is full of overlaps, meaning objects partially covering other objects. Lines are broken up if something, such as couch pillows, lies in front of it.

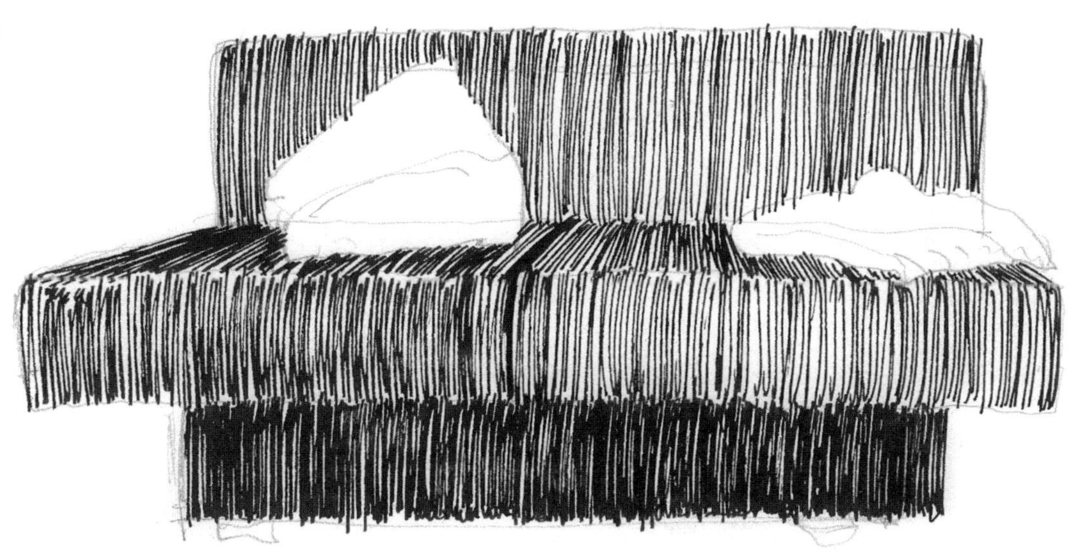

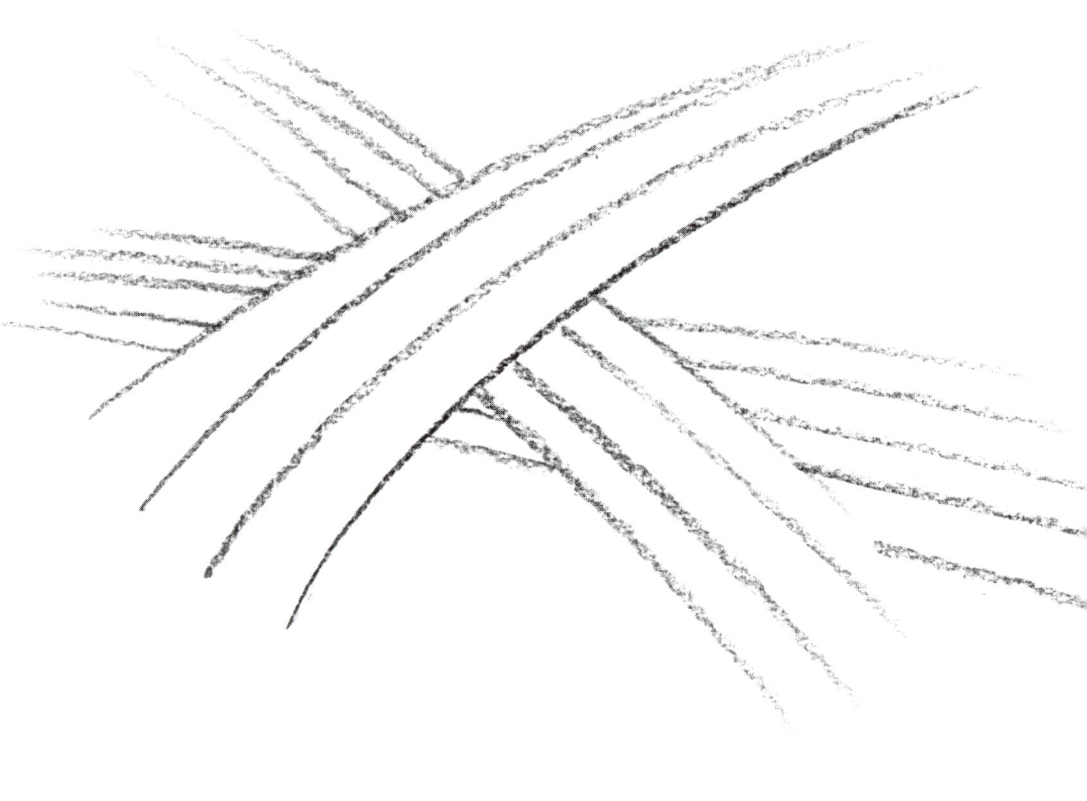

Overlaps are generated where something lies
in front of another object.

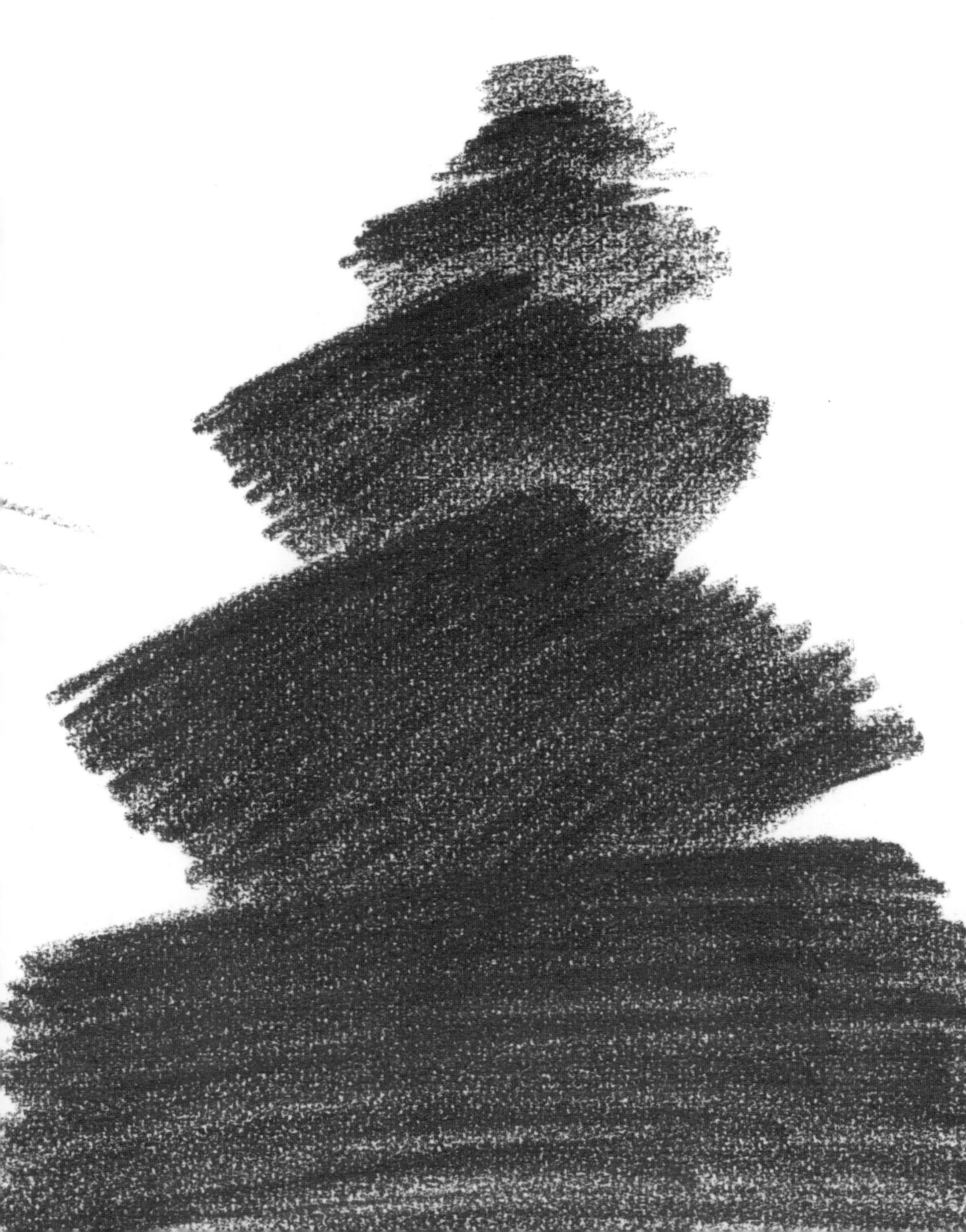

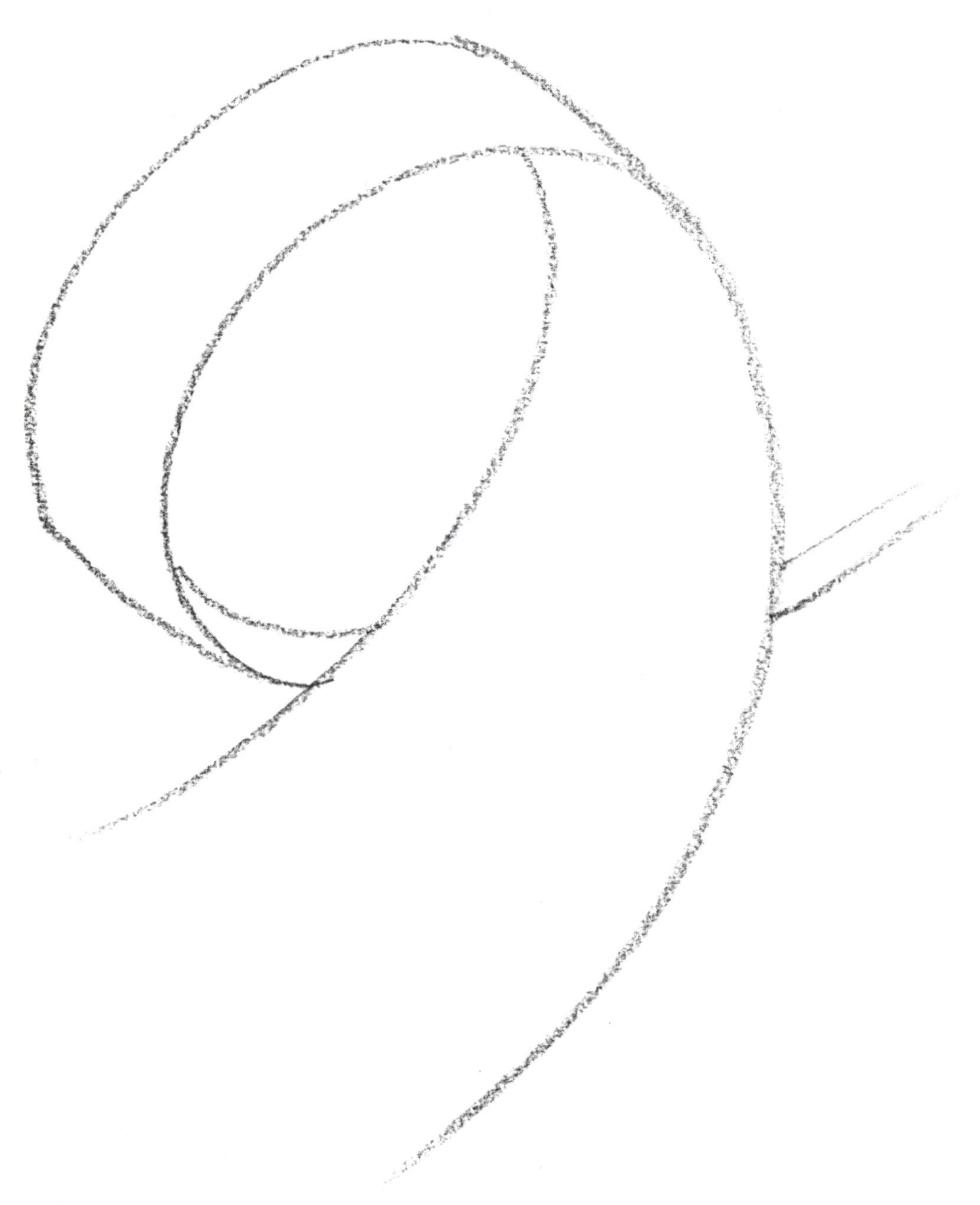

A loop alternates the inside and outside.

A white stripe lies on top of a single dark area because
both parts are perceived as one unit.

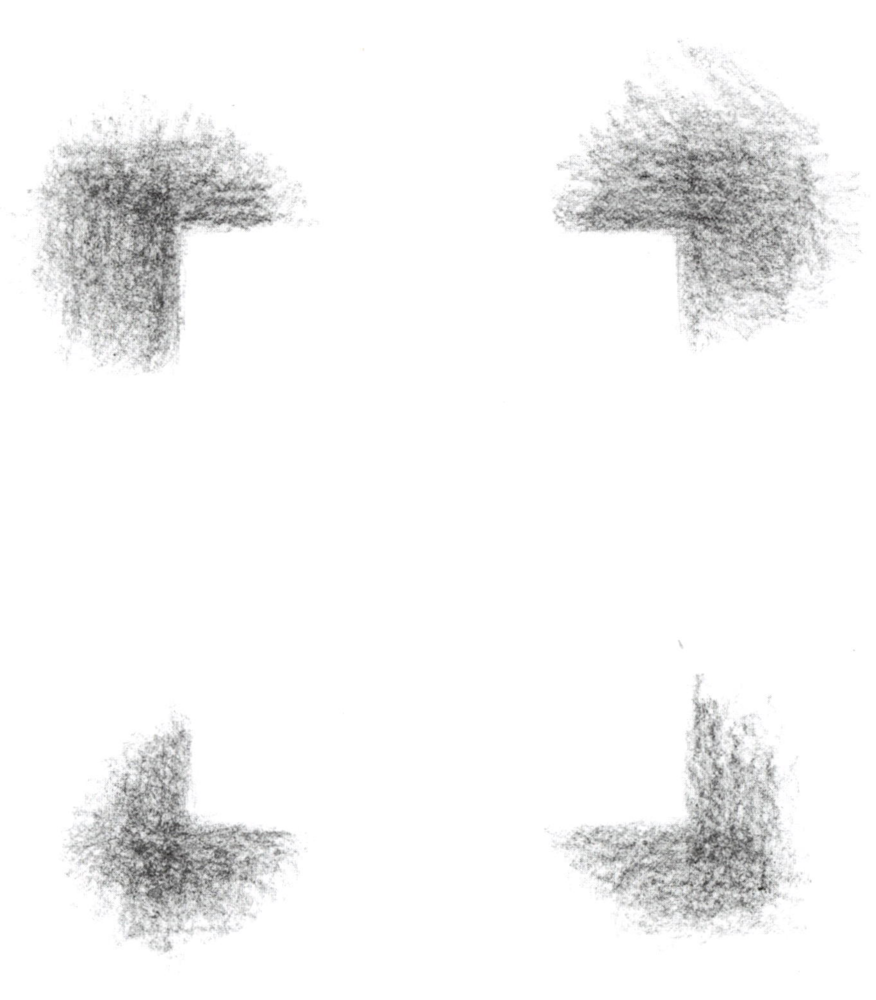

Obviously a rectangle is lying in front of the image plane.
The dark spots move into the background because our
perception prefers crisp, concise shapes.

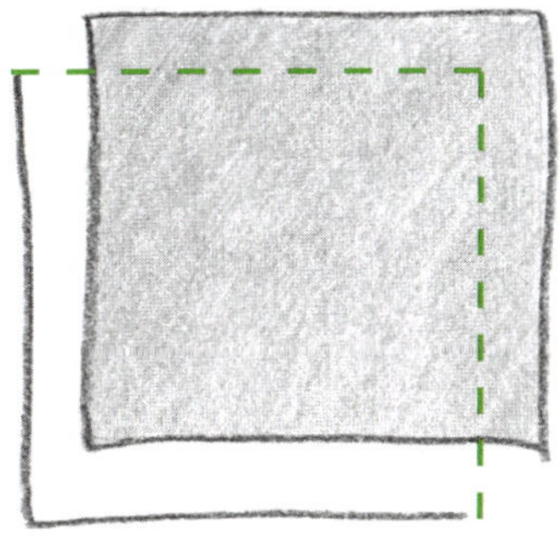

Just a few lines are enough to convey that these identical
shapes overlap. Our imagination completes the missing lines.

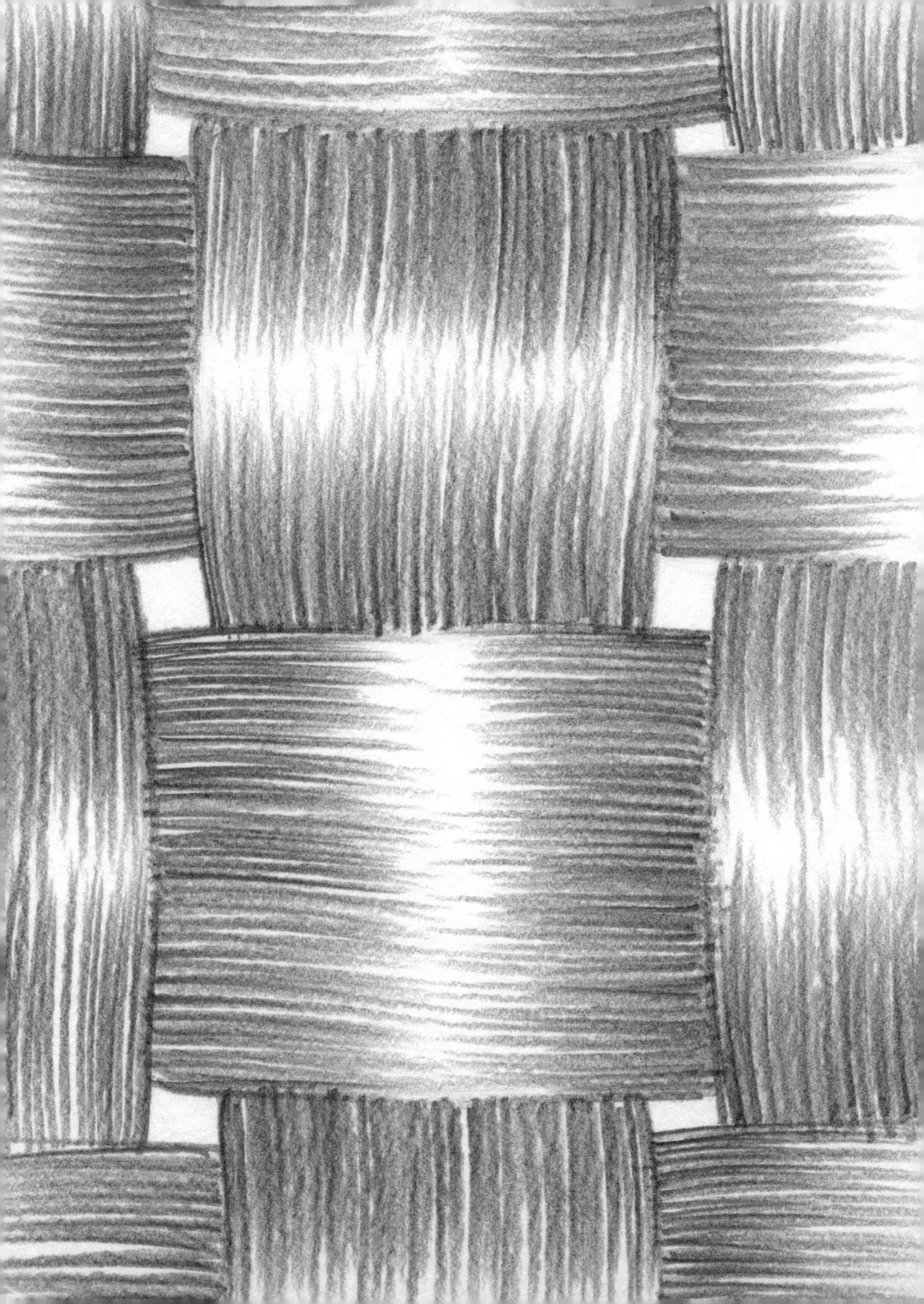

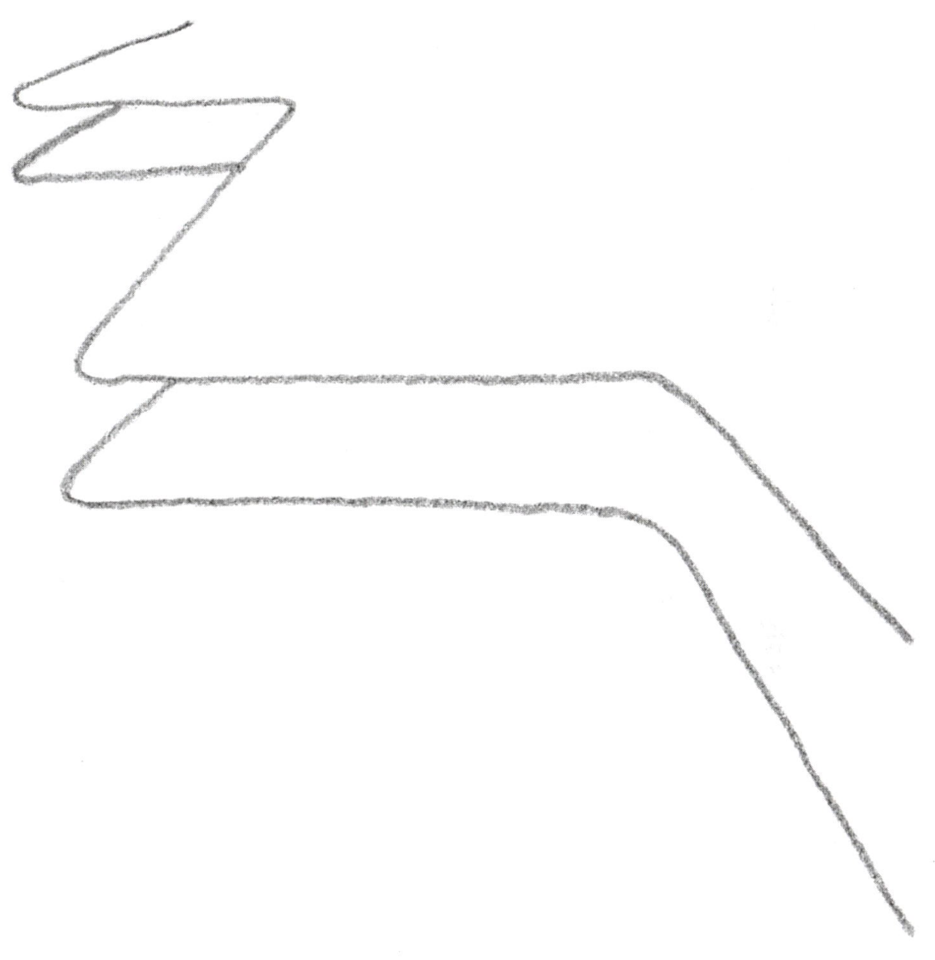

With the help of overlaps, the lines become borders of areas.

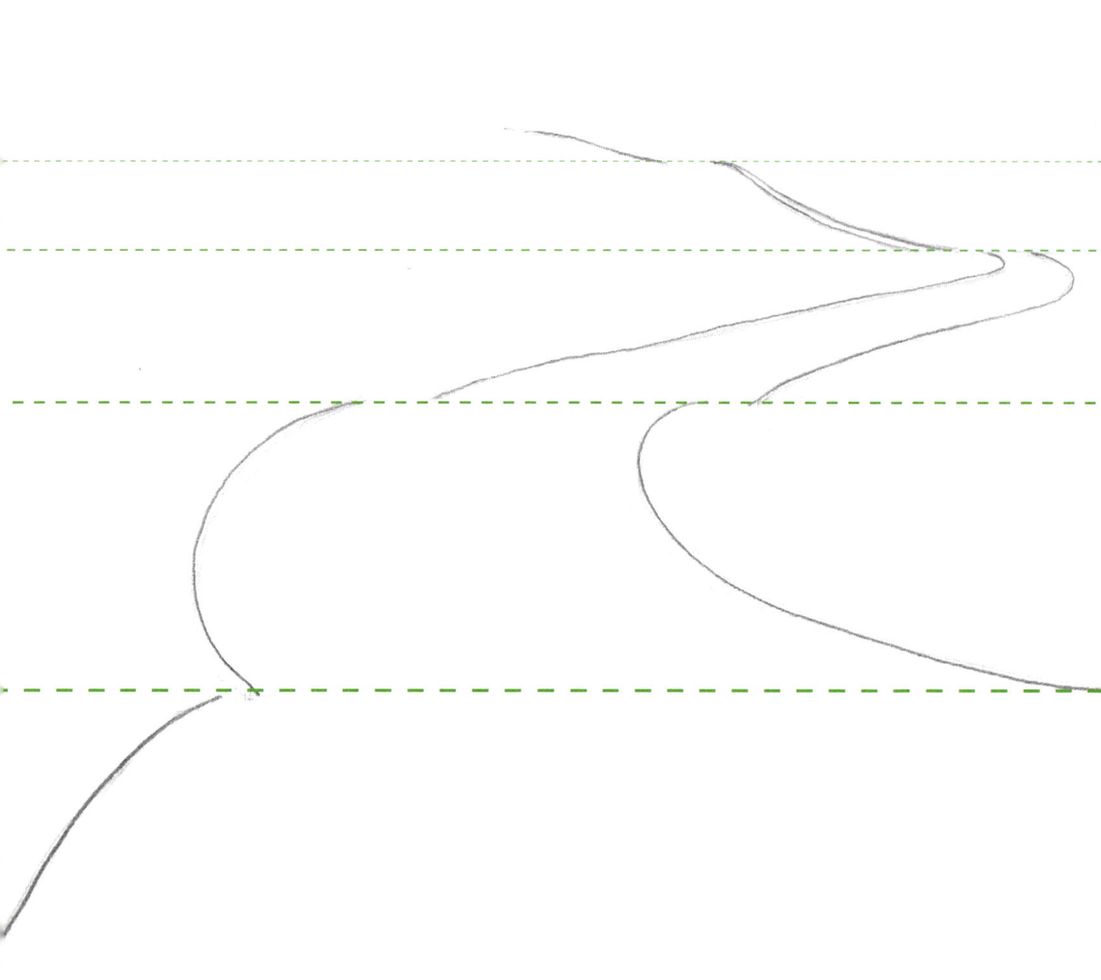

The street disappears behind the bulges of the terrain
and then reappears. That's how hills emerge
in the flow of the lines.

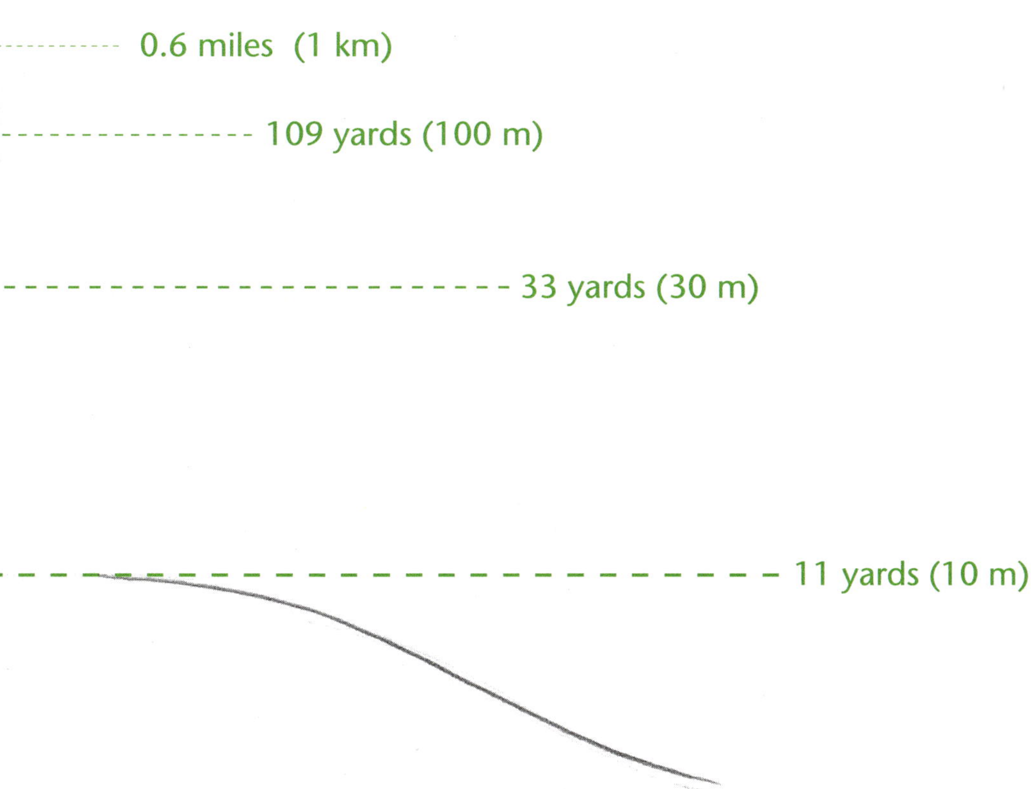

0.6 miles (1 km)
109 yards (100 m)
33 yards (30 m)
11 yards (10 m)

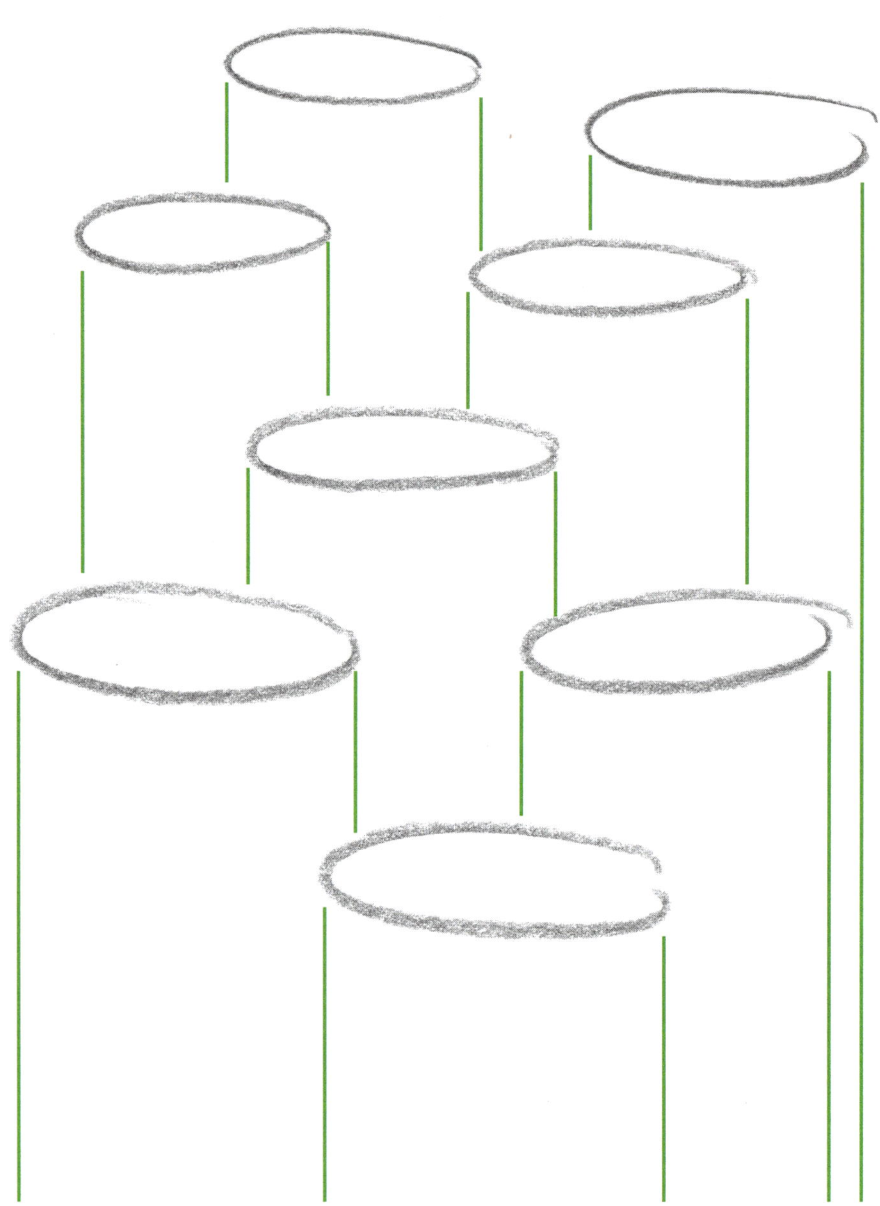

The tubes are drawn in parallel perspective. They're all the same size, whether they're close or far away. The spatial array is clear because of the overlaps.

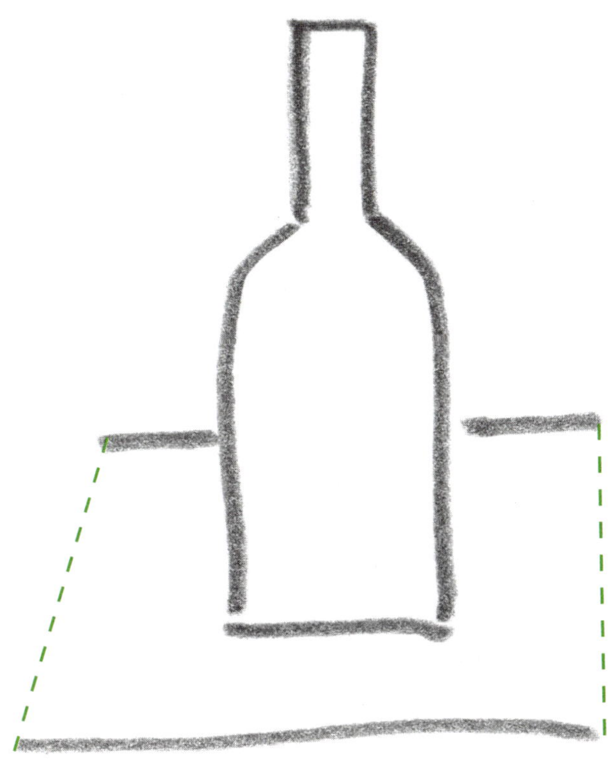

How necessary are the missing lines
to create the impression of space?

3. Folds and Waves

In paintings from the Middle Ages, the fall of the folds in a garment worn by a figure were an expression of emotionality and spirituality. The old masters understood how to make fabric appear highly sculptural through the folds. Folds and creases are basically directional changes. A directional change without a sharp crease becomes a wave.

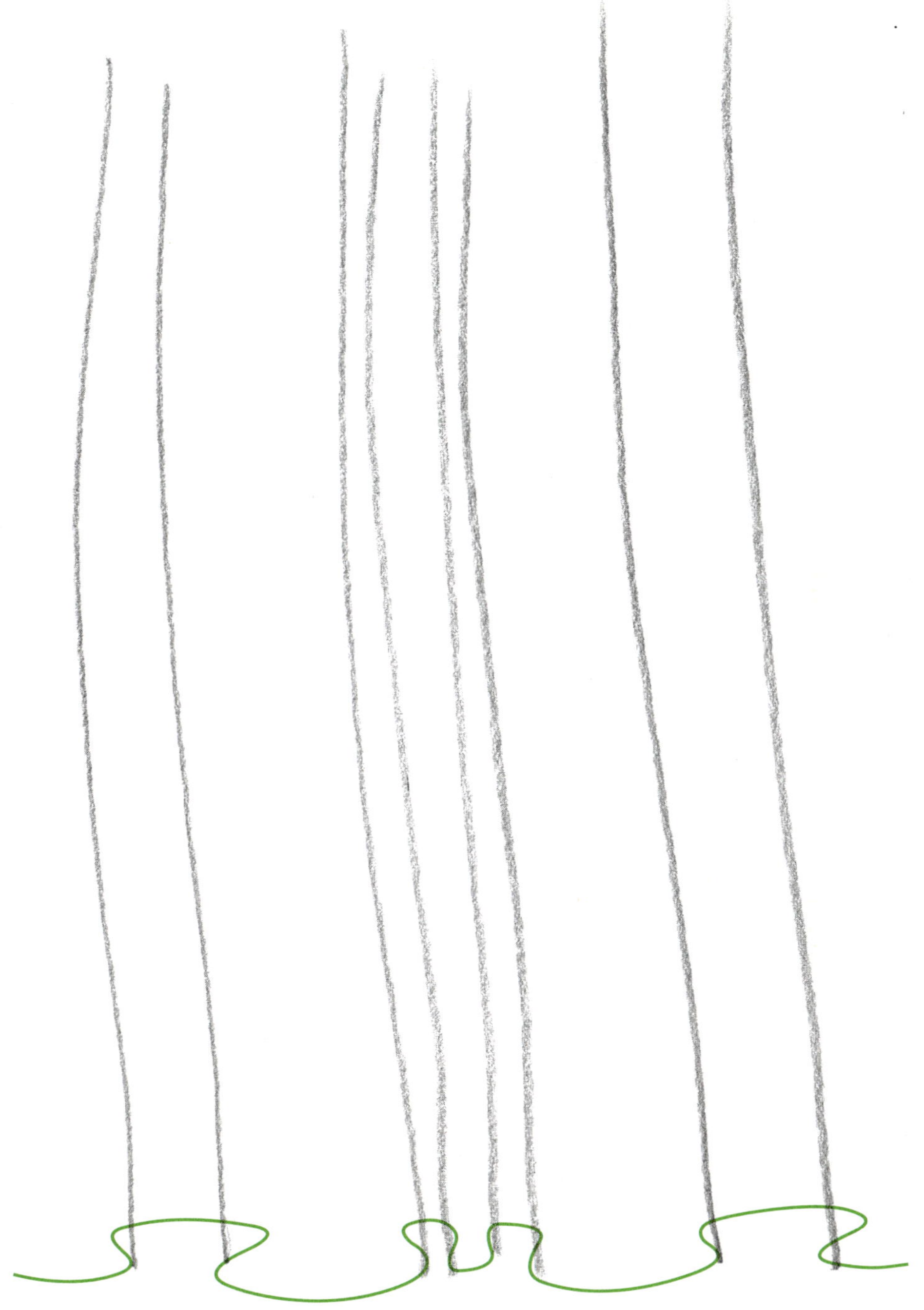

The wavy line at the bottom gives the fabric movement.

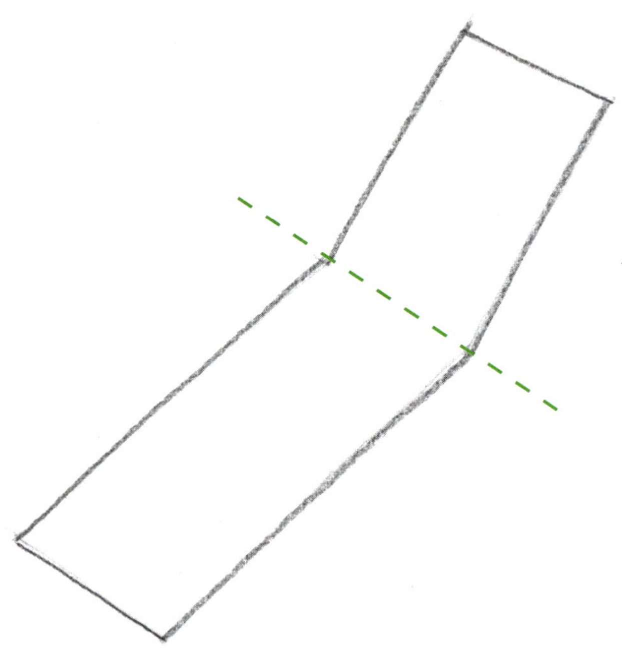

A slight fold creates a small directional change.

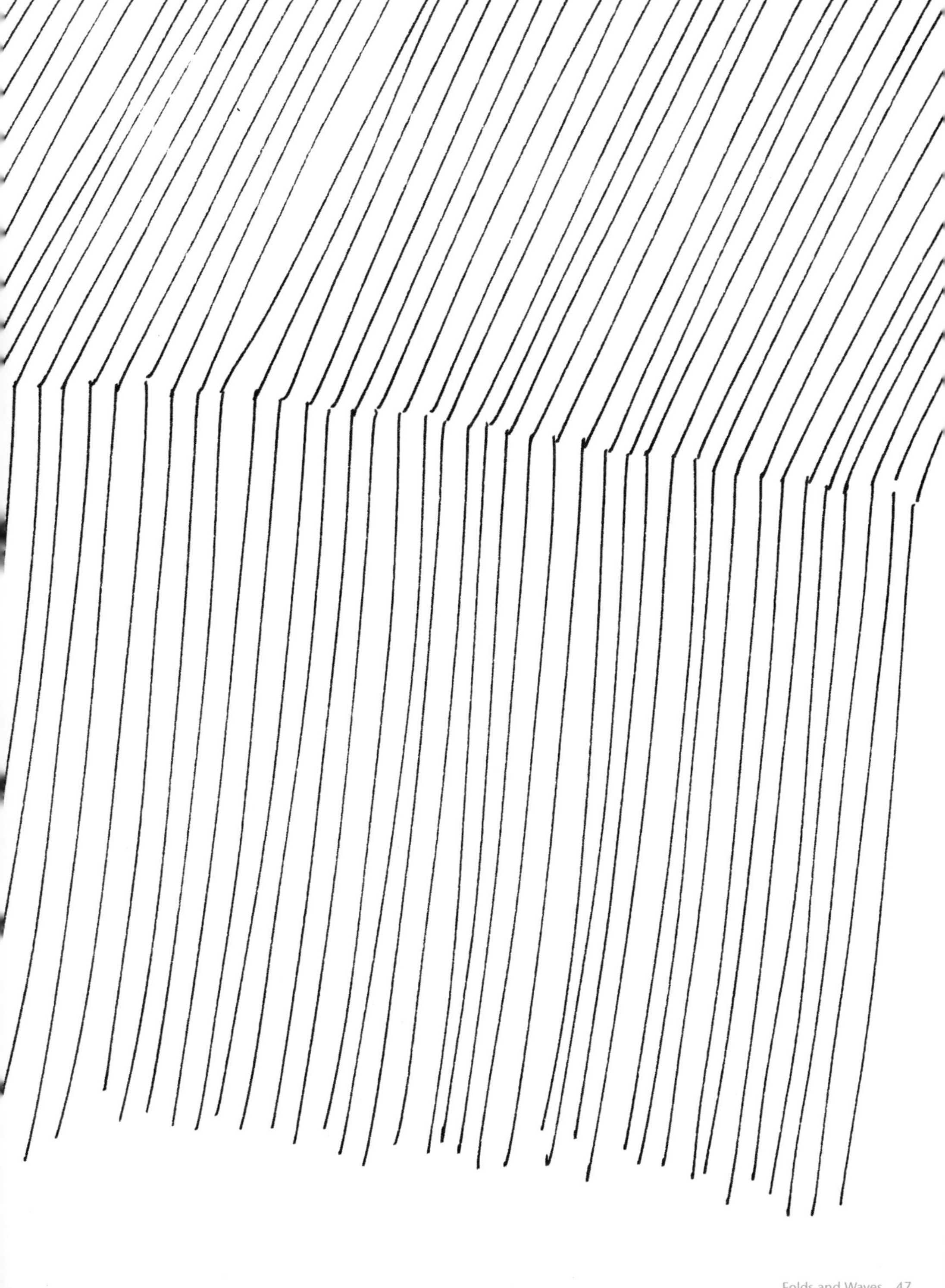

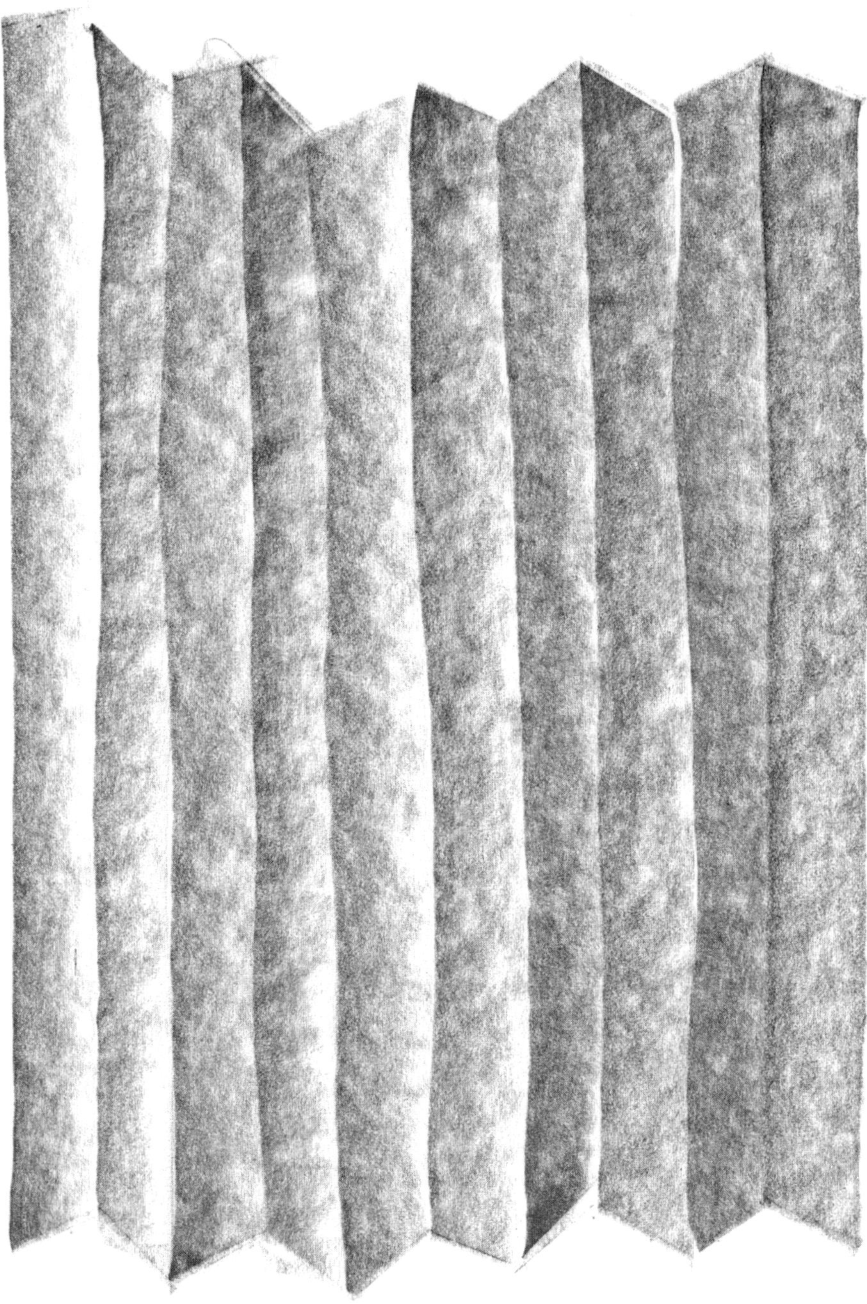

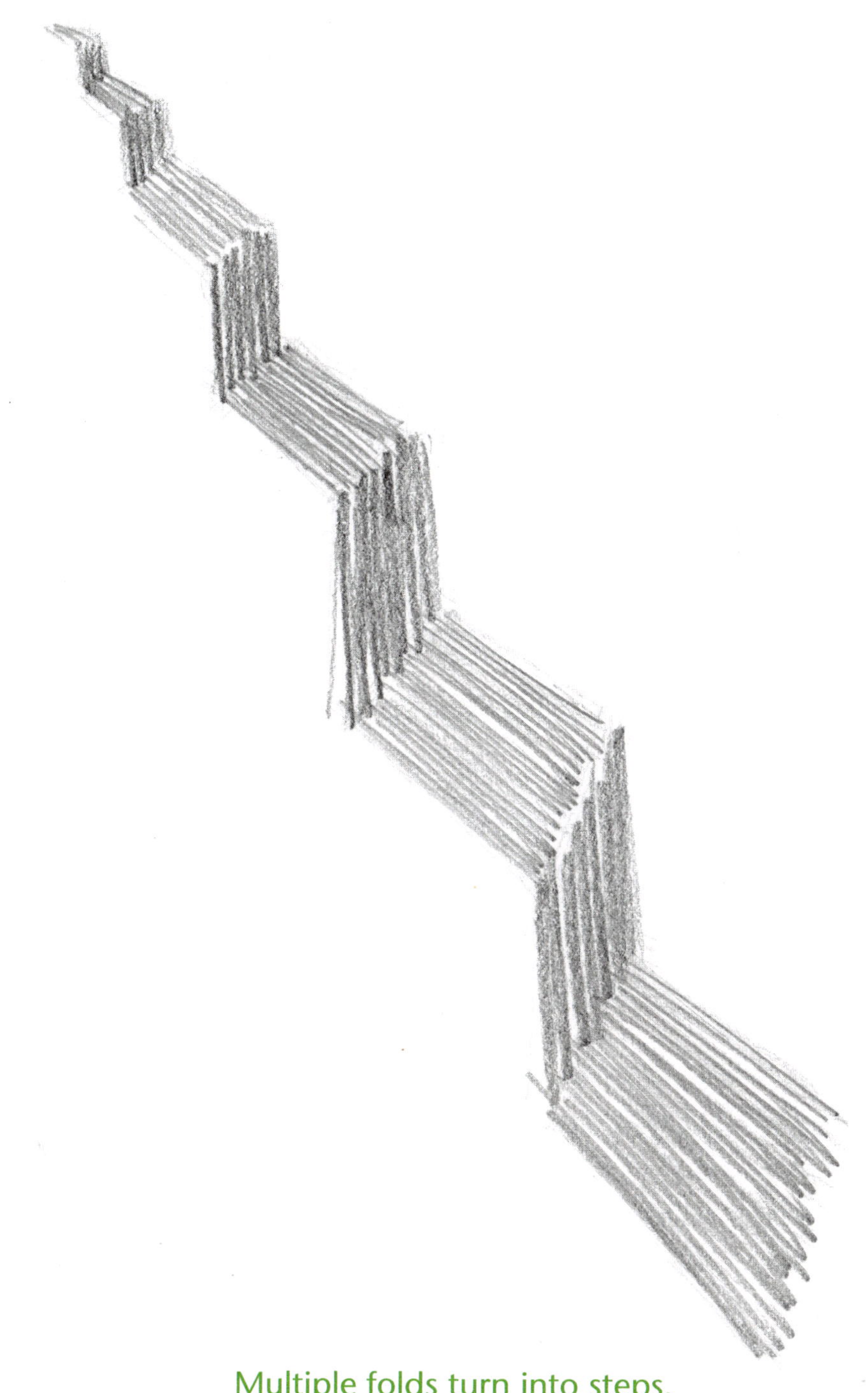

Multiple folds turn into steps.

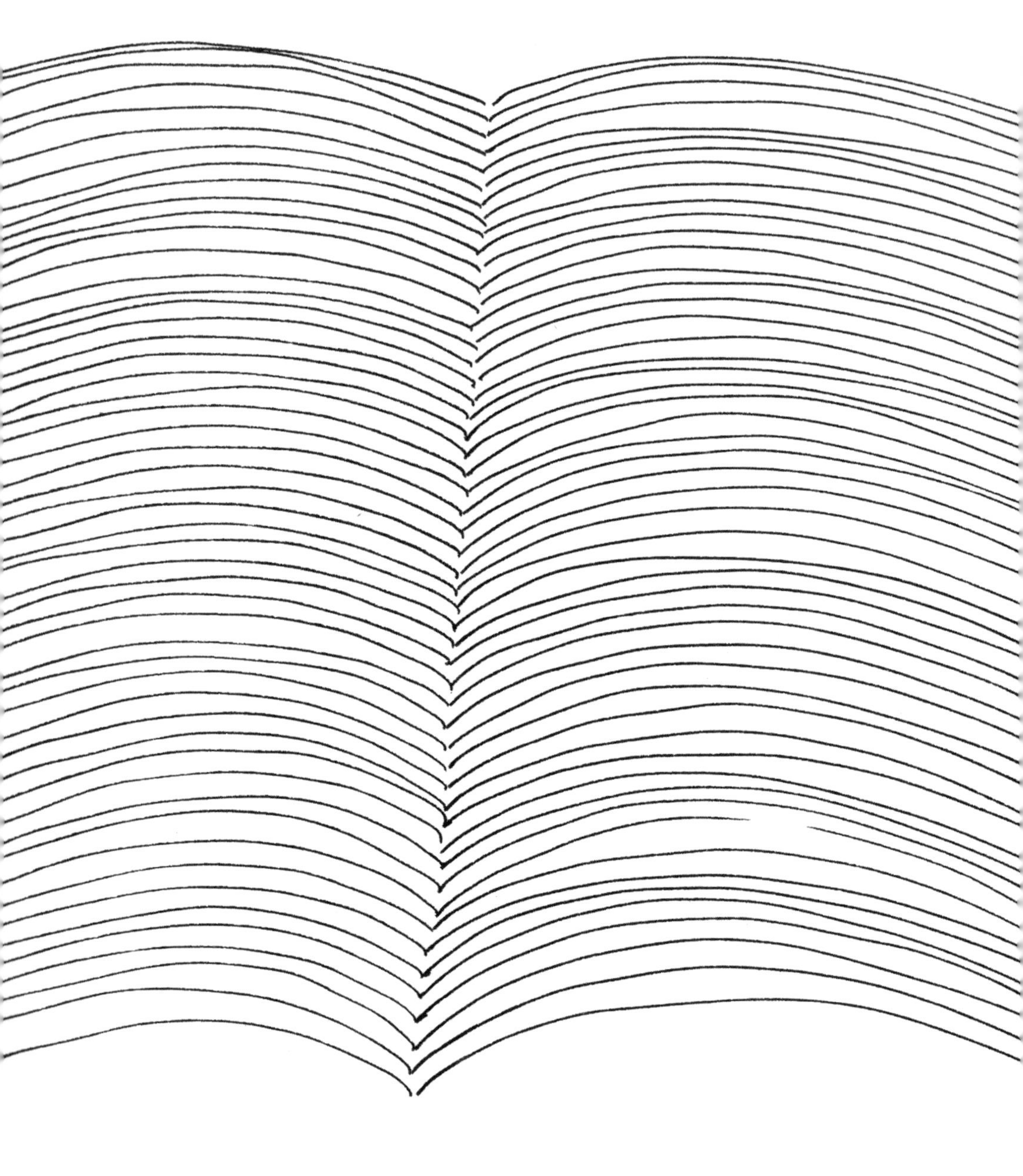

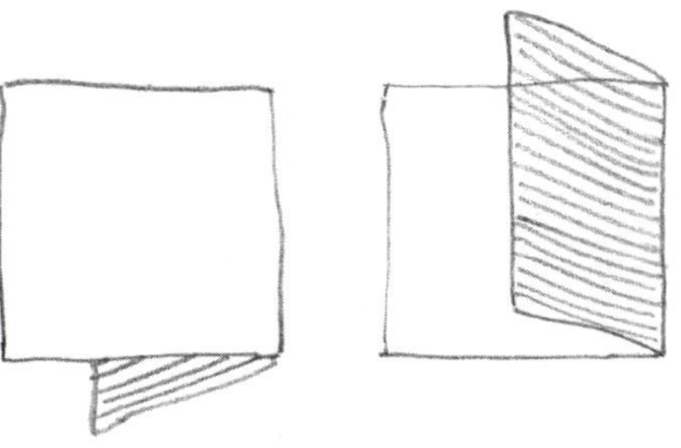

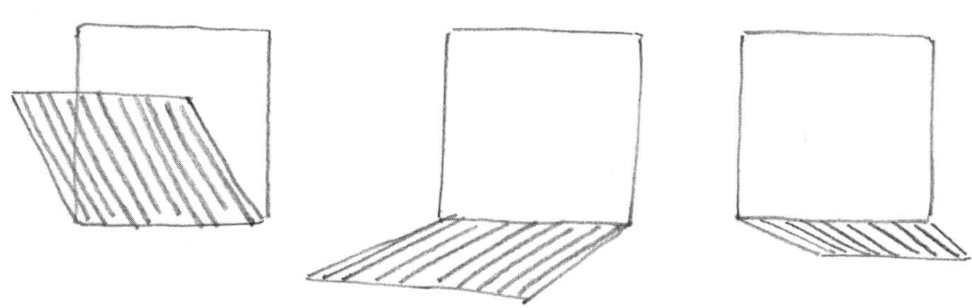

The square appears in the same plane every time.
The flap opens sometimes in the front and
sometimes in the back.

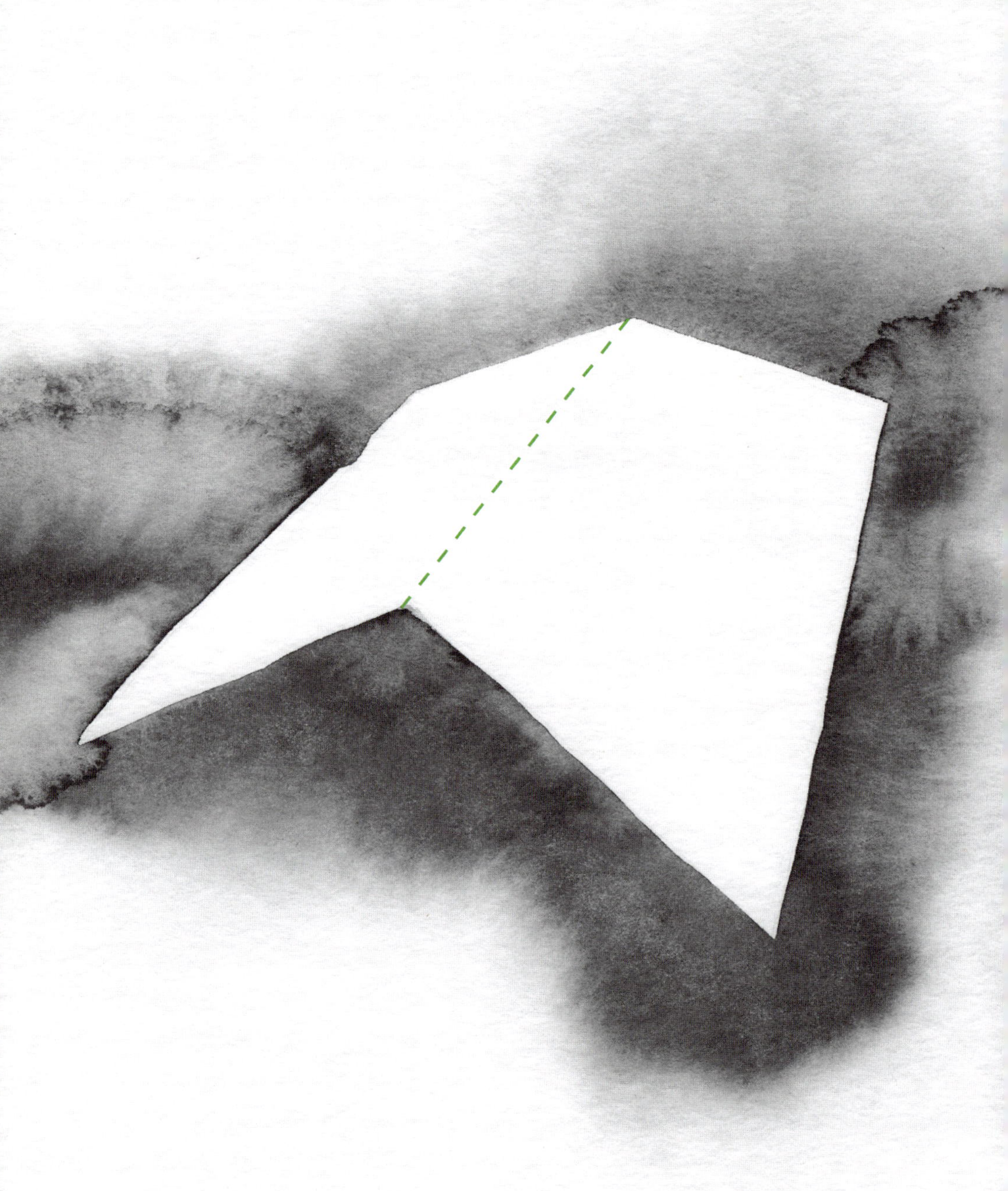

This folded square becomes a six-cornered shape.

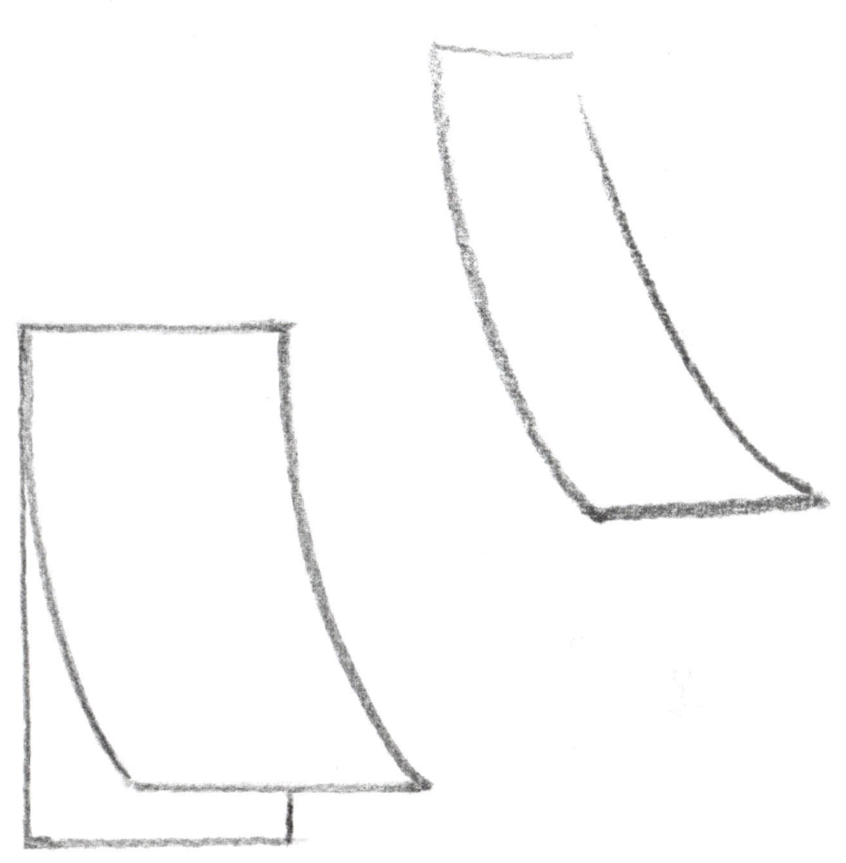

A piece of paper curls upward.
If you narrow the paper as it ascends,
it almost turns into a ski jump.

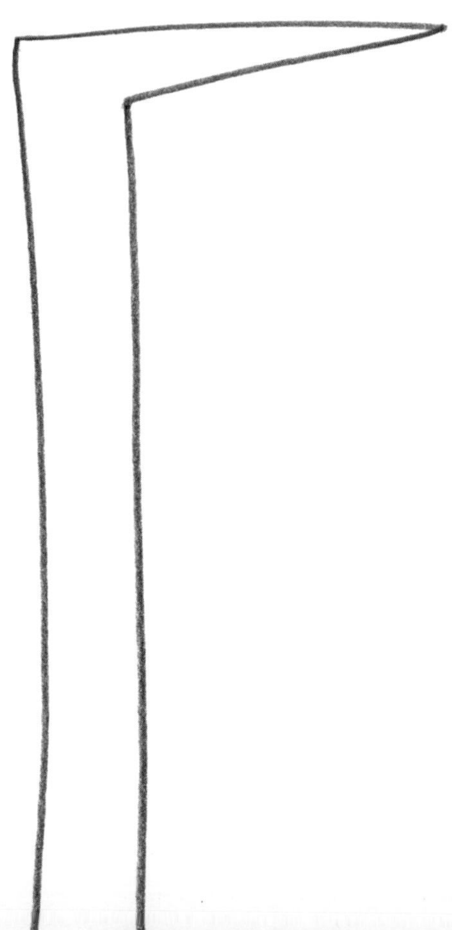

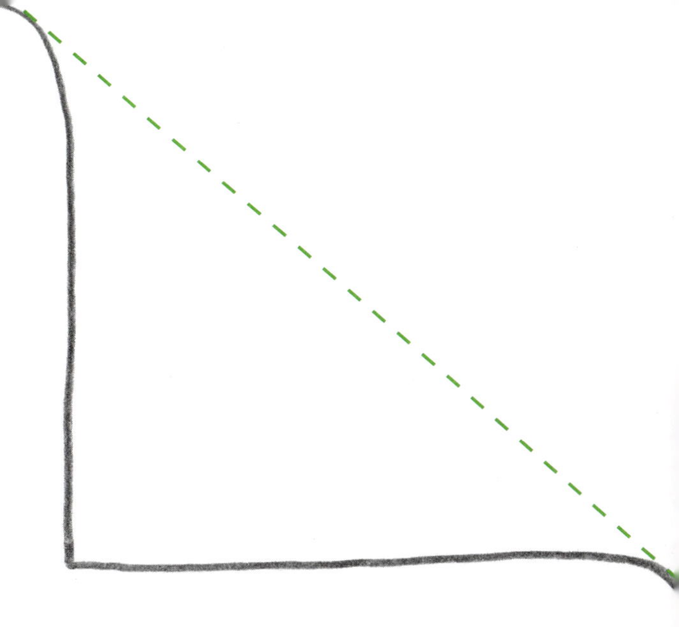

A folded piece of paper is already a spatial object.

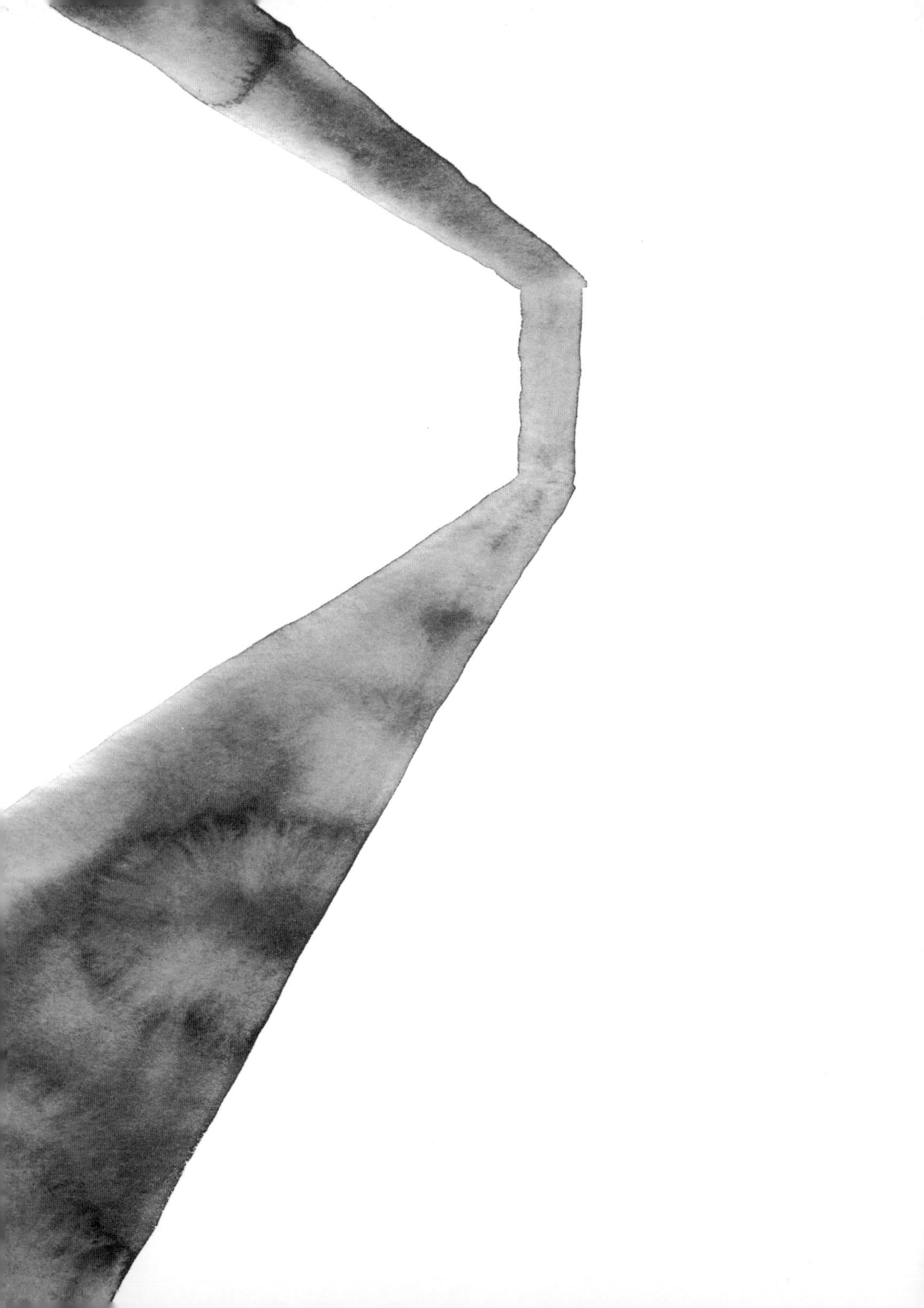

The more skewed the lines, the more sculptural the drawing.

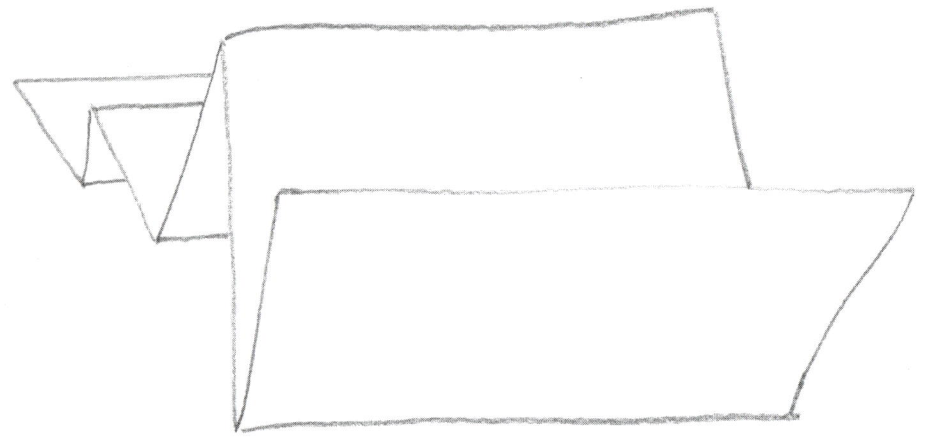

Folded areas are not completely visible
because of the overlaps.

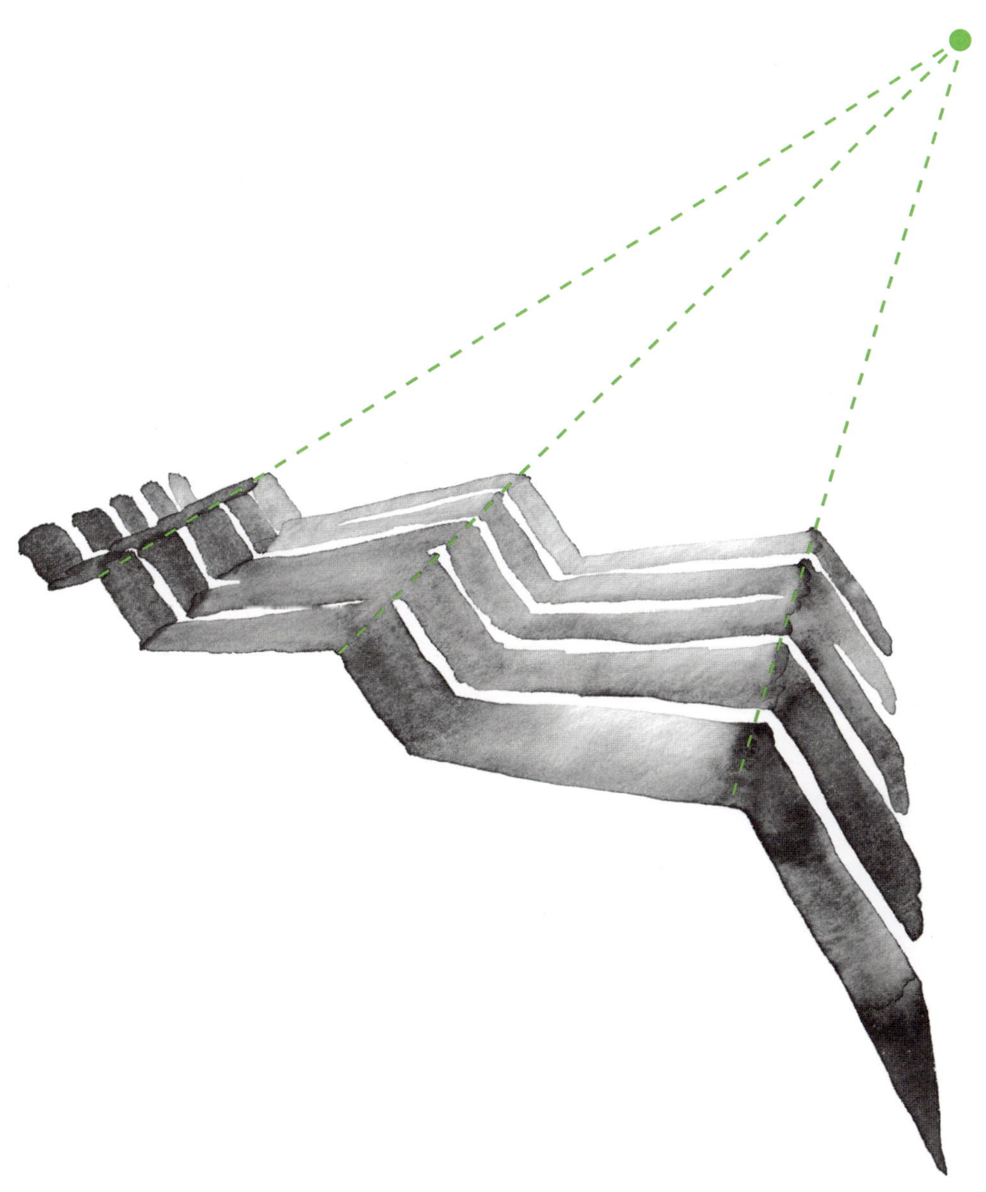

The folded edges are not parallel to the drawing plane because they meet at the vanishing point (see page 64).

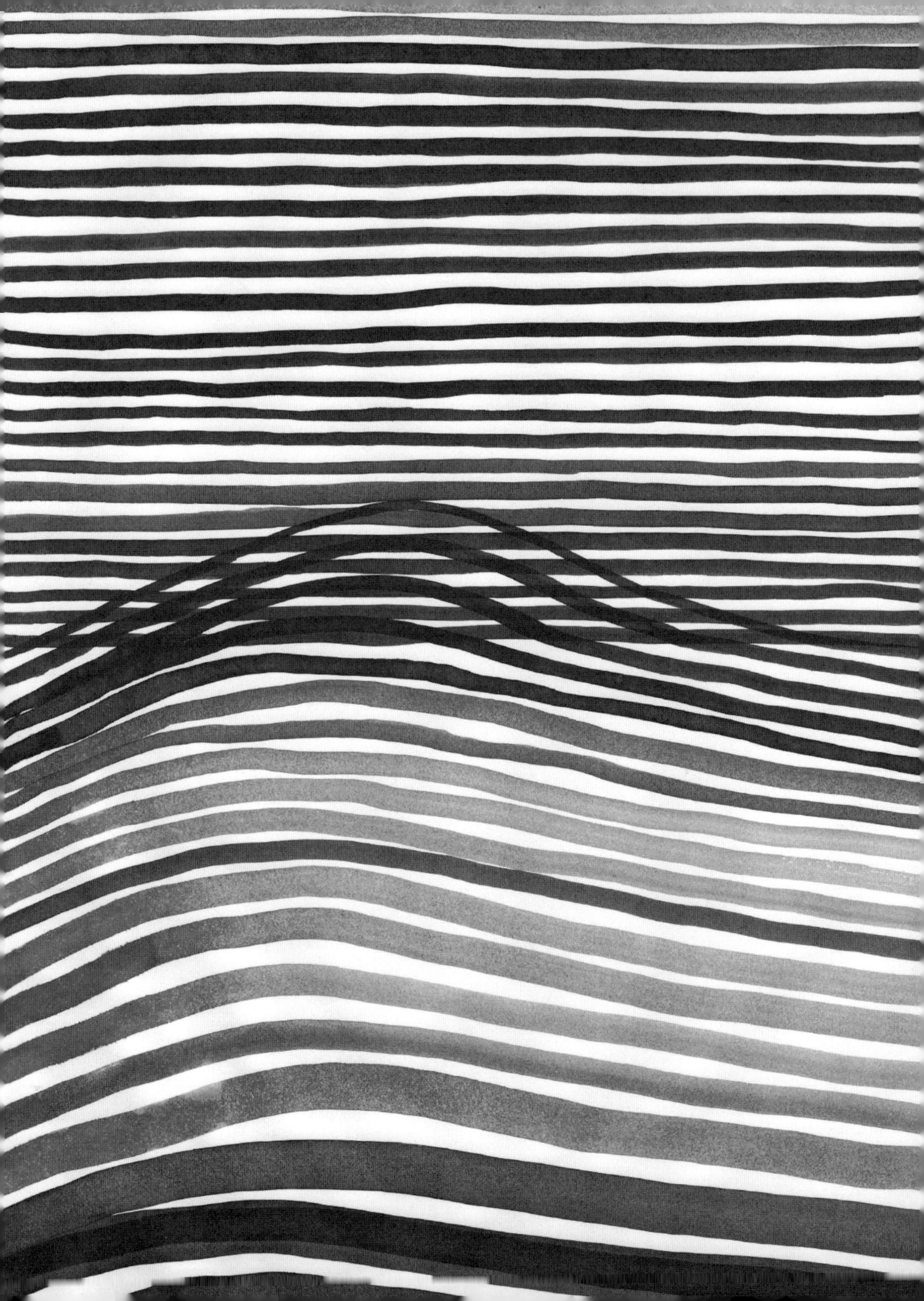

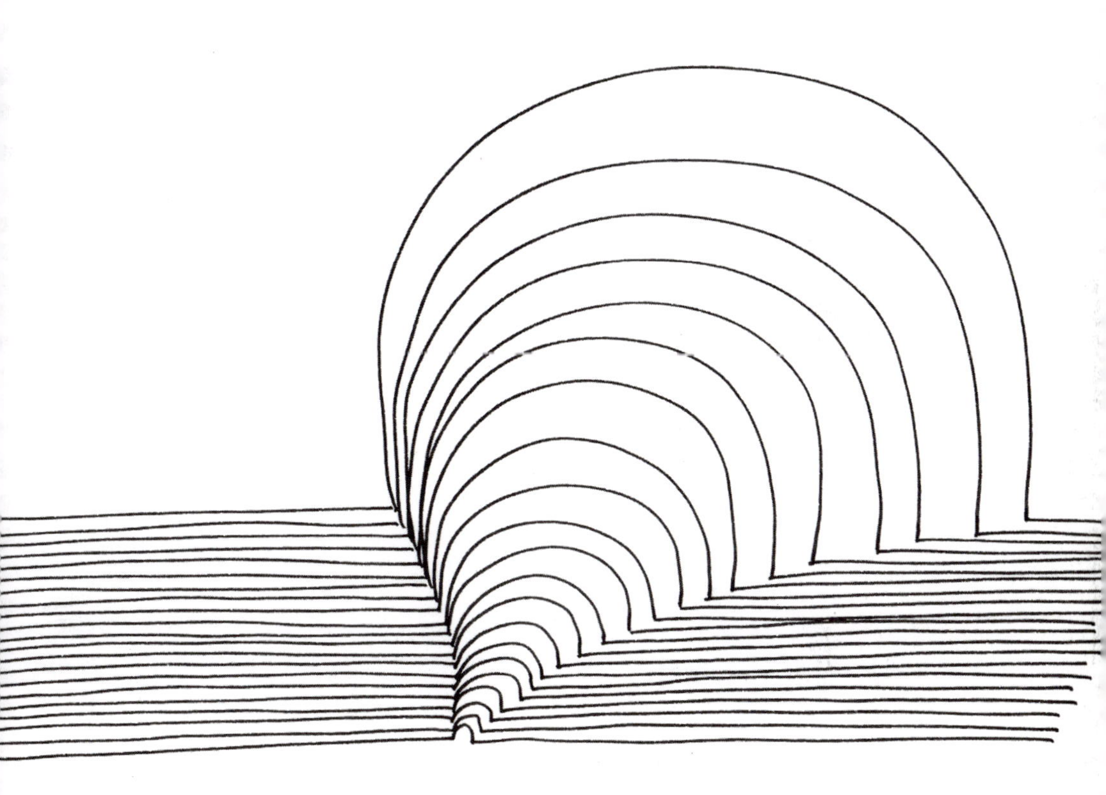

Waves take as much space as they need.

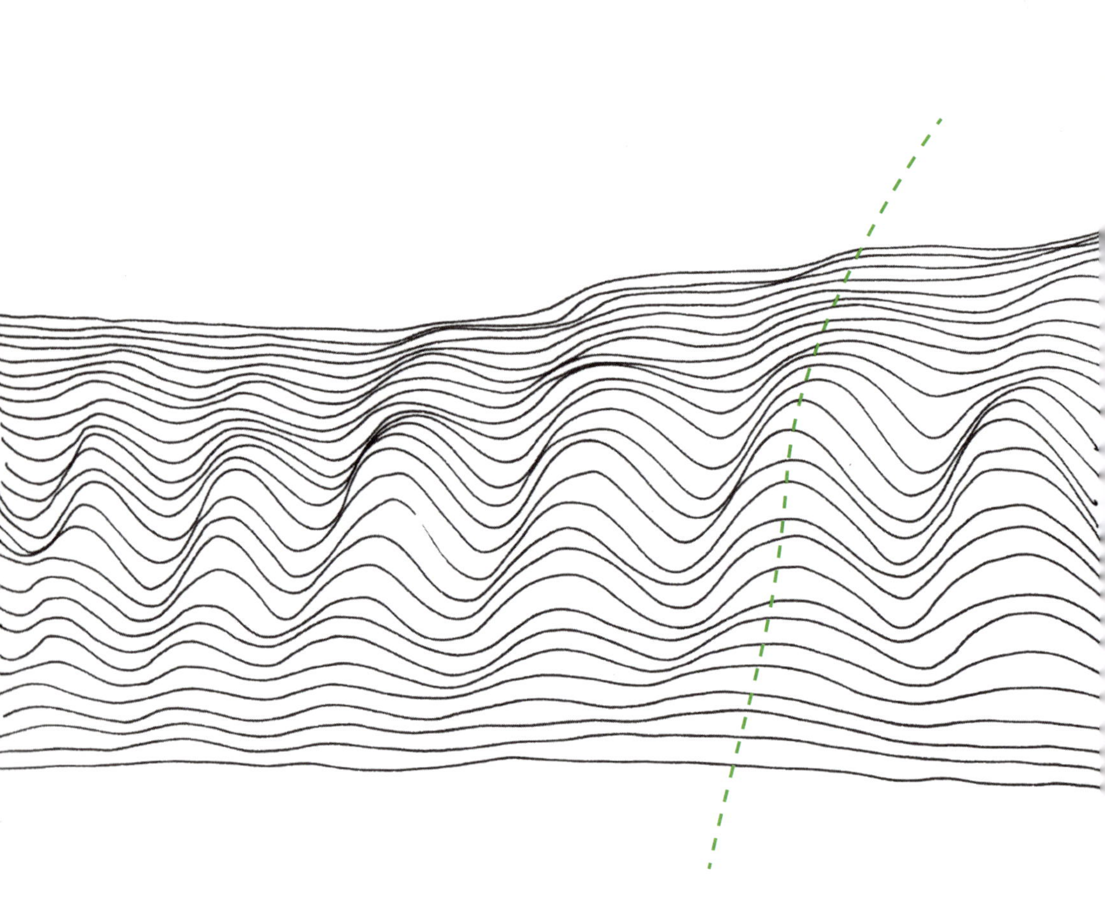

Wave lines are repeated in a consistent fashion.

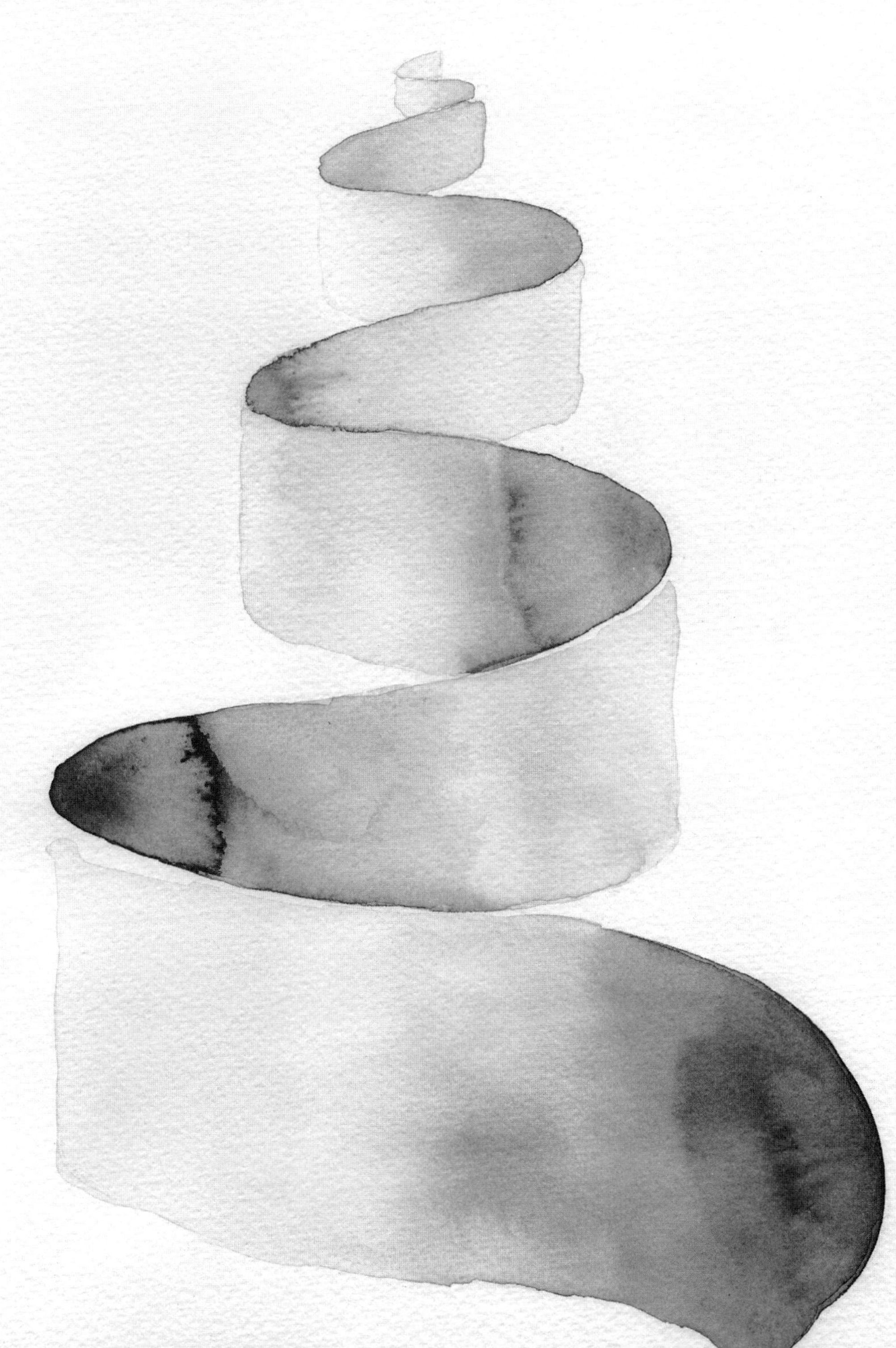

4. Vanishing Points

When looking at railroad tracks, it seems the tracks meet in the distance. This imaginary point is called a *vanishing point*. The alignment of lines toward one or multiple vanishing points is an effective way to create the appearance of three dimensions while drawing architectural subjects, streets, and furniture. Vanishing lines are lines that move away from the observer and meet at one point, even though, in reality, they're parallel to each other, such as a building's balconies and windows, street edges, or table edges. In addition, constant shapes and the distances between them become smaller the farther away they are.

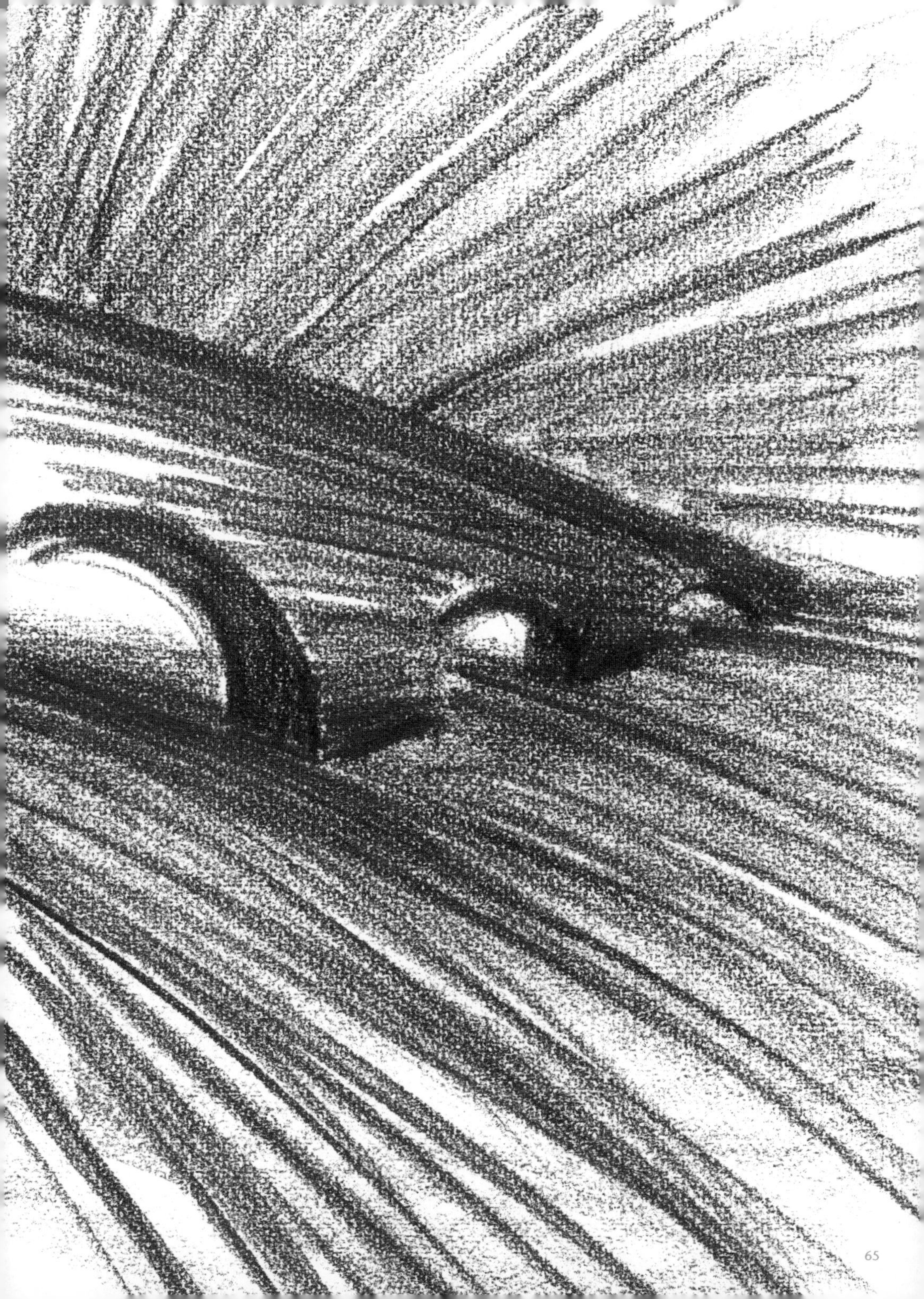

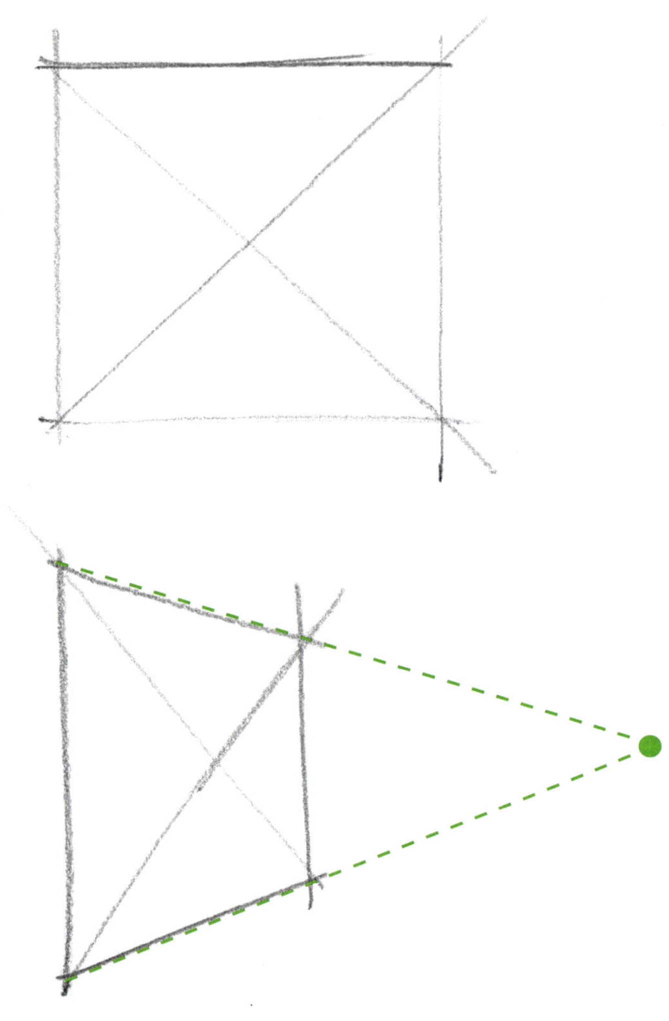

A square becomes a trapezoid.

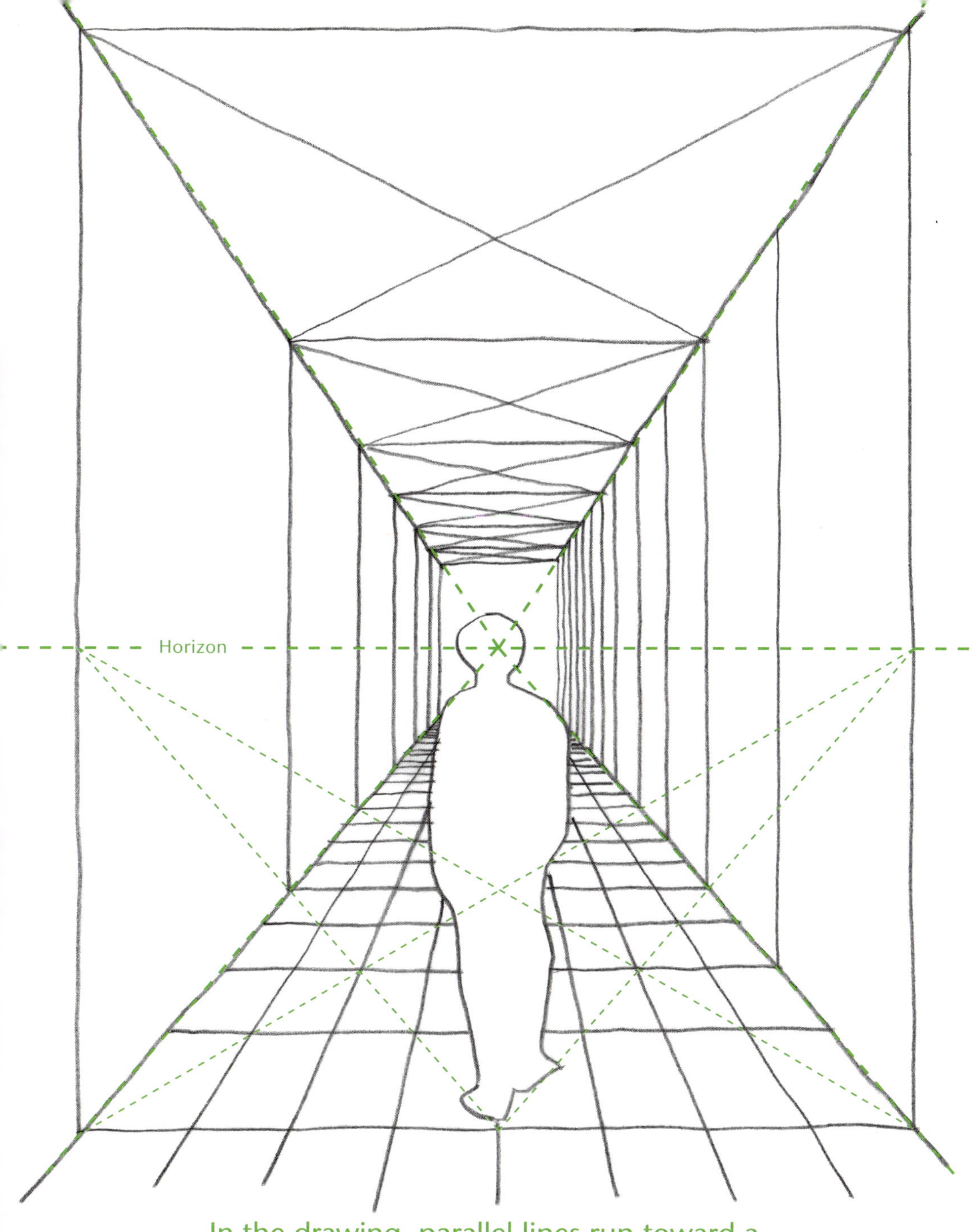

In the drawing, parallel lines run toward a
vanishing point at the eye level of the viewer.

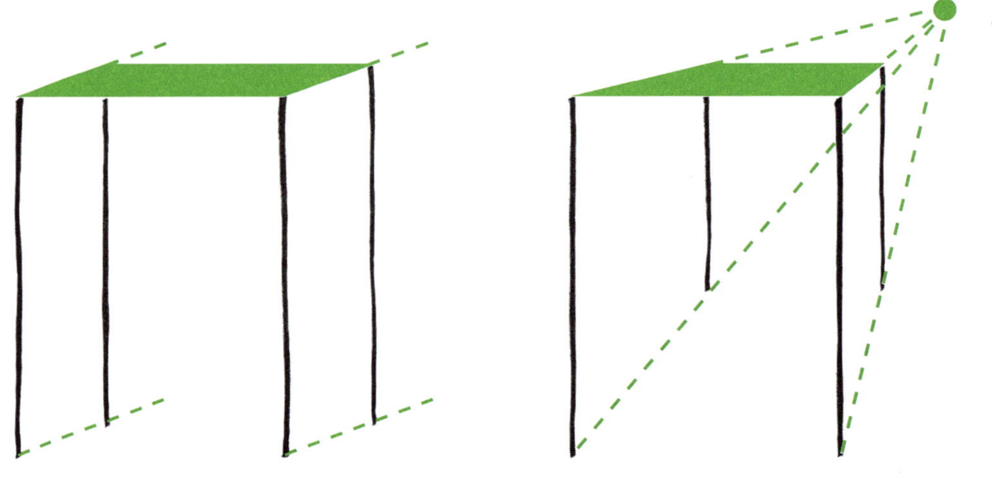

Left: Parallel perspective—the diagonals are parallel.
Right: Vanishing point perspective—
the diagonals all lead to a vanishing point.

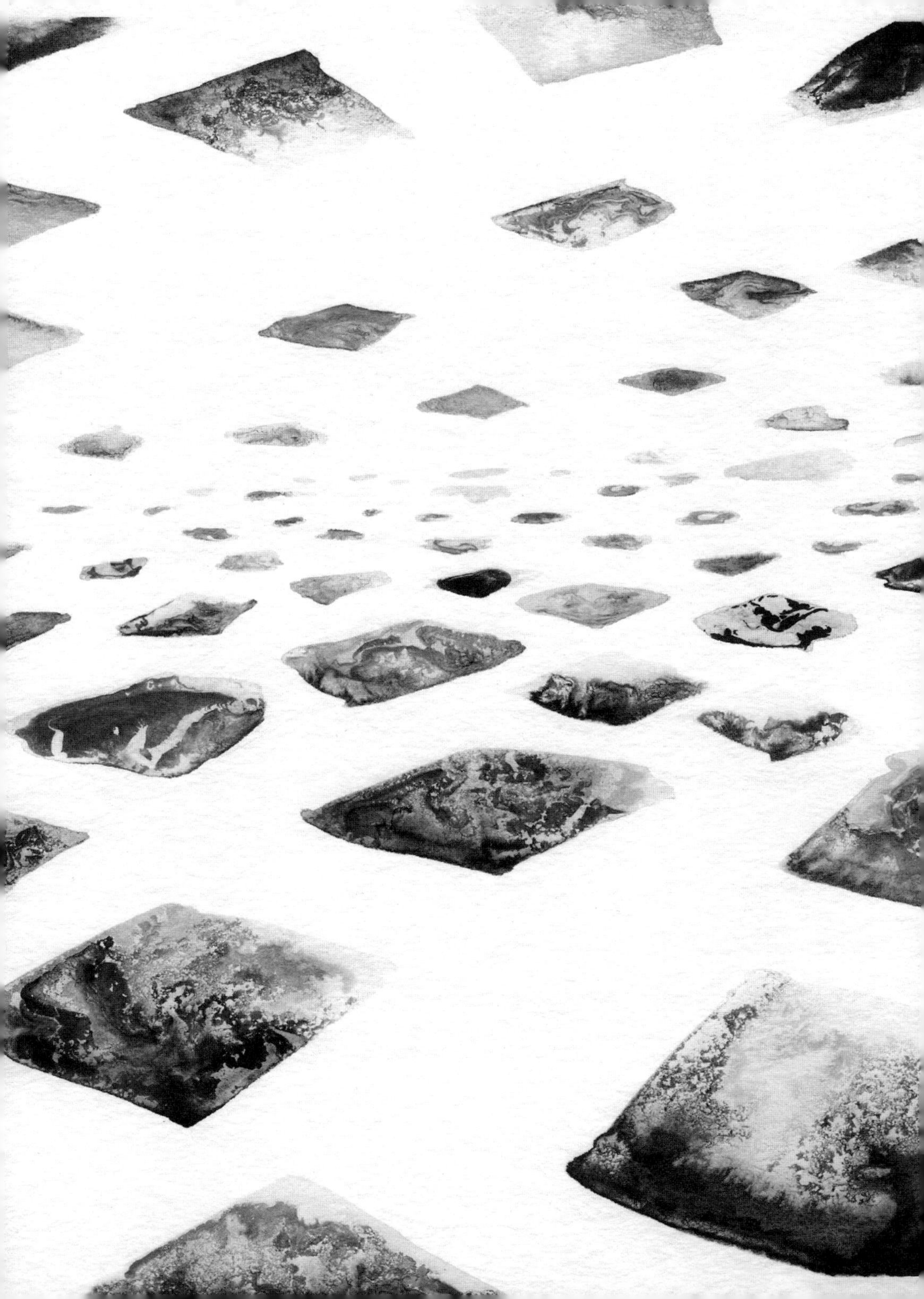

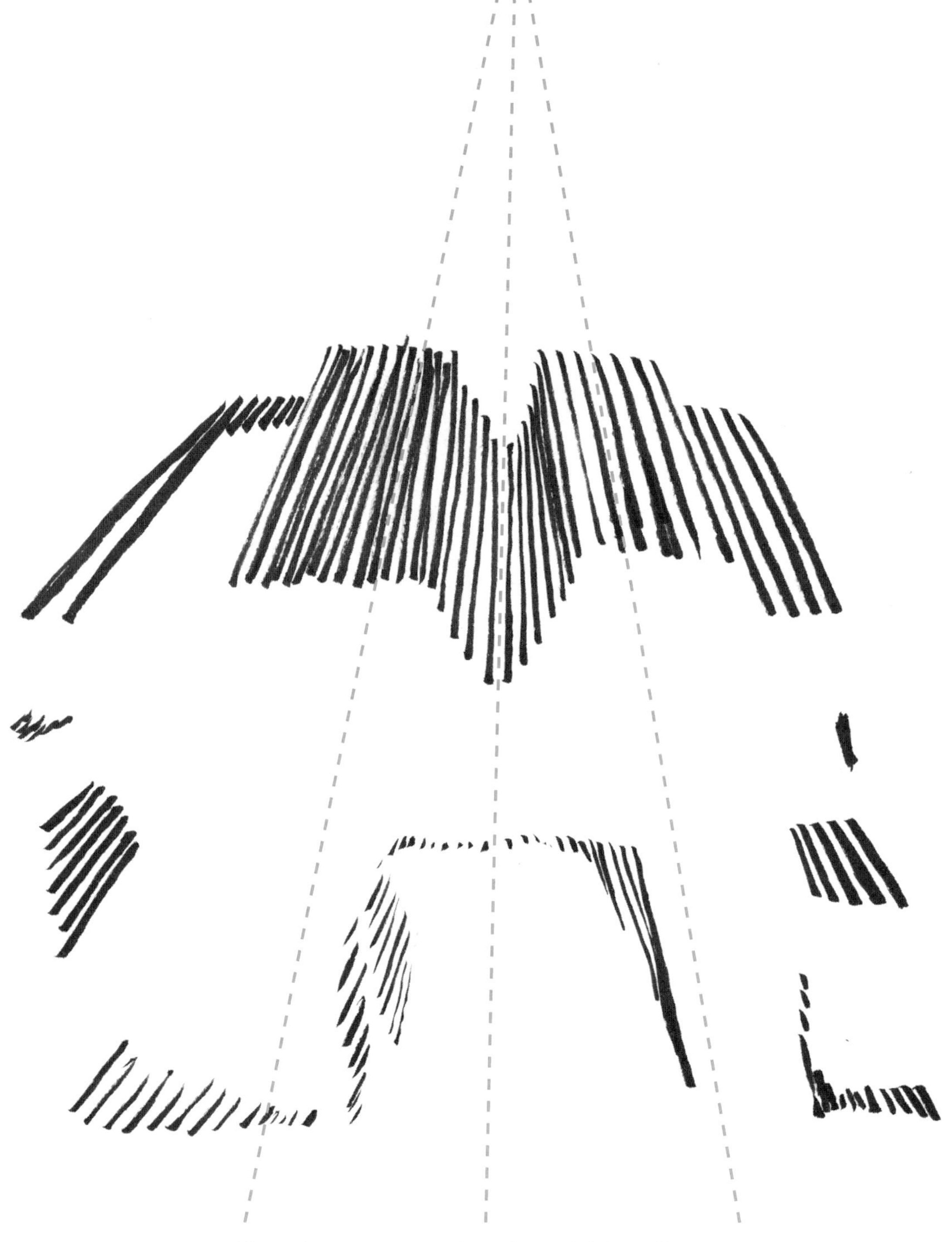Here is an example of vanishing lines.

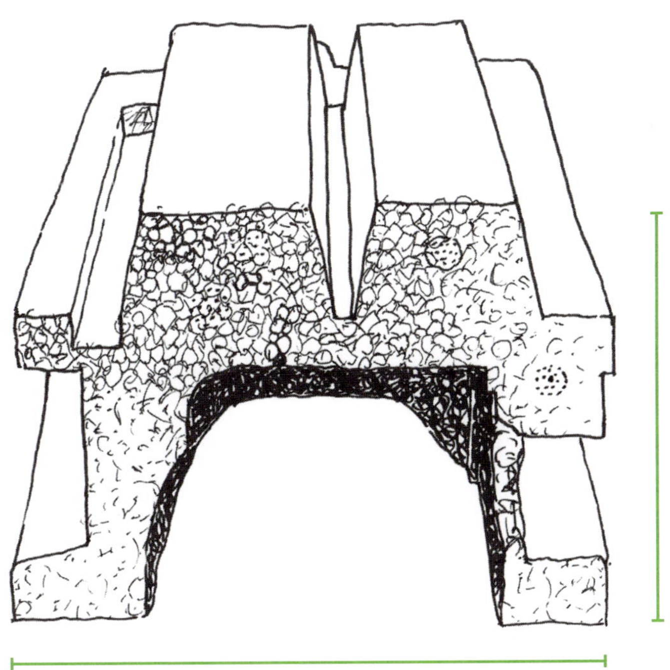

The cross section is flat like a panel and
parallel to the image plane.

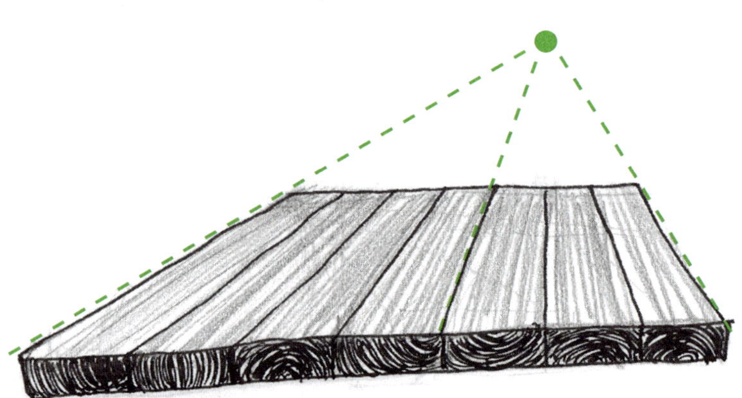

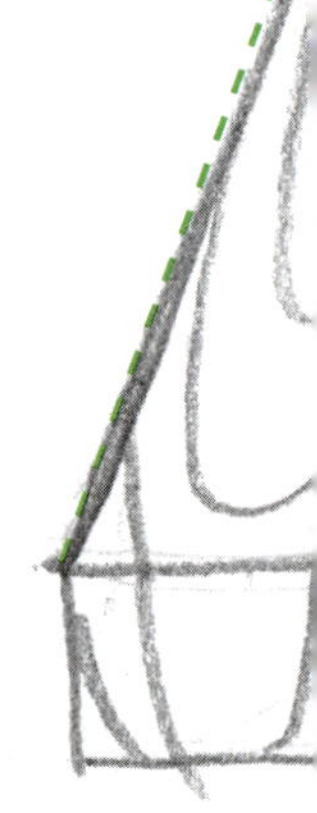

A worm's-eye perspective is when an object is viewed from below with a low vanishing point.

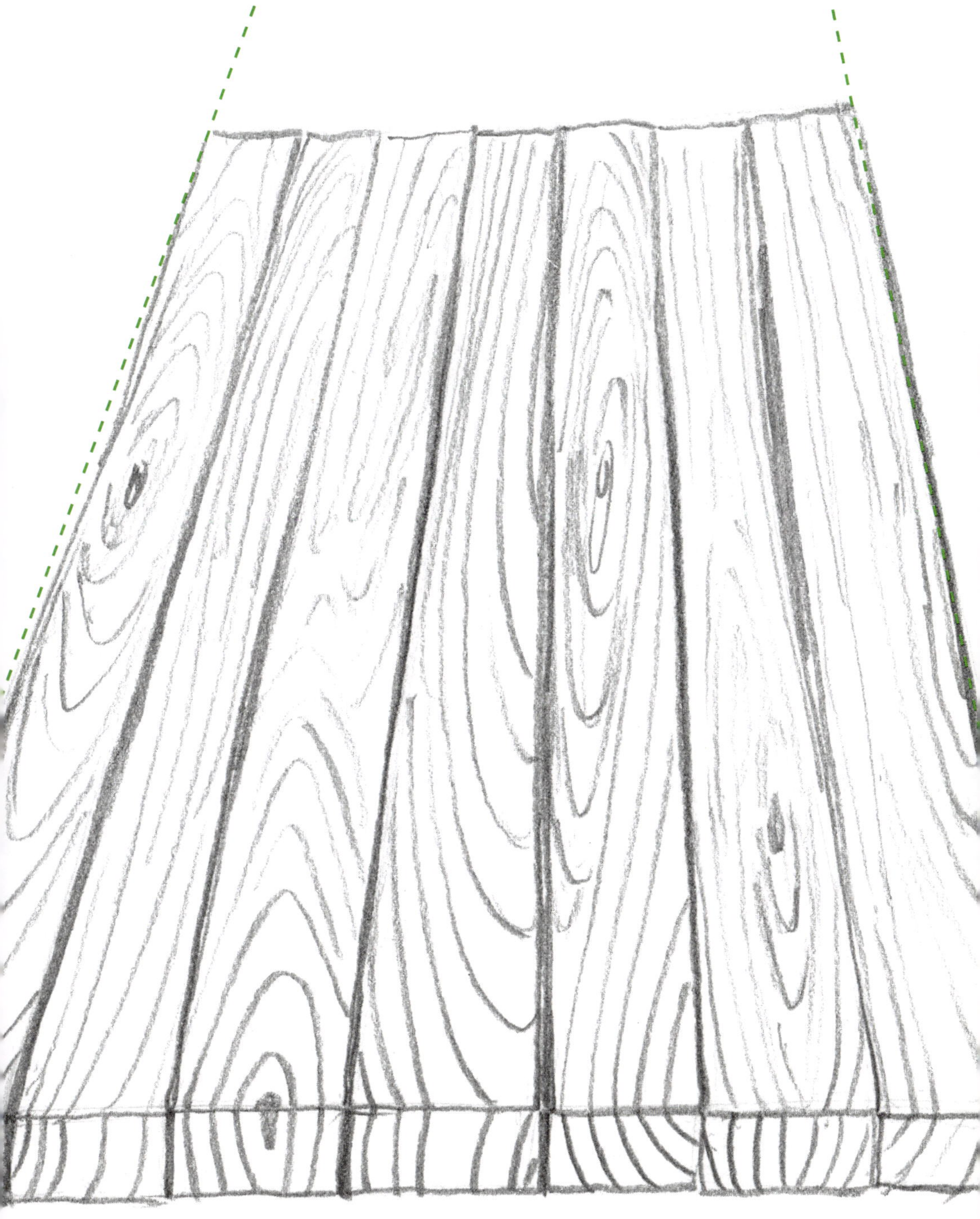

A bird's-eye perspective is when an object is viewed from
above, with a high vanishing point.

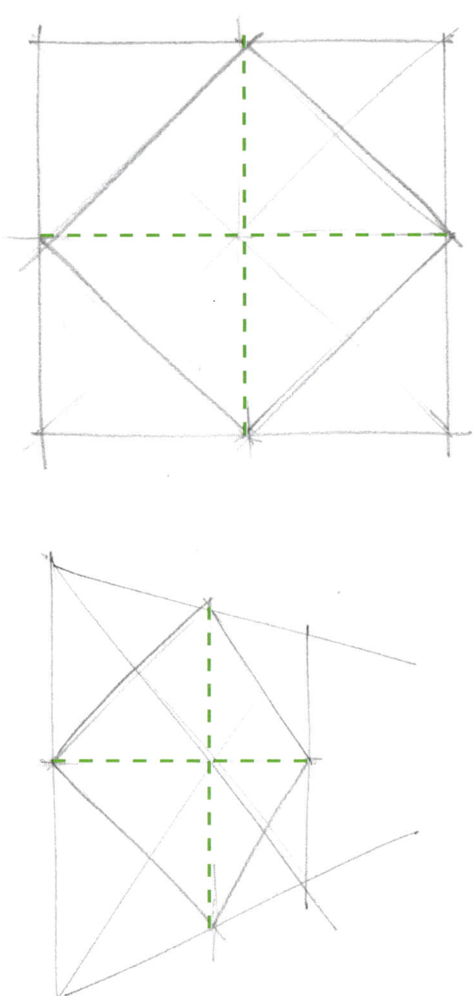

The center point of an area is found at the intersection of the diagonals. In perspective, the center follows the diagonal lines. In the example above, the center point moves farther back, as shown by the intersecting diagonals.

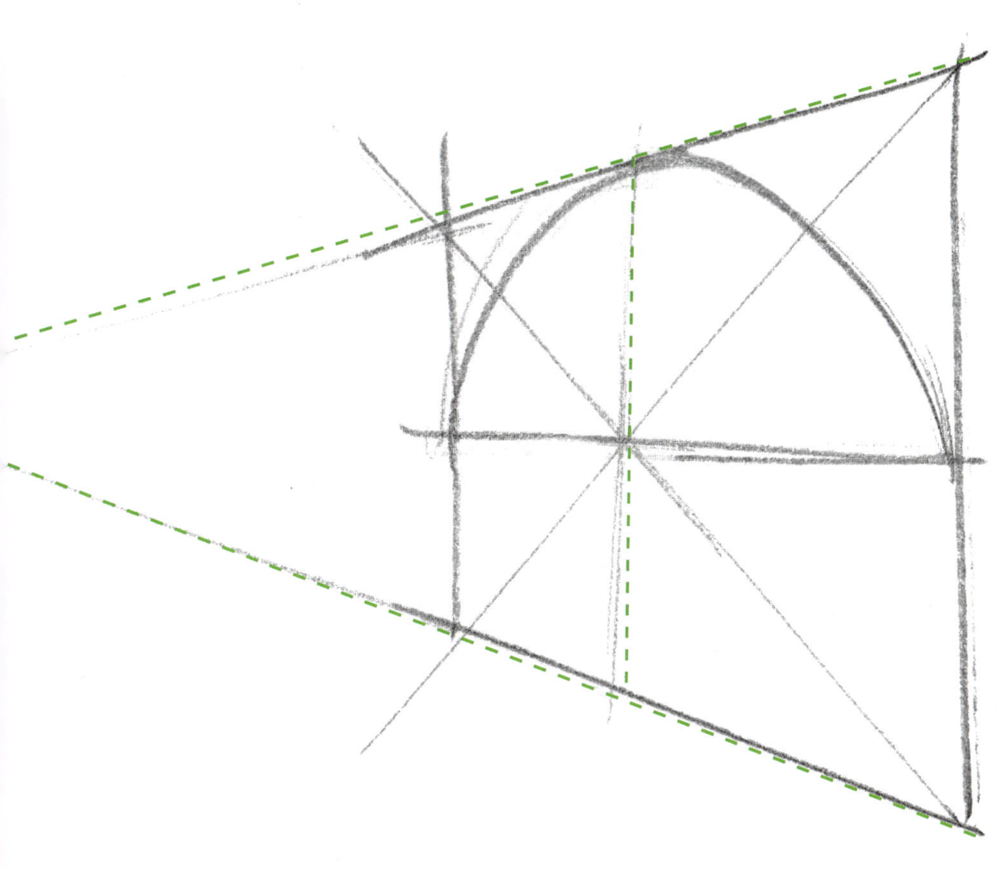

The intersection of the diagonals can also be useful when
drawing an object with curved lines in perspective.
The intersection above marks the vertex of the arch.

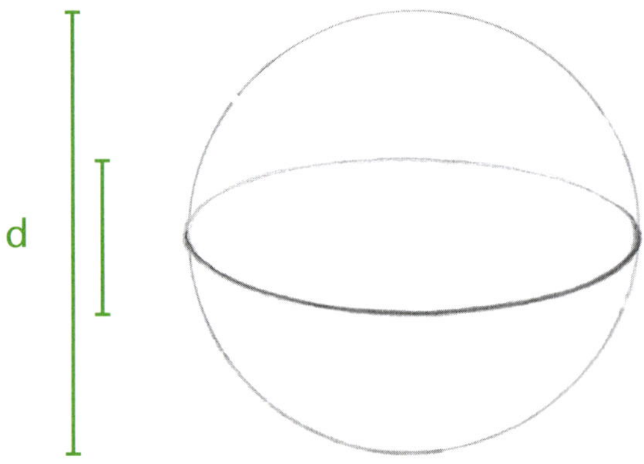

A circle becomes an ellipse.

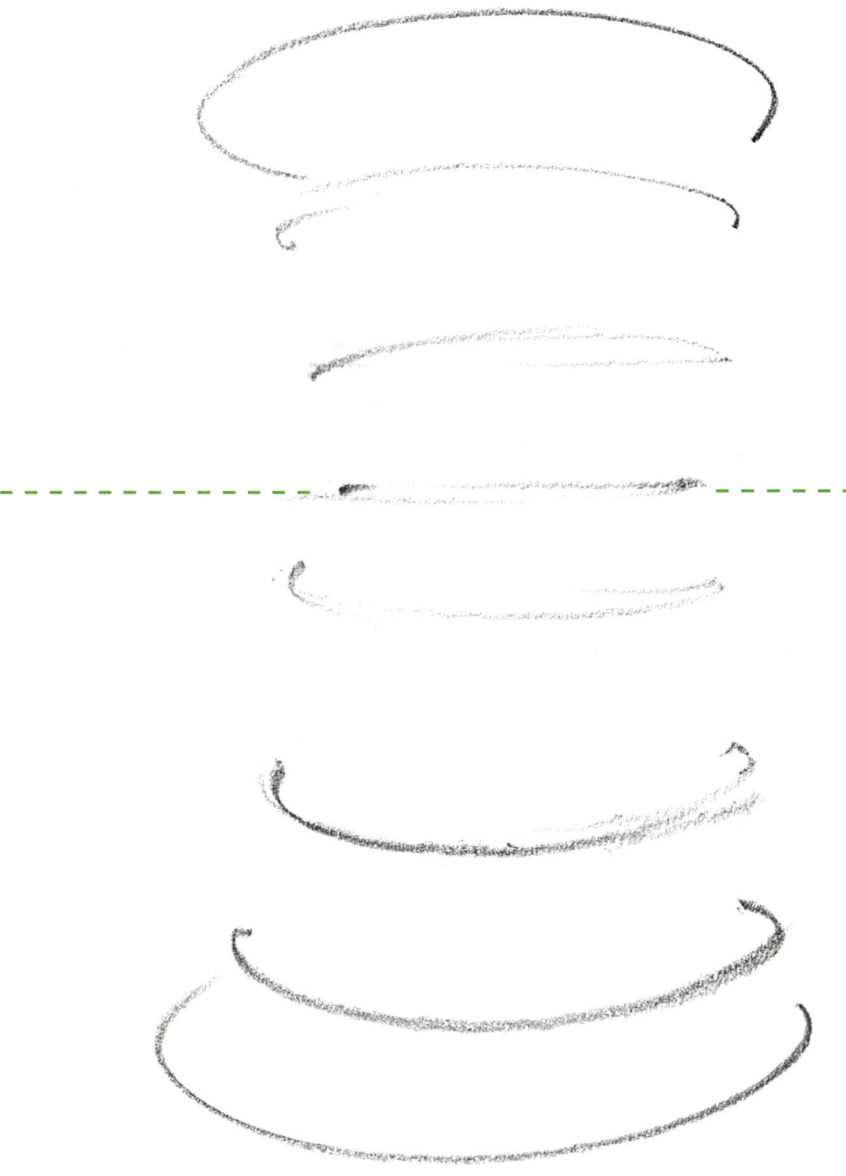

The rounding becomes shallower the closer it gets to eye level.

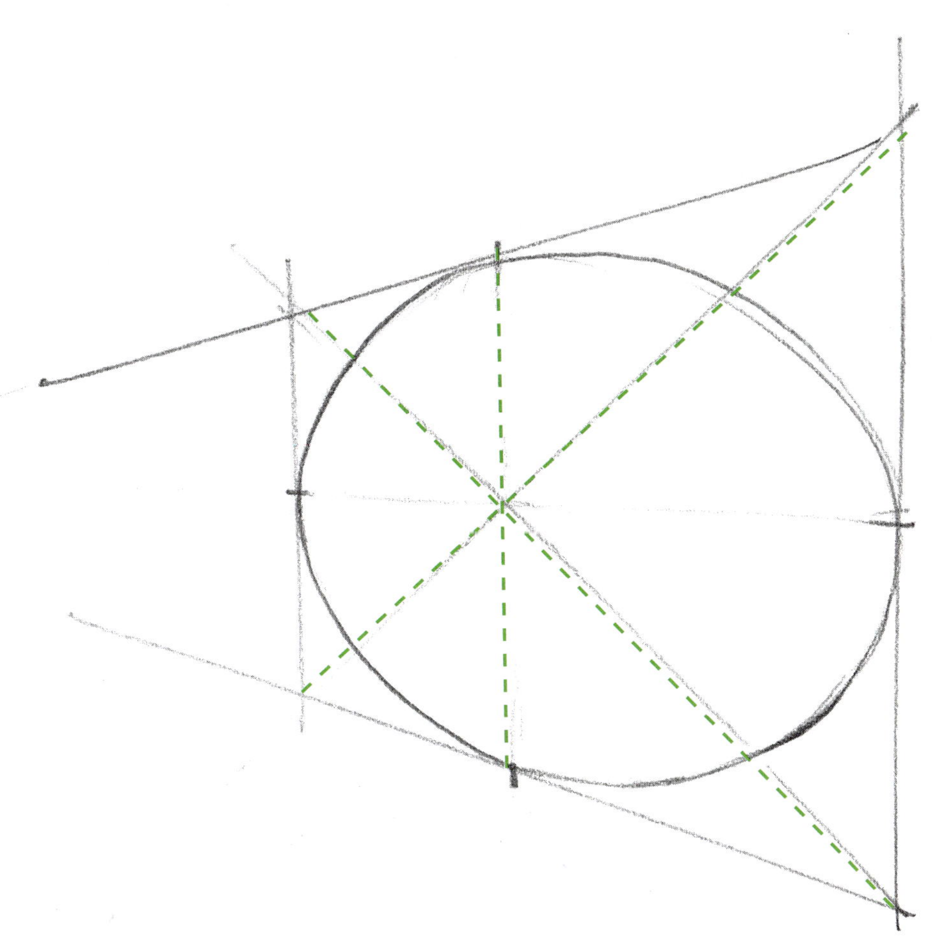

To construct an ellipse, first draw a trapezoid and then draw
the diagonals from corner to corner, as shown above. Once
you locate the center, you can find the points of the ellipse
that touch the trapezoid.

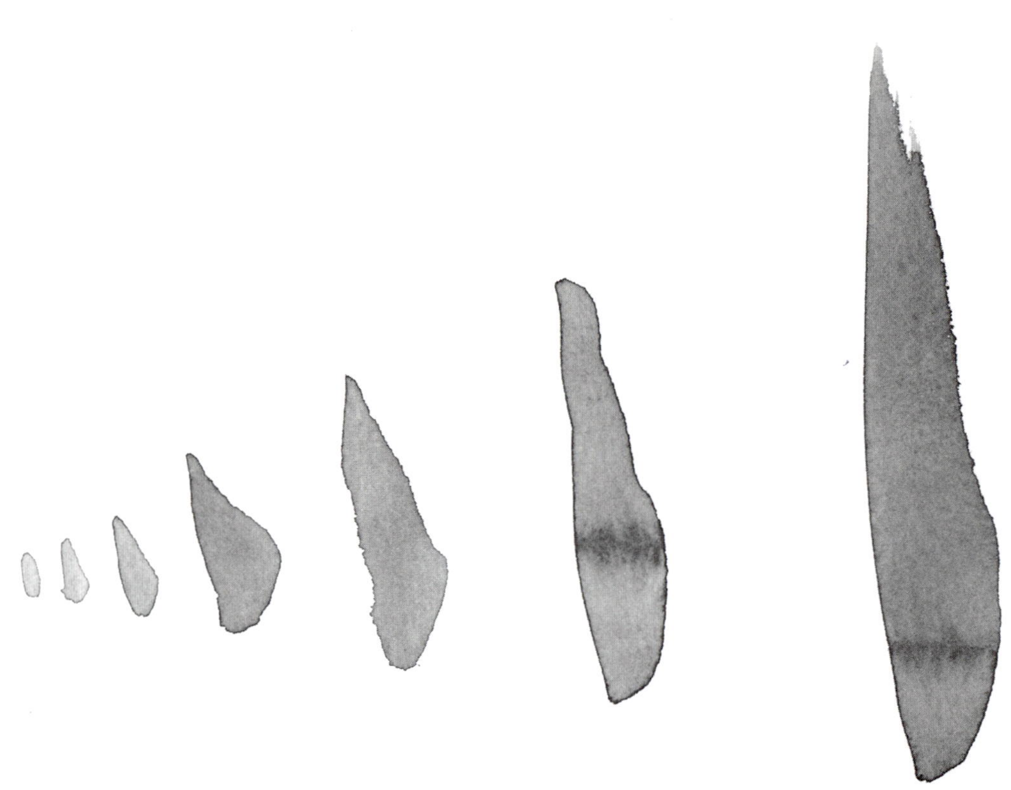

For one-point perspective, the distance between
the shapes gets smaller and smaller the closer it
gets to the vanishing point. It is best to draw this
while standing, to get more of an overview.

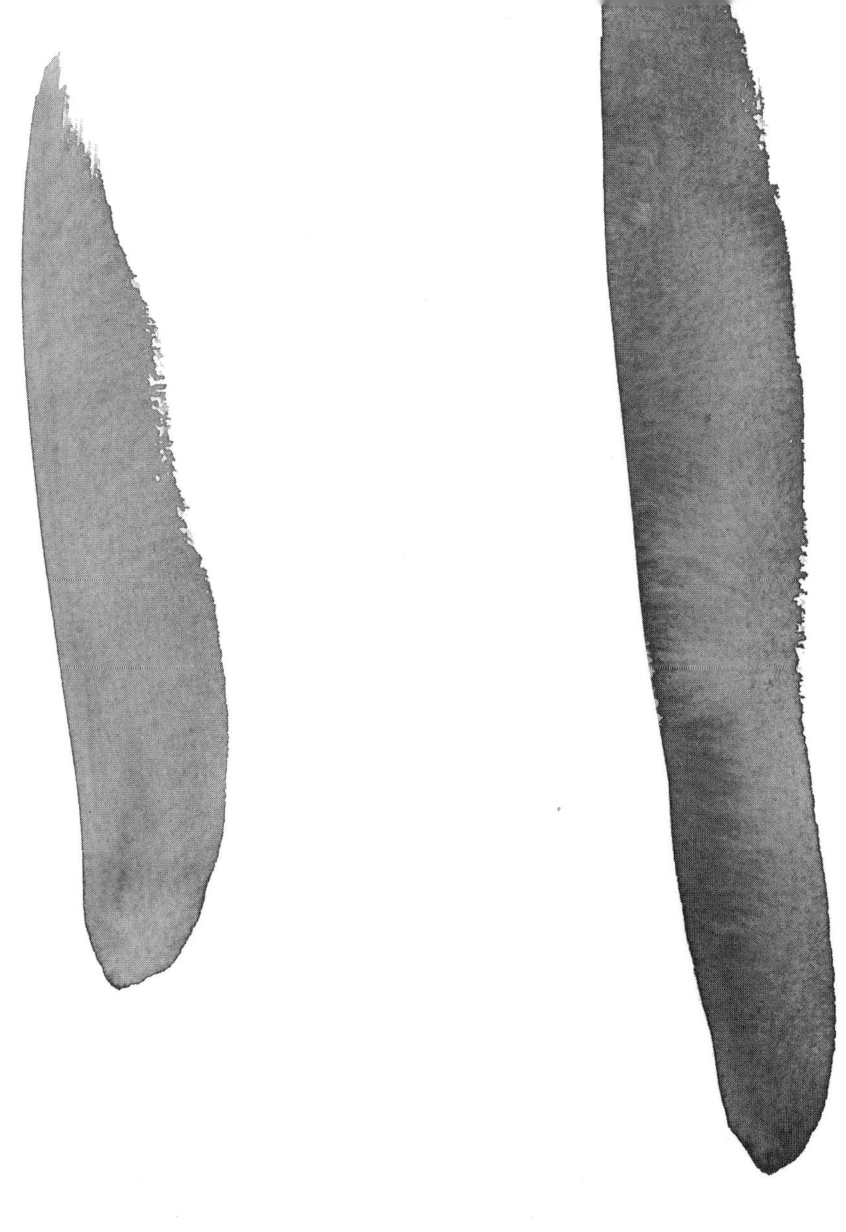

How much do the successive gaps between lines become
smaller the closer they get to the vanishing point? You can
guess, but you'll be more precise by using diagonal lines.
Lightly draw a diagonal line across the largest gap, as shown.
(You'll erase the diagonals when done.) Then bring that line
left, straight across the gap, parallel to the first straight line.
This is the point where the next diagonal line begins.
You can use this quick method when drawing rows
of street lights, storefronts, and trains.

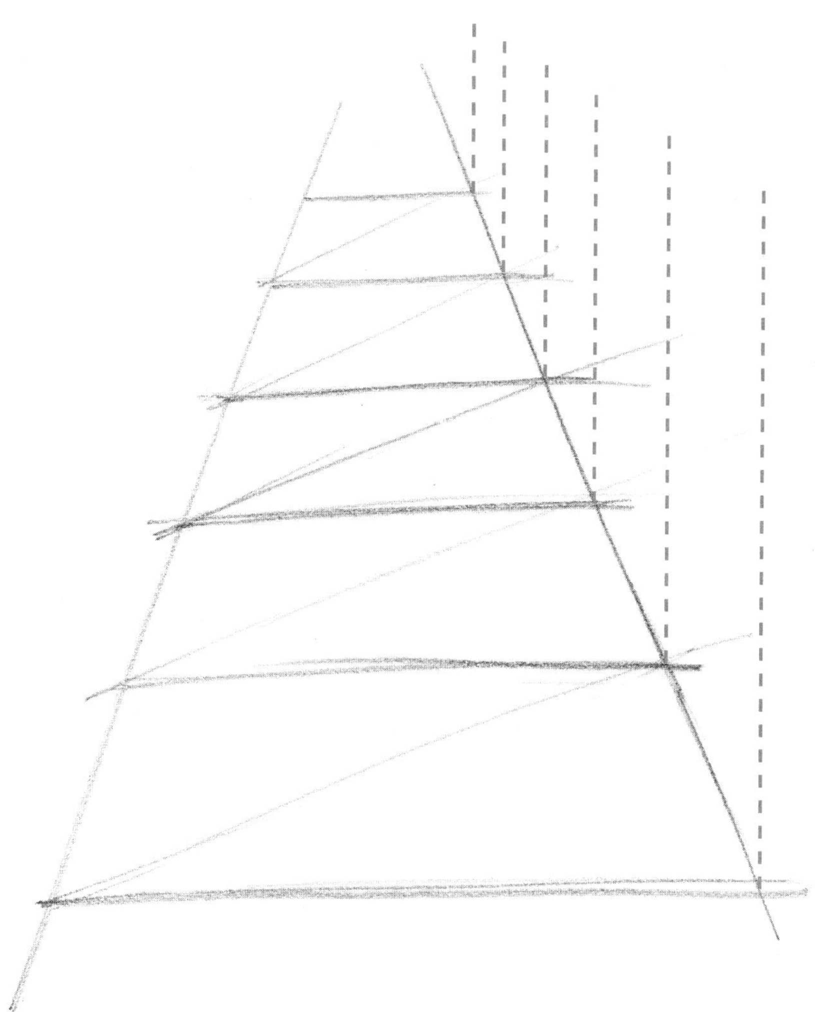

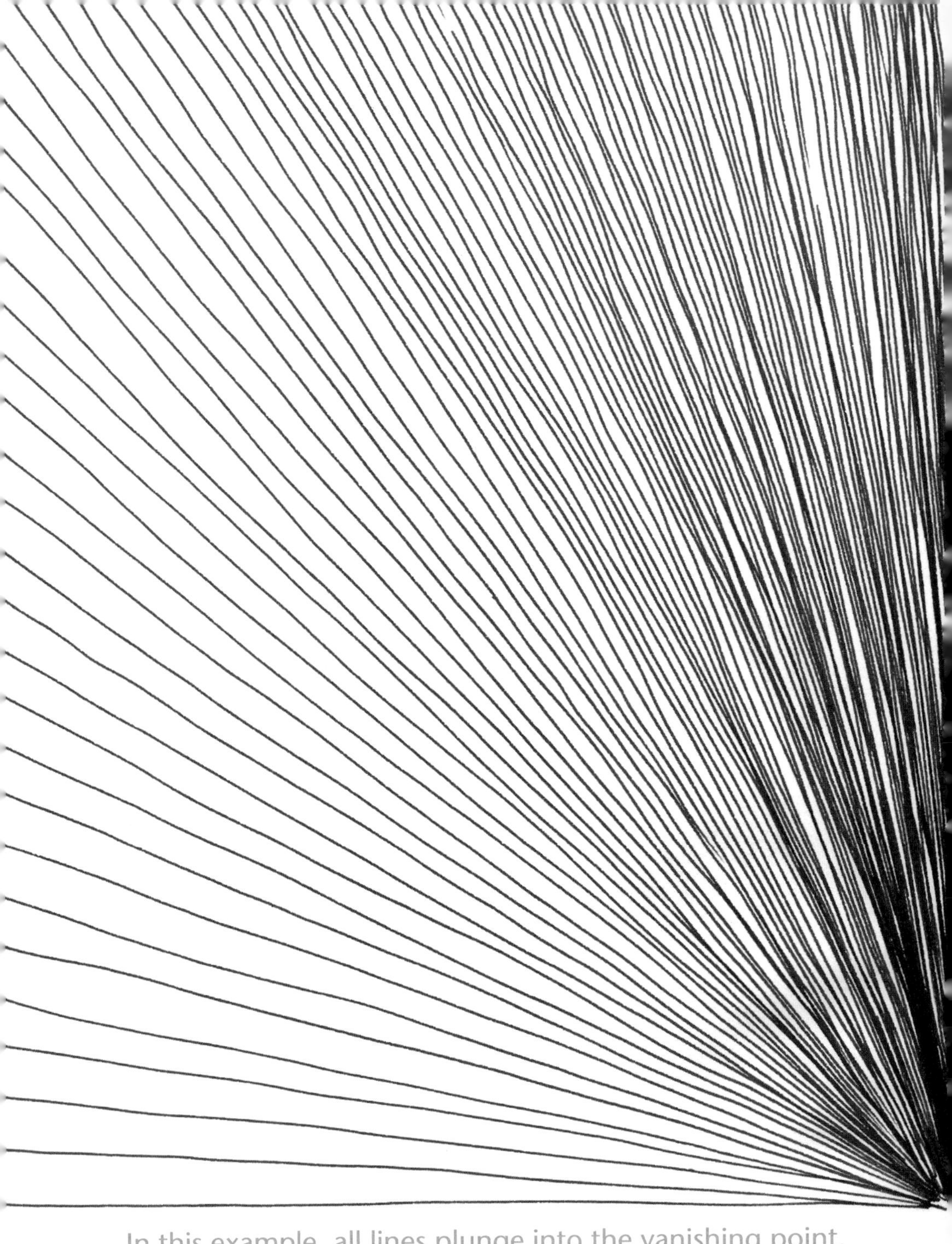

In this example, all lines plunge into the vanishing point.

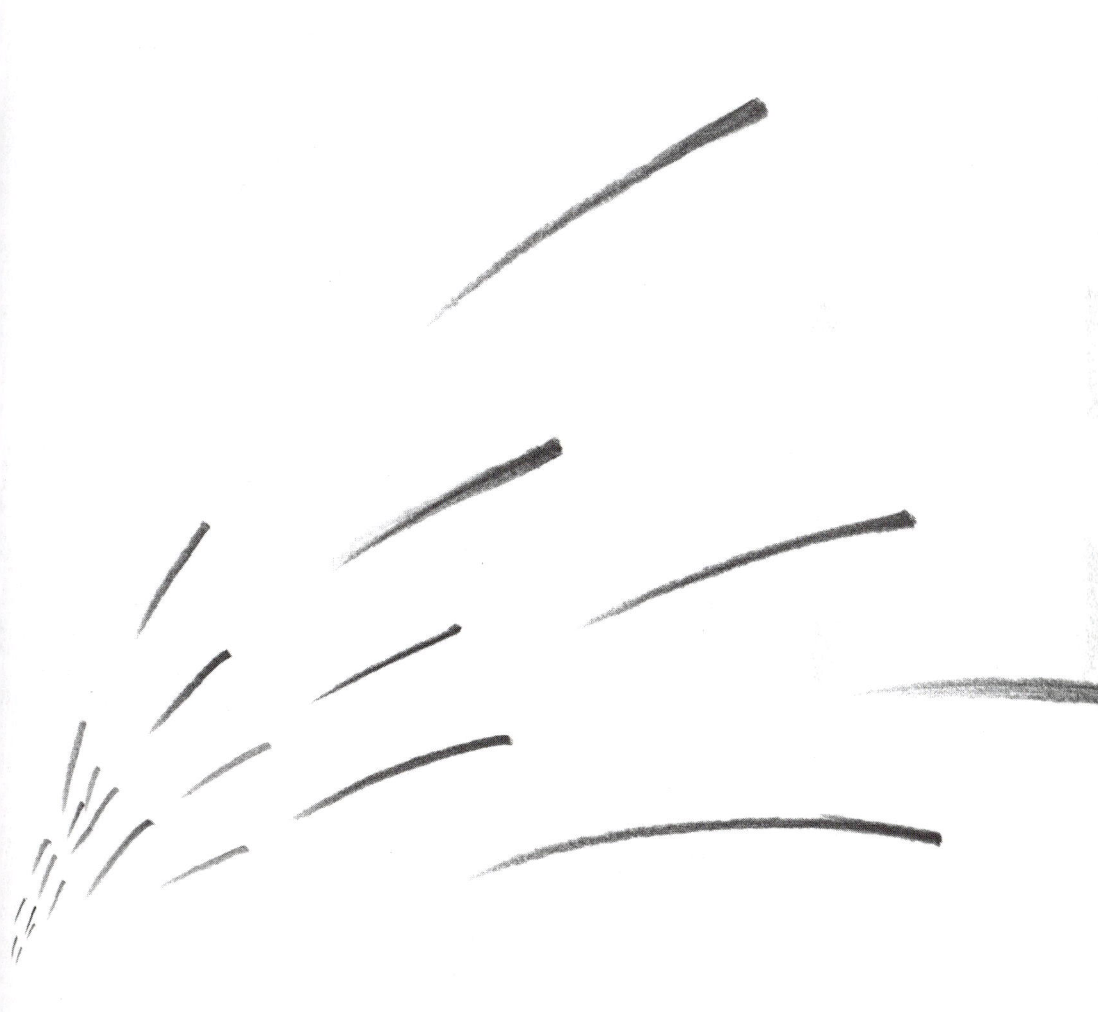

Here the lines move in the
opposite direction in which they're drawn.

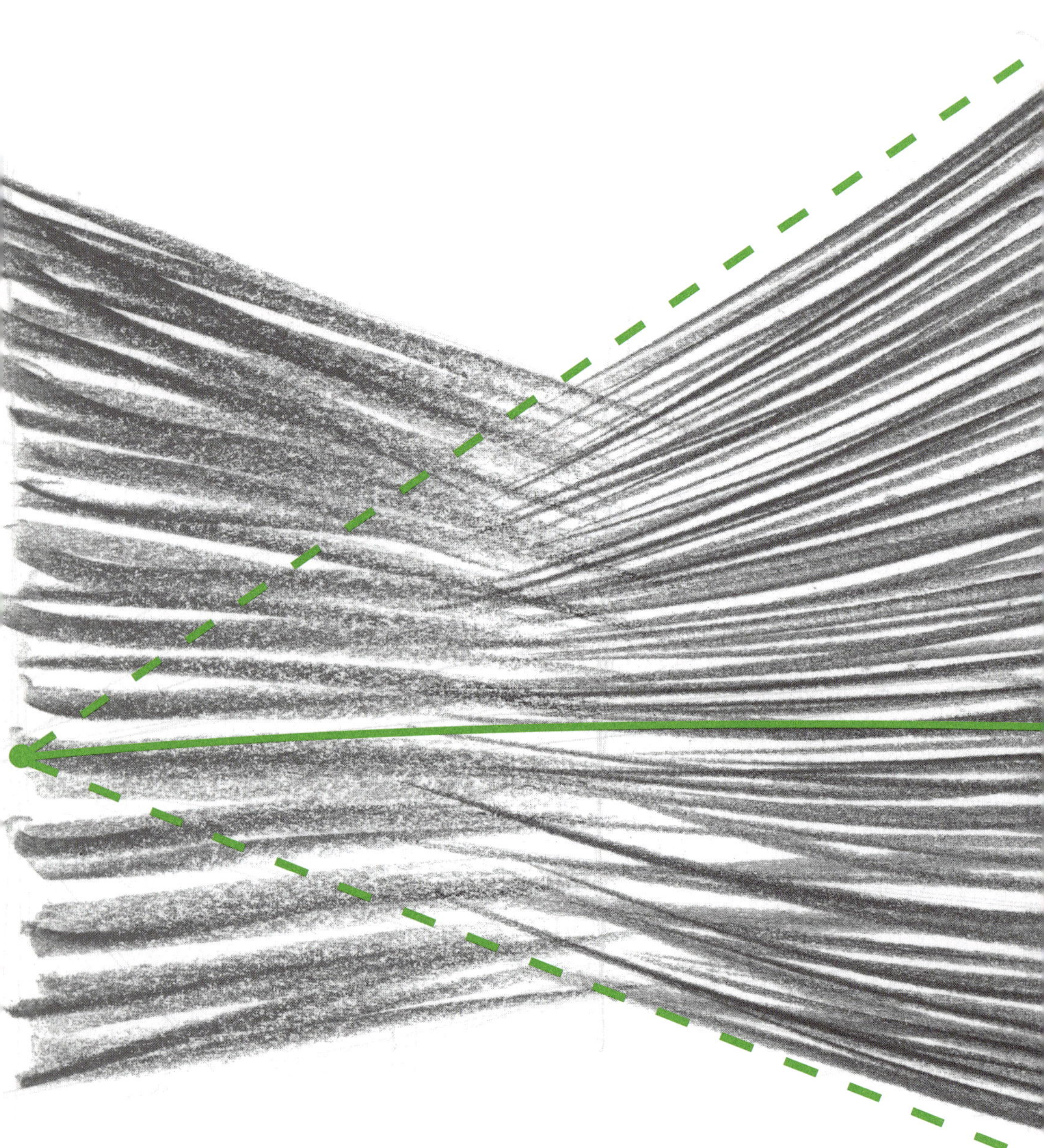

If a rectangular object is turned so that the viewer looks directly at the corner, the image plane that previously showed a parallel front turns into an area with additional vanishing lines.

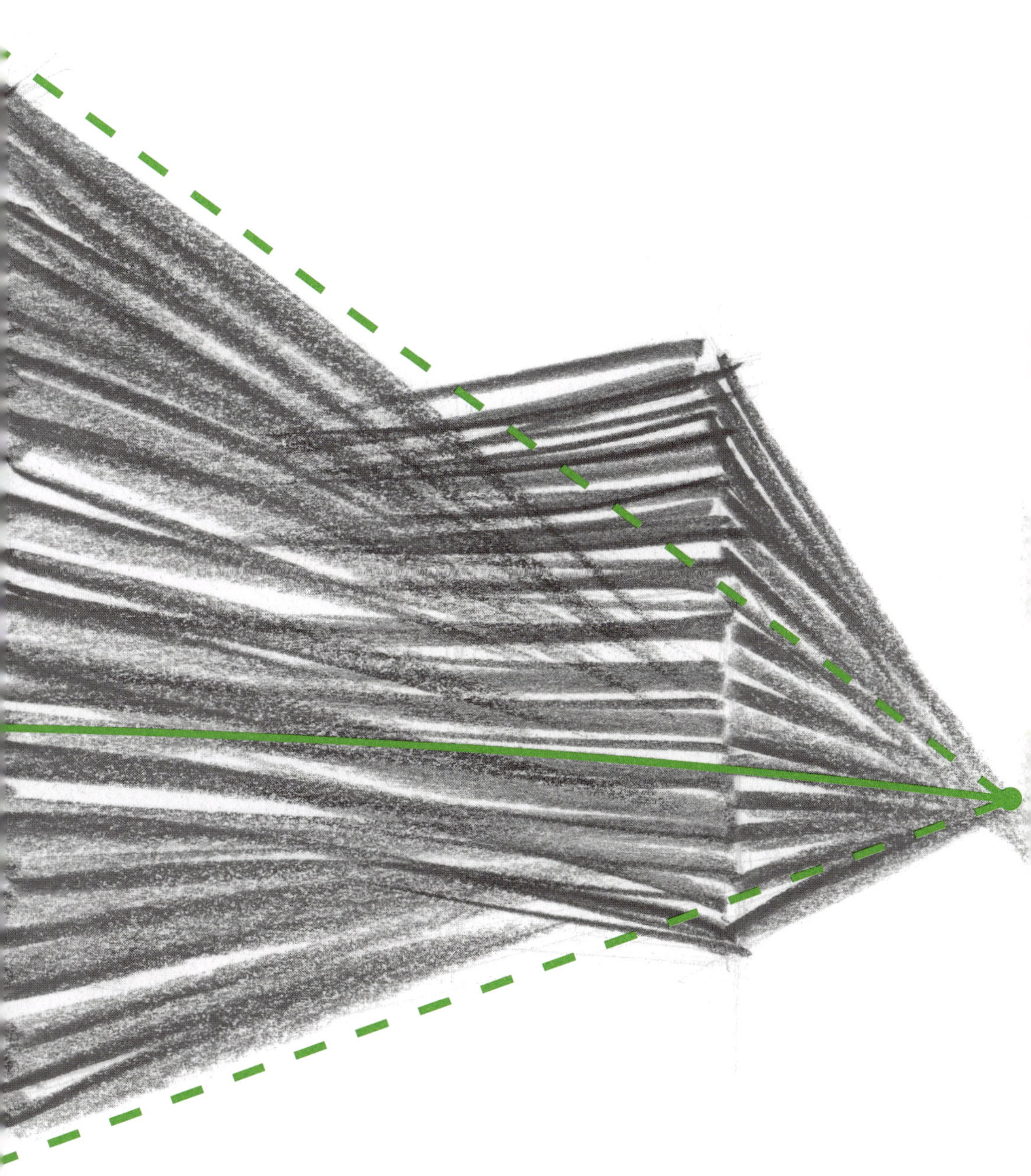

That's how a view of an object with two vanishing points is created. Here they're located at the edges of the paper.

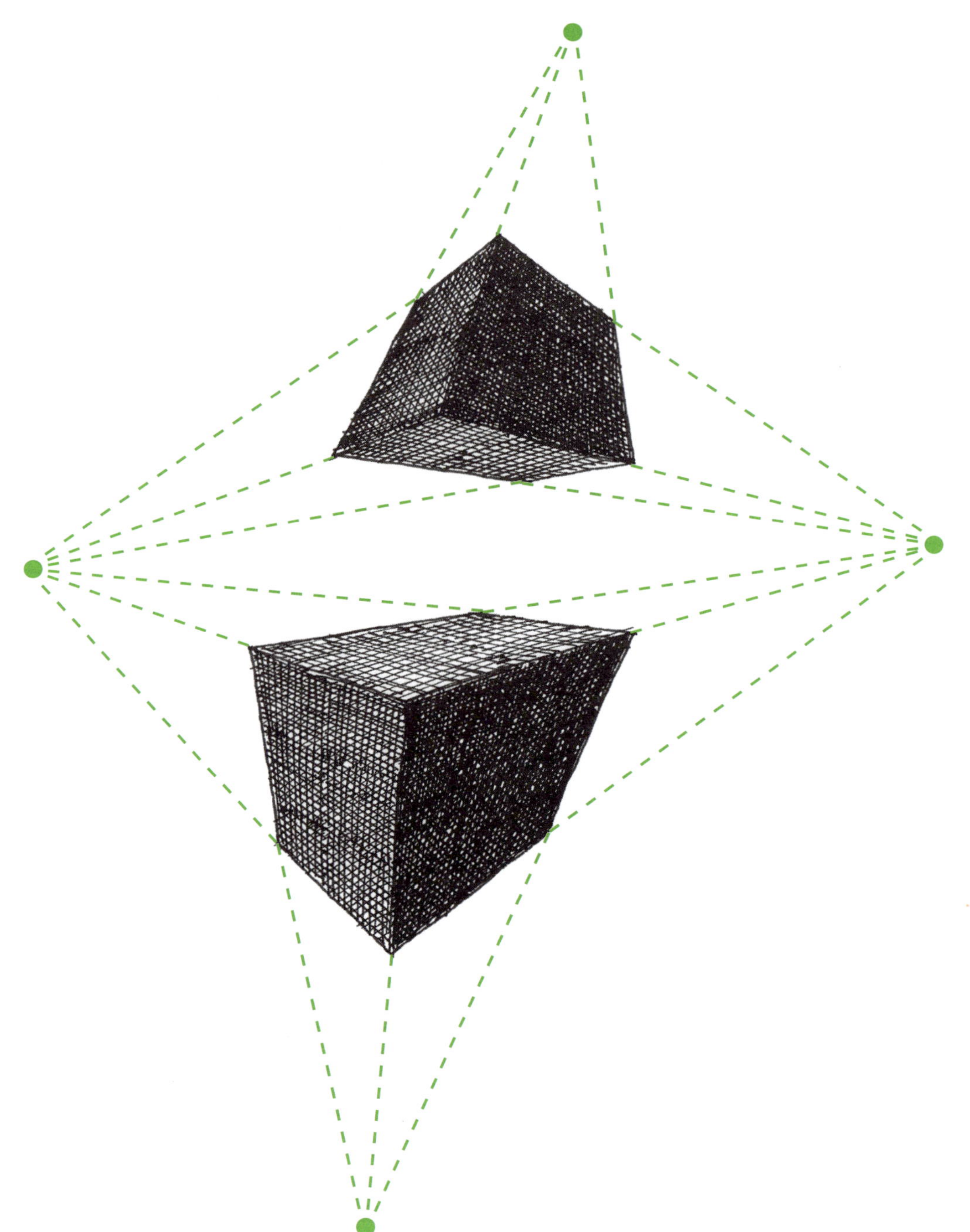

The free placement of the vanishing points gives the illusion
of the cubes—or the viewer—turning and floating.

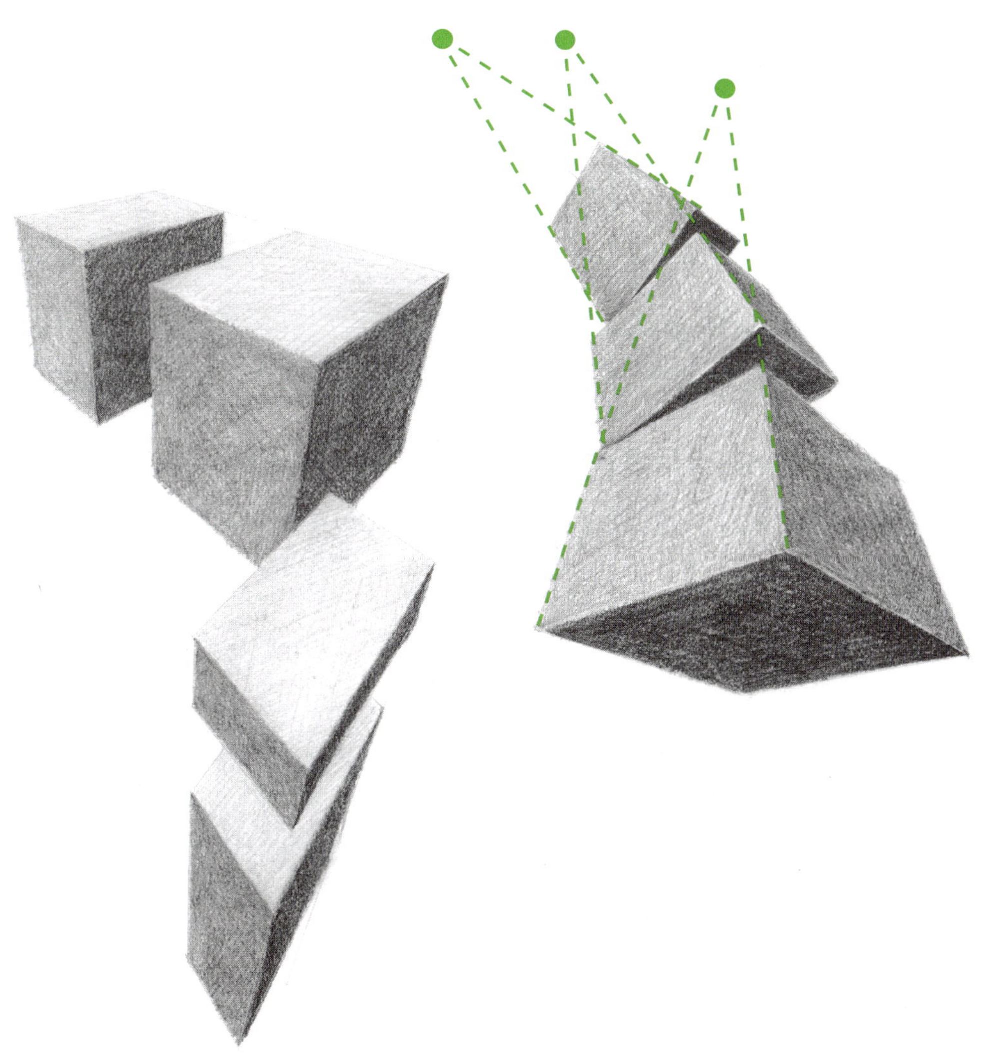

Here is an exercise for drawing with three vanishing points:
Cubes aligned with the same vanishing points are in reality
rectangular to each other. If the vanishing points are
moved, the alignment of the cubes is also moved.

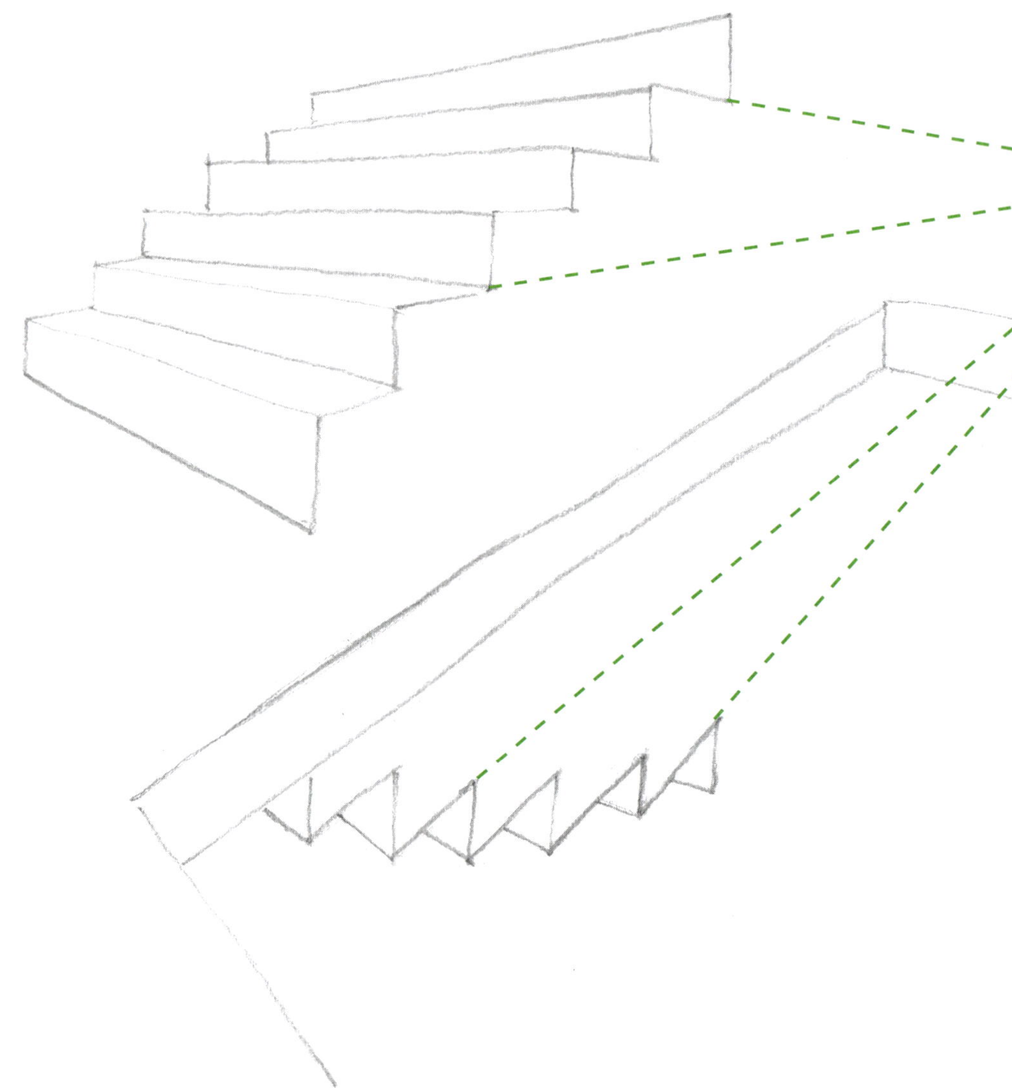

Verticals are mirrored on the symmetrical axis,
and all vanishing lines are oriented toward the
same vanishing point as the original points were.

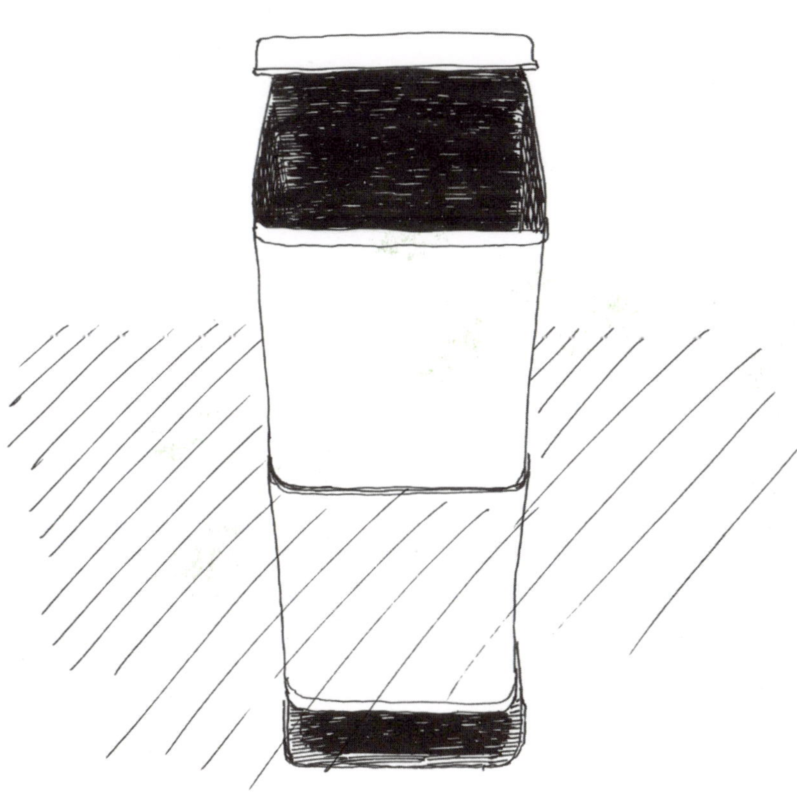

The vanishing points of the reflection
are the same as the ones of the object.

5. Shape

Light and shadow create corporality and volume. Bulges and curves are created through the change from white to gray to black.

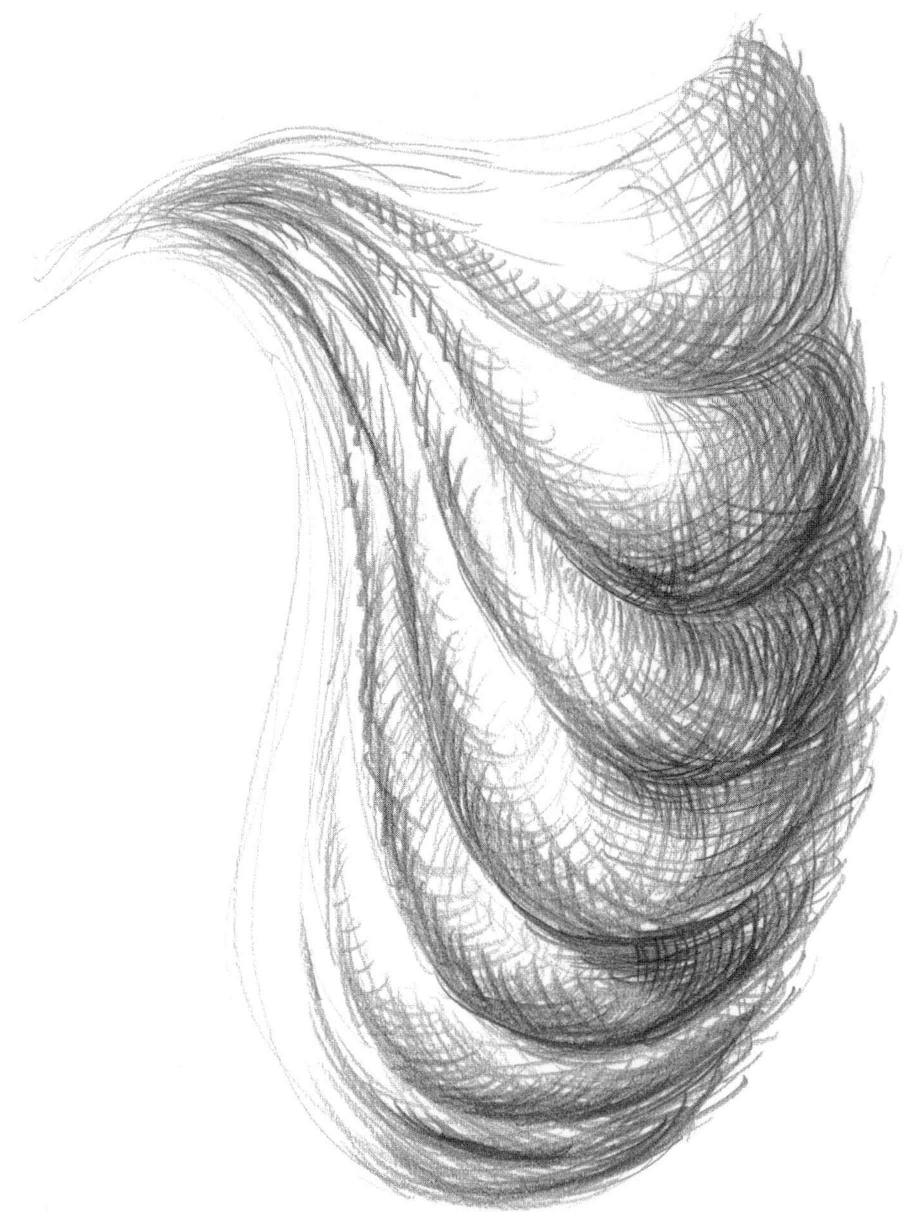

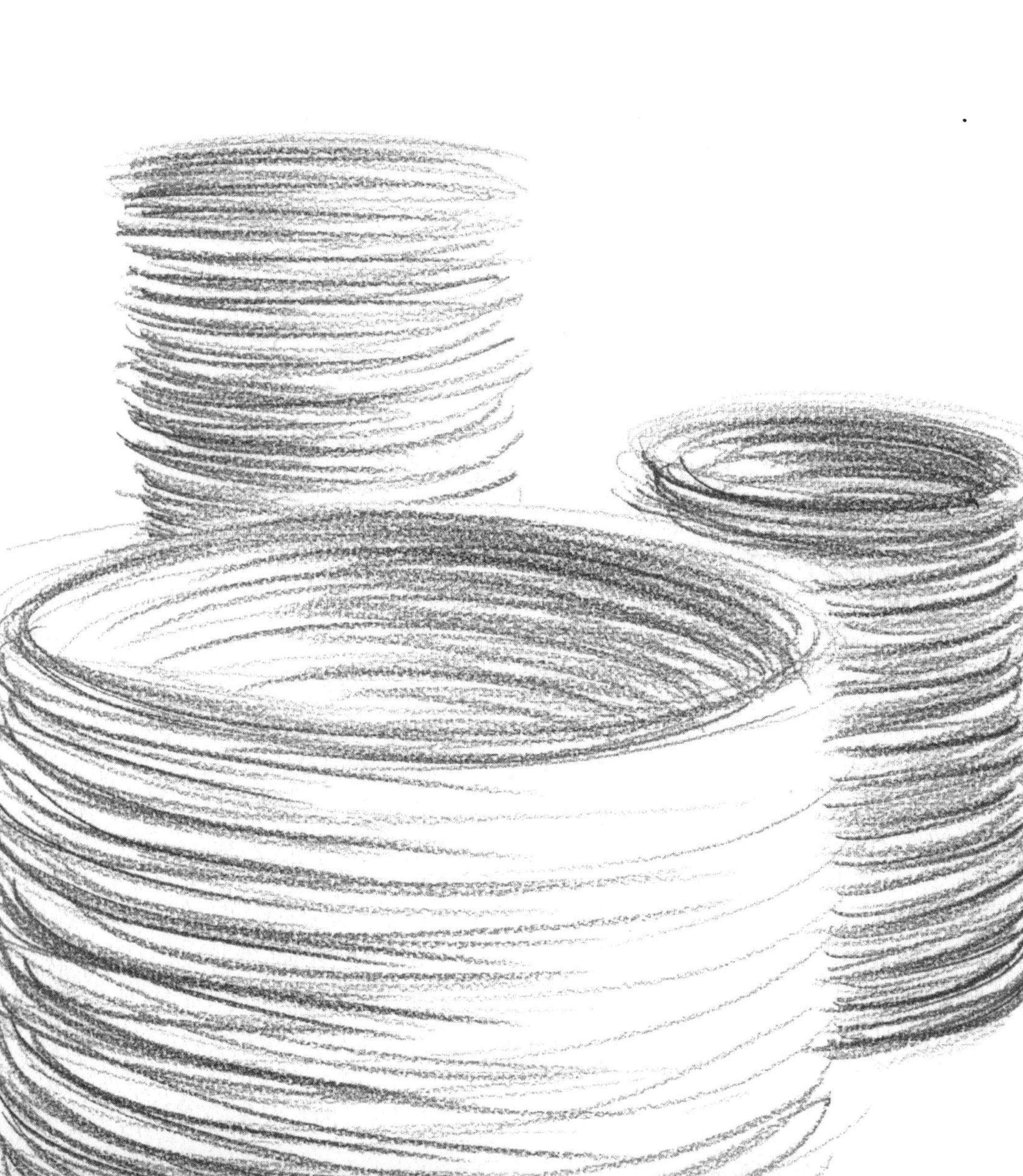

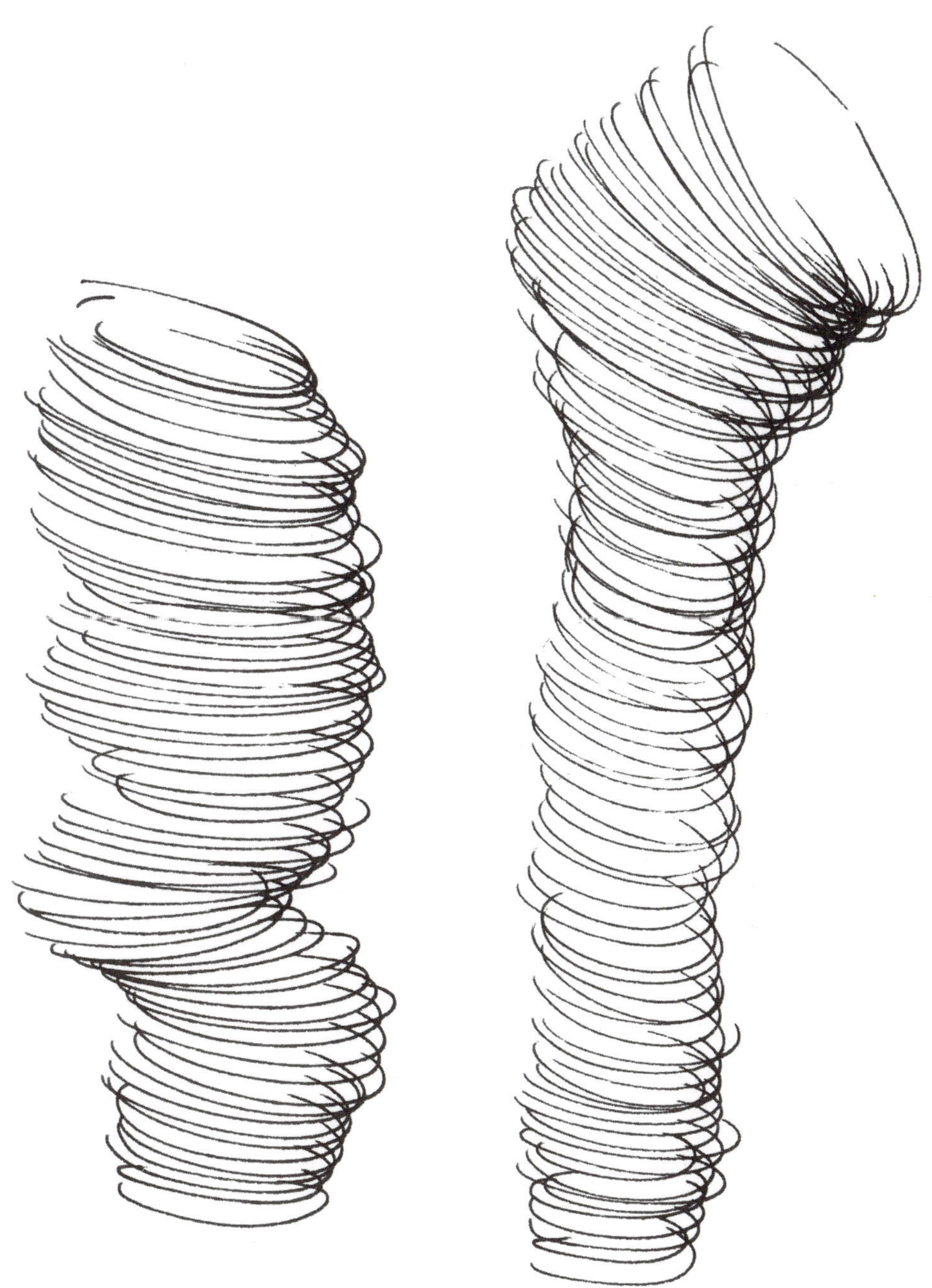

Here is an exercise for shaping: With quick, circular motions,
set half ellipses on top of or next to each other.

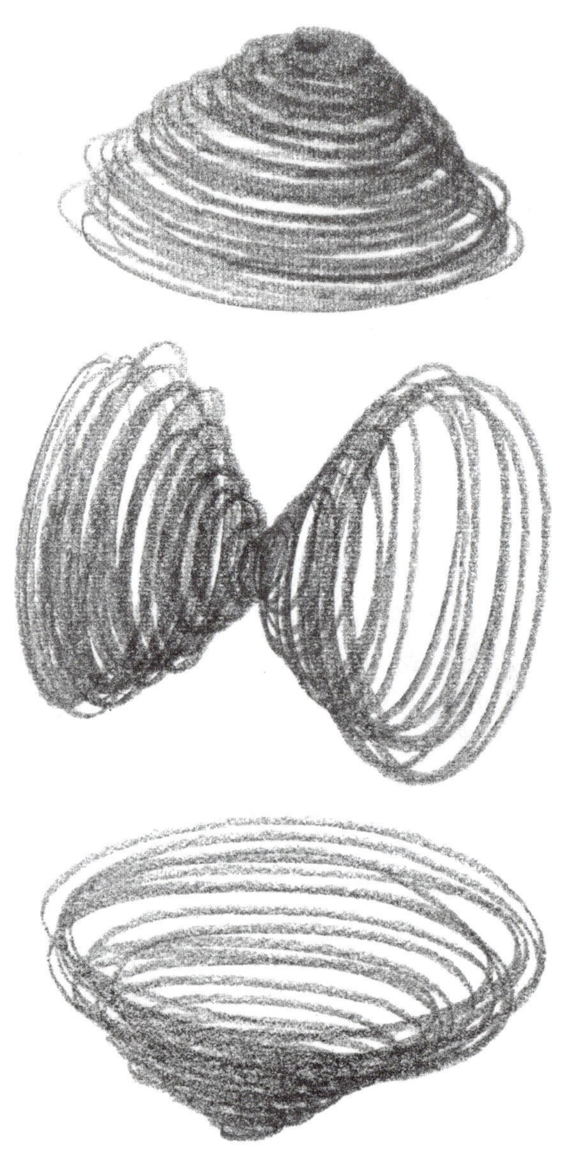

These become smaller when turning around an axis

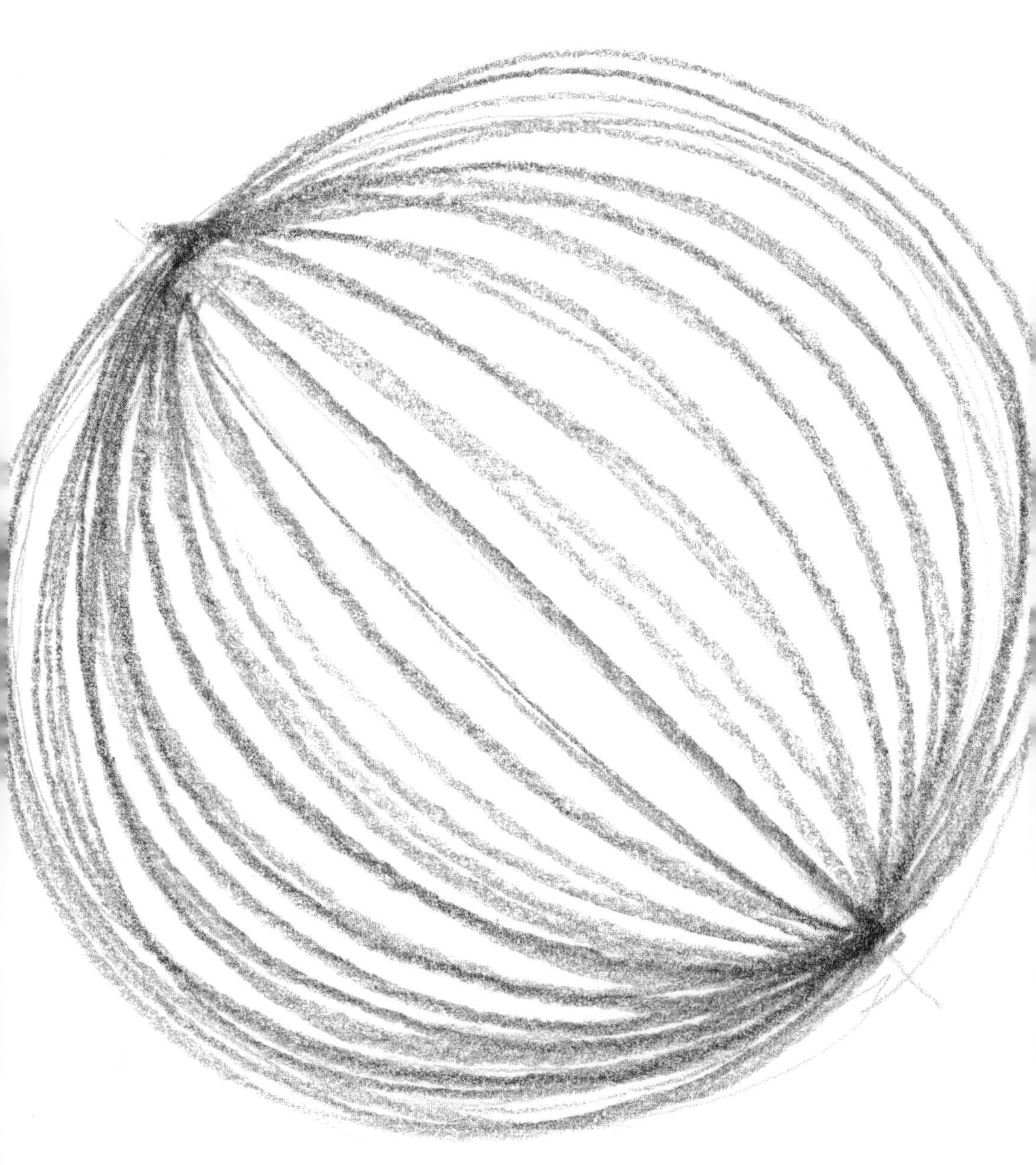

or circling around a ball.

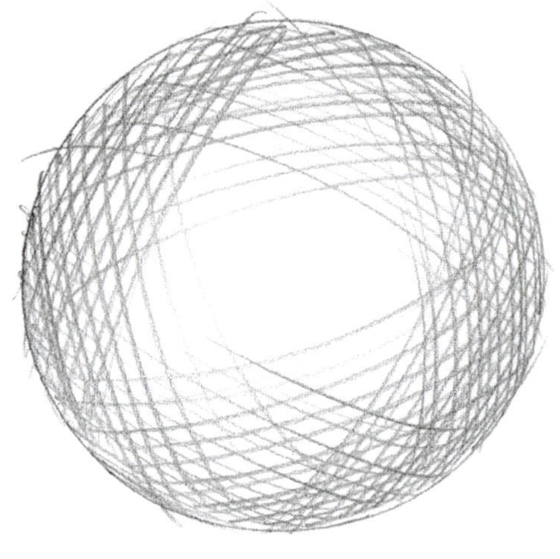

In general, the lightest parts move forward—
in this case, creating a ball.

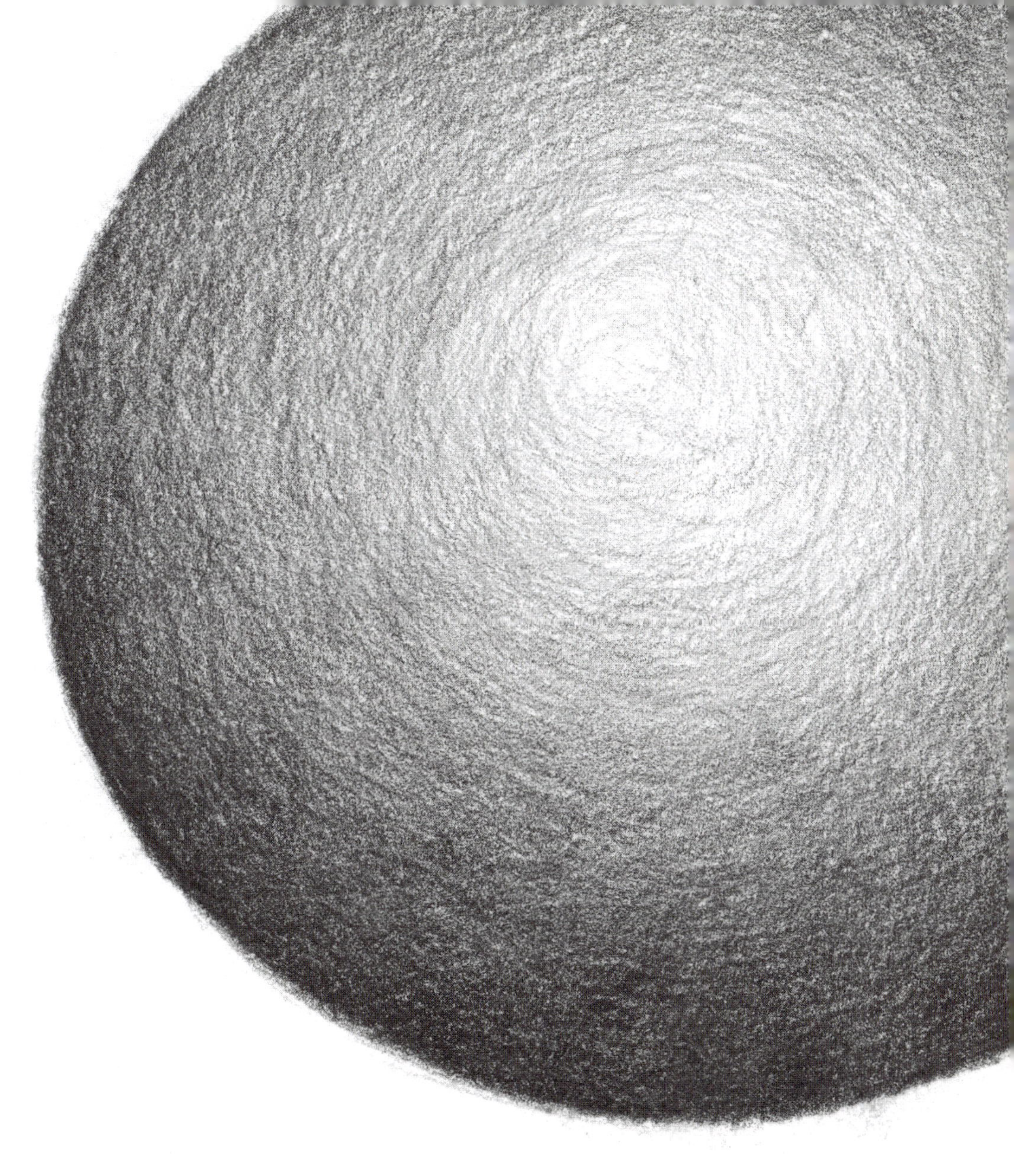

However, light areas can also appear to be farther away,
as in a tunnel view.

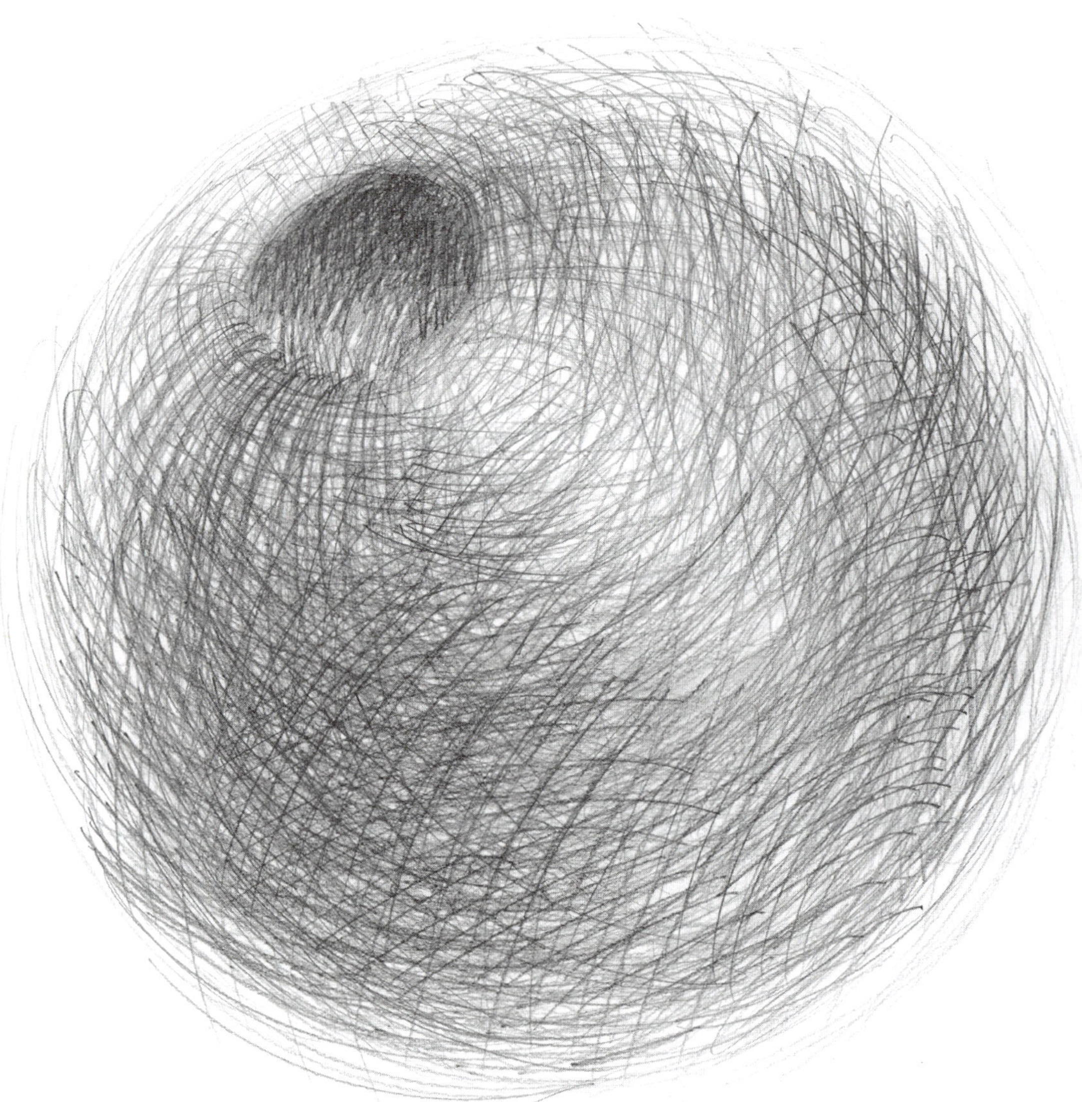

The shaping of hatching doesn't have to follow
a hard rule to create a spatial impact.

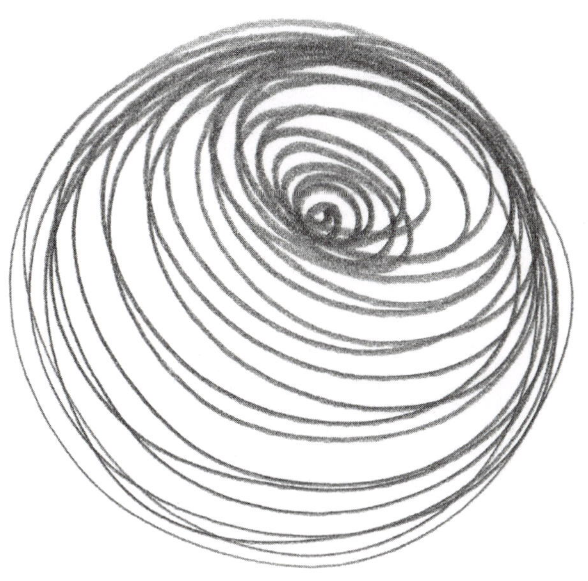

The shifting of the spinning center
creates the bulge of the ball.

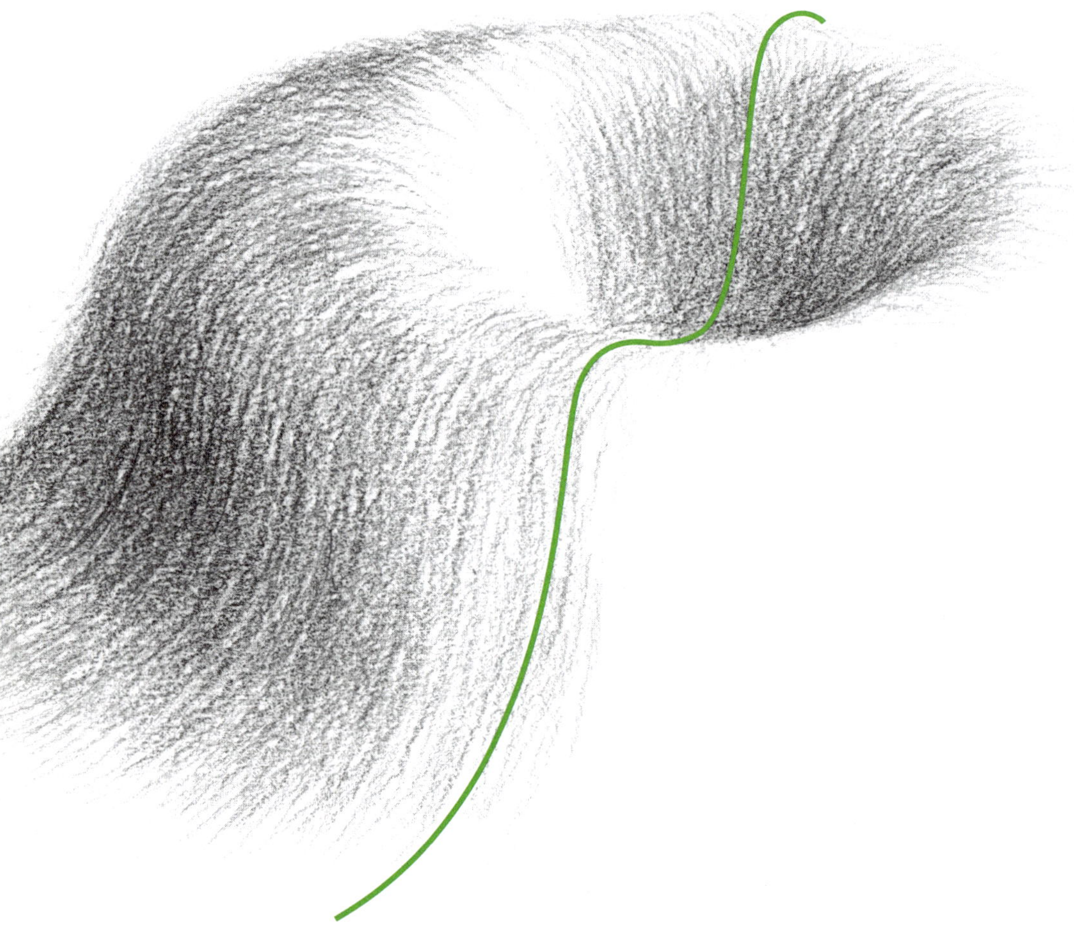

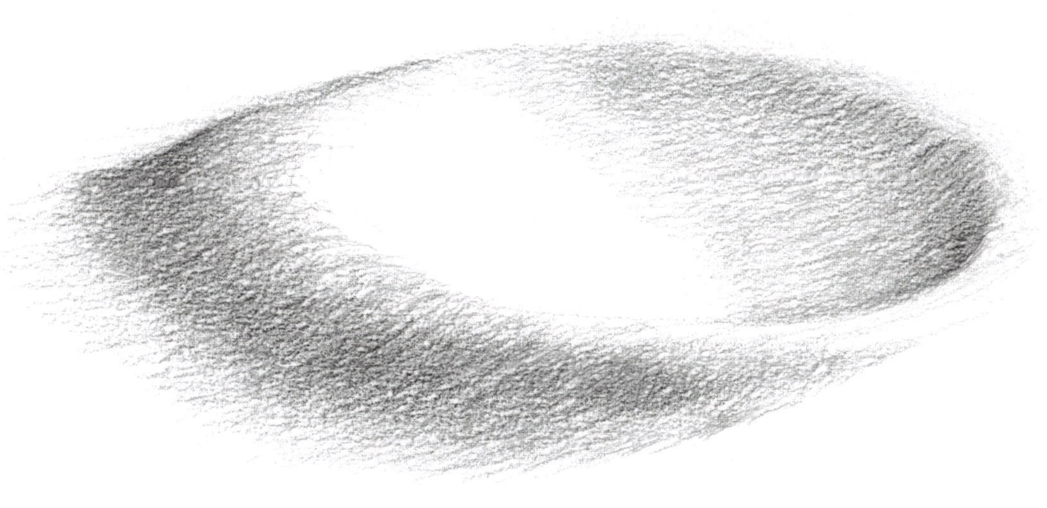

Slopes and bulges are created with soft hatching.
The shaping lines describe the volume as if the
pencil is feeling along the outside of the object.

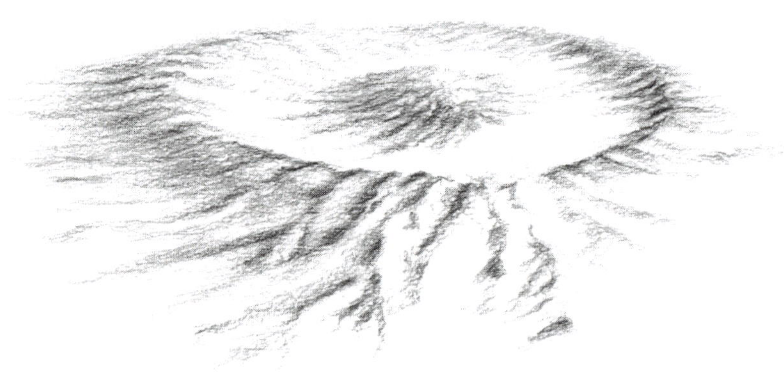

A bulge can be either a dip or a bump

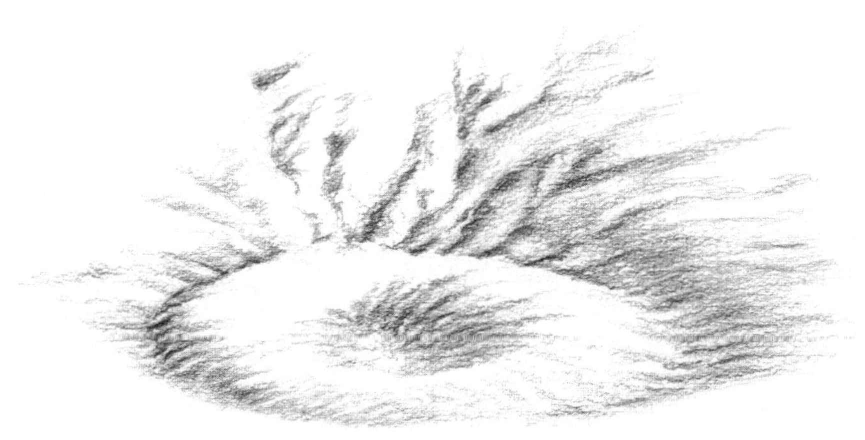

depending on the point of view.

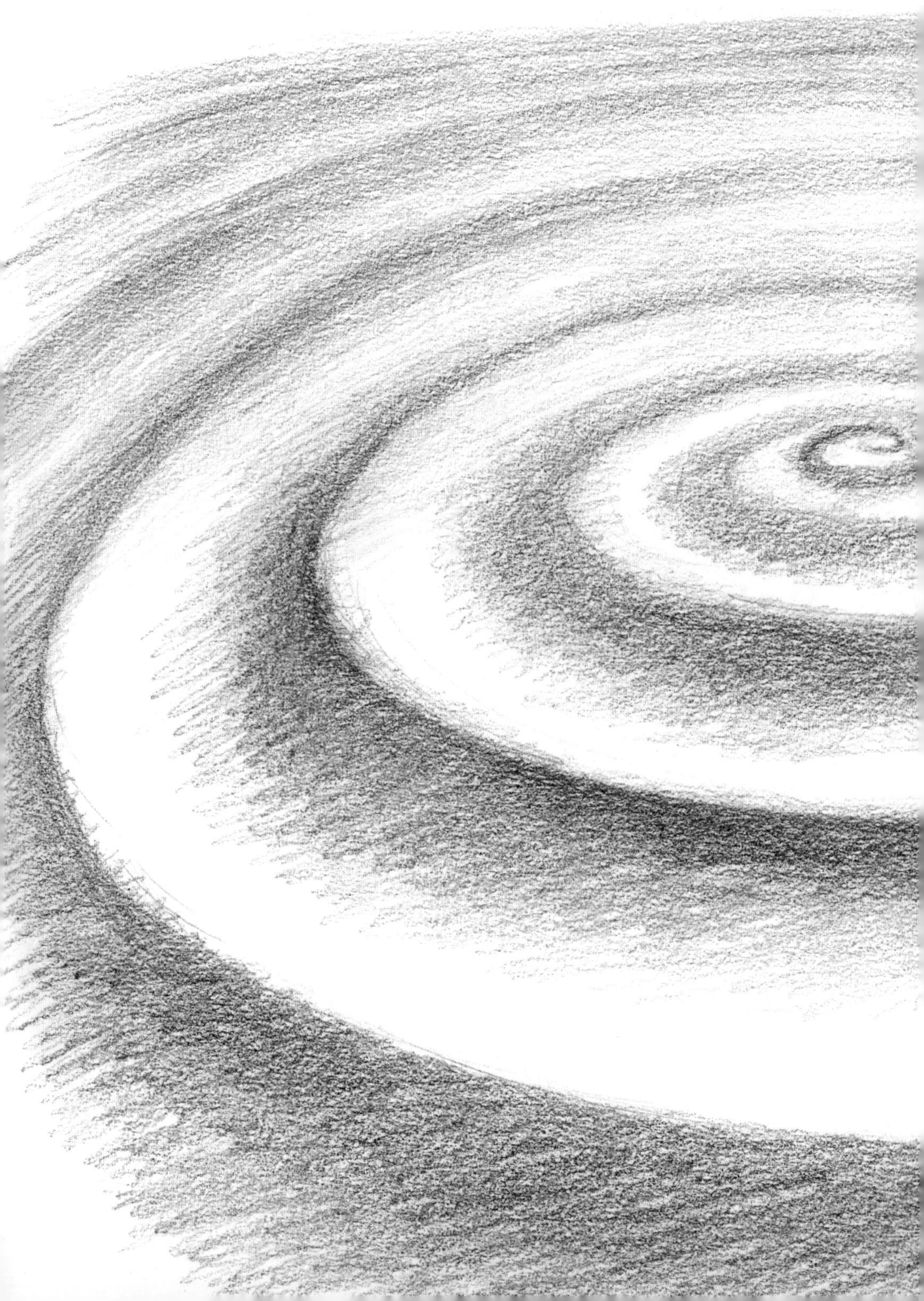

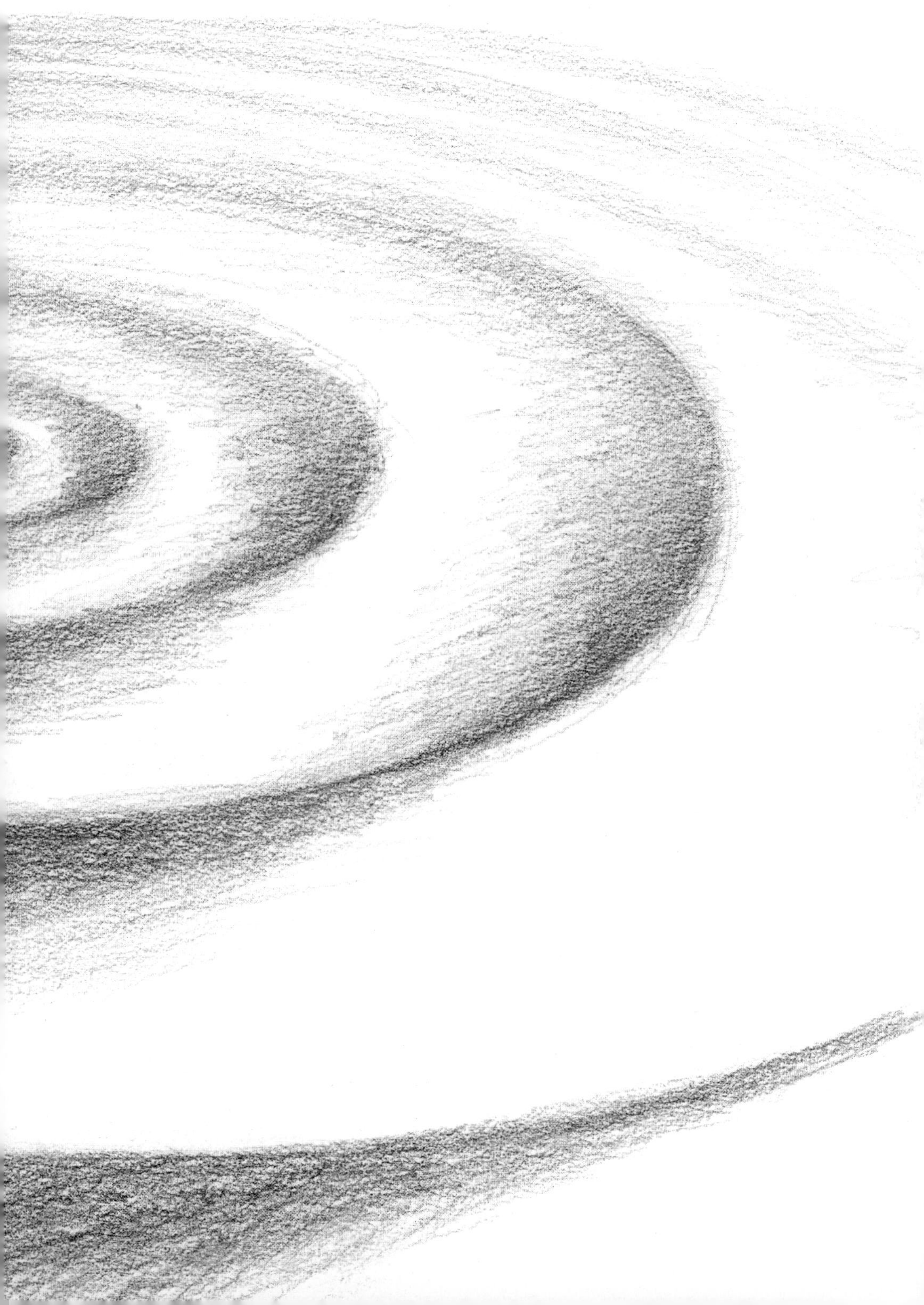

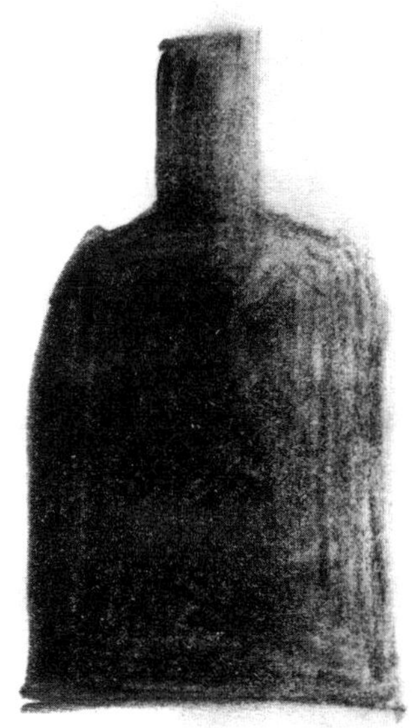

Plasticity is accomplished by adding highlights.

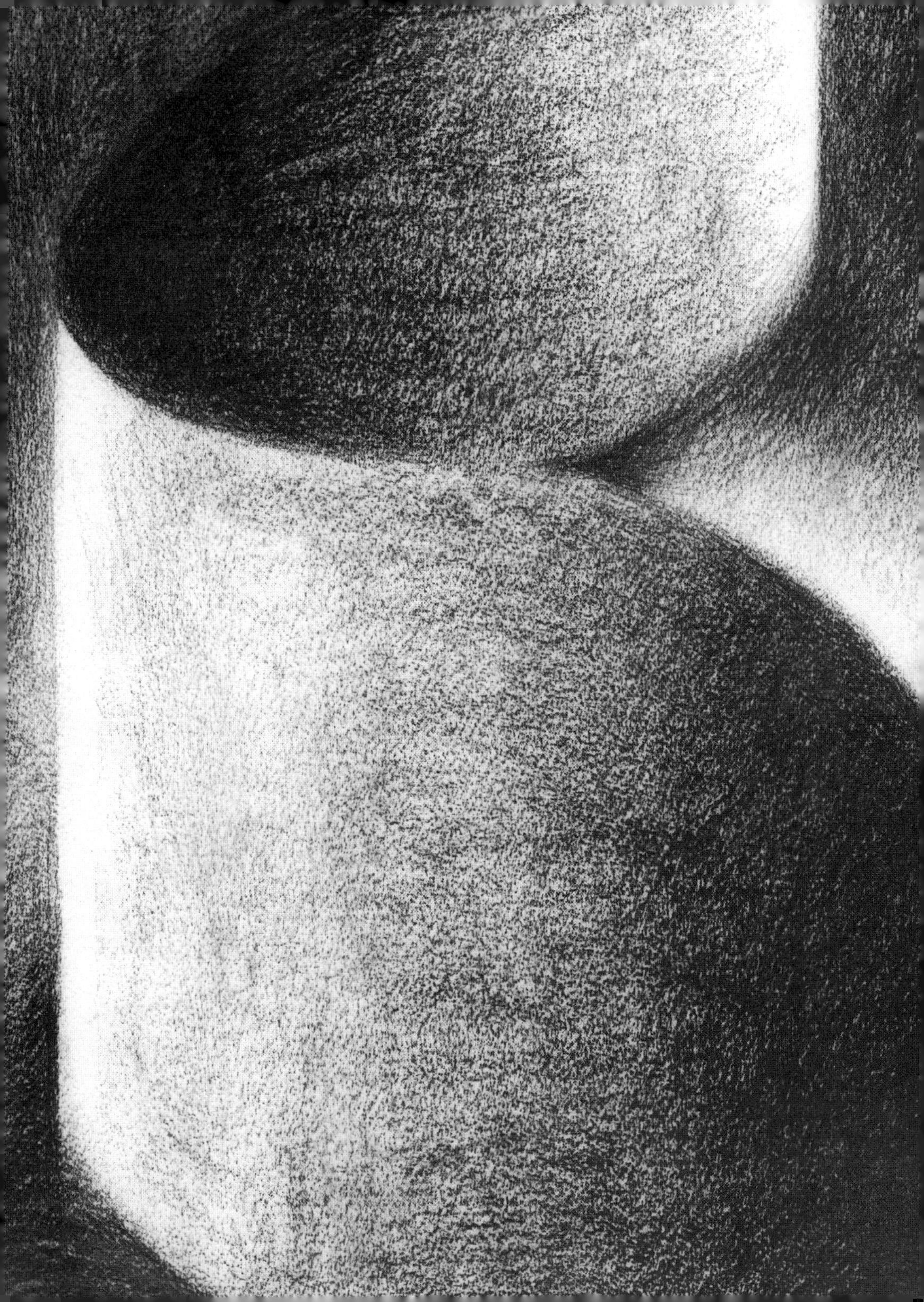

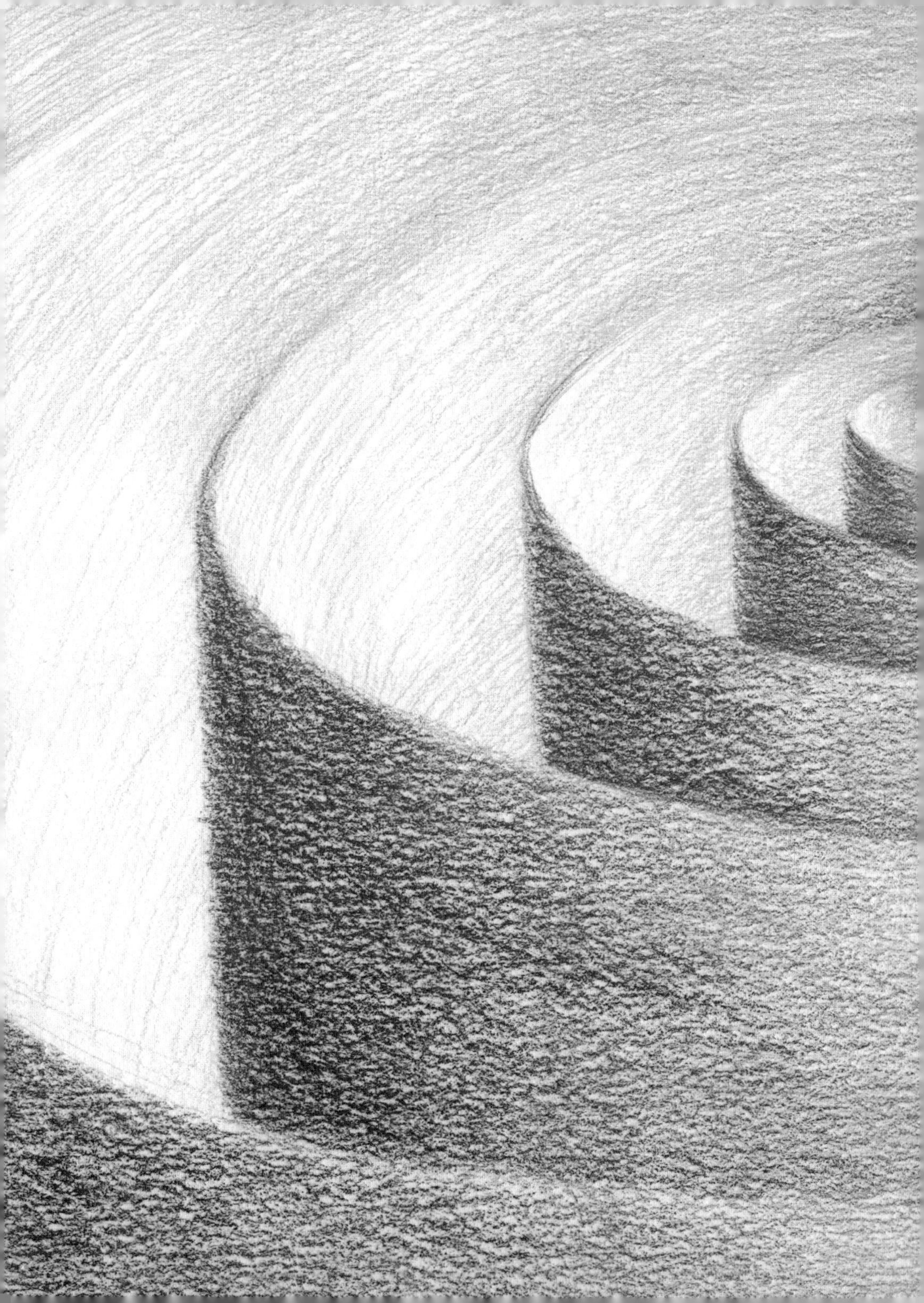

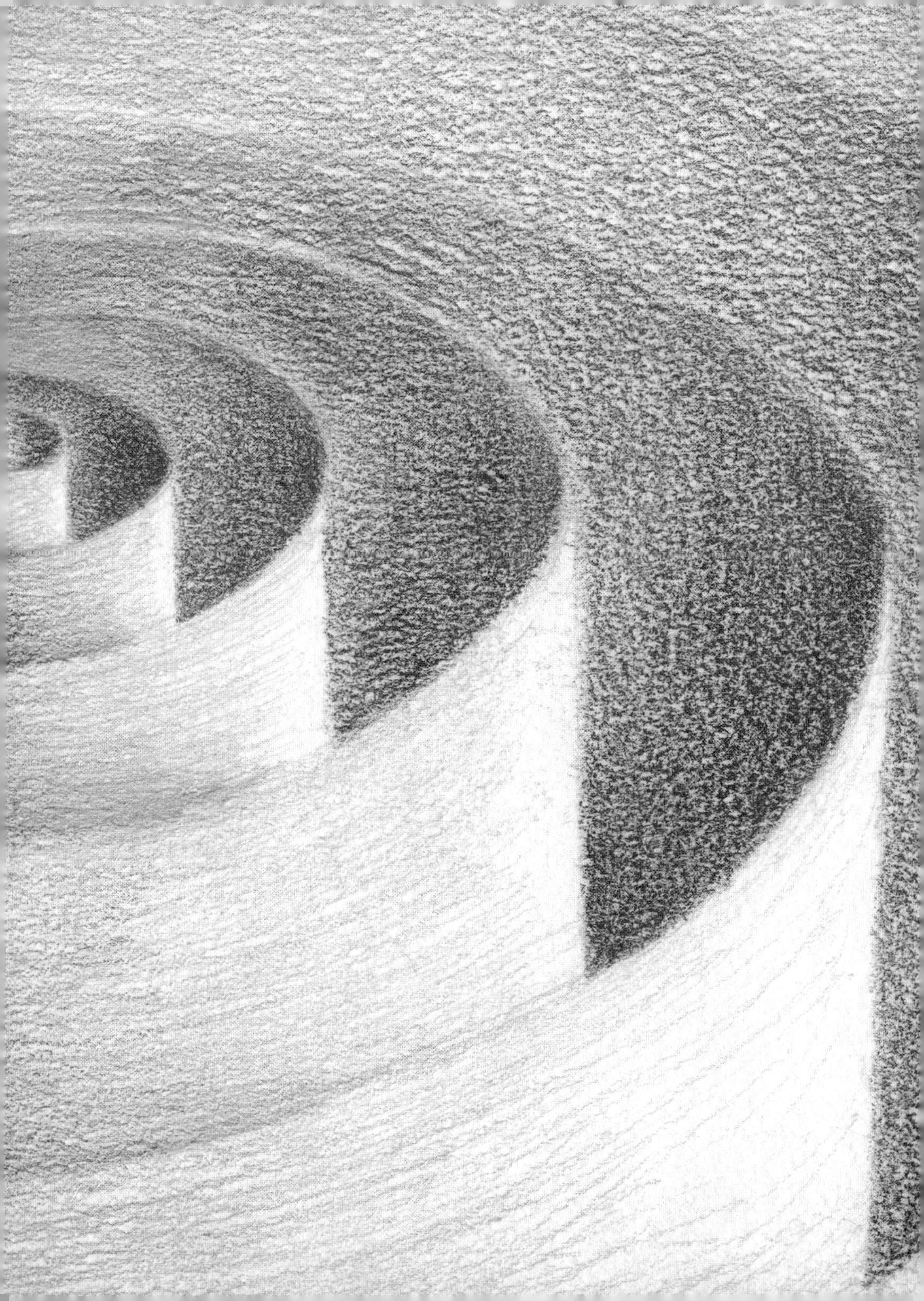

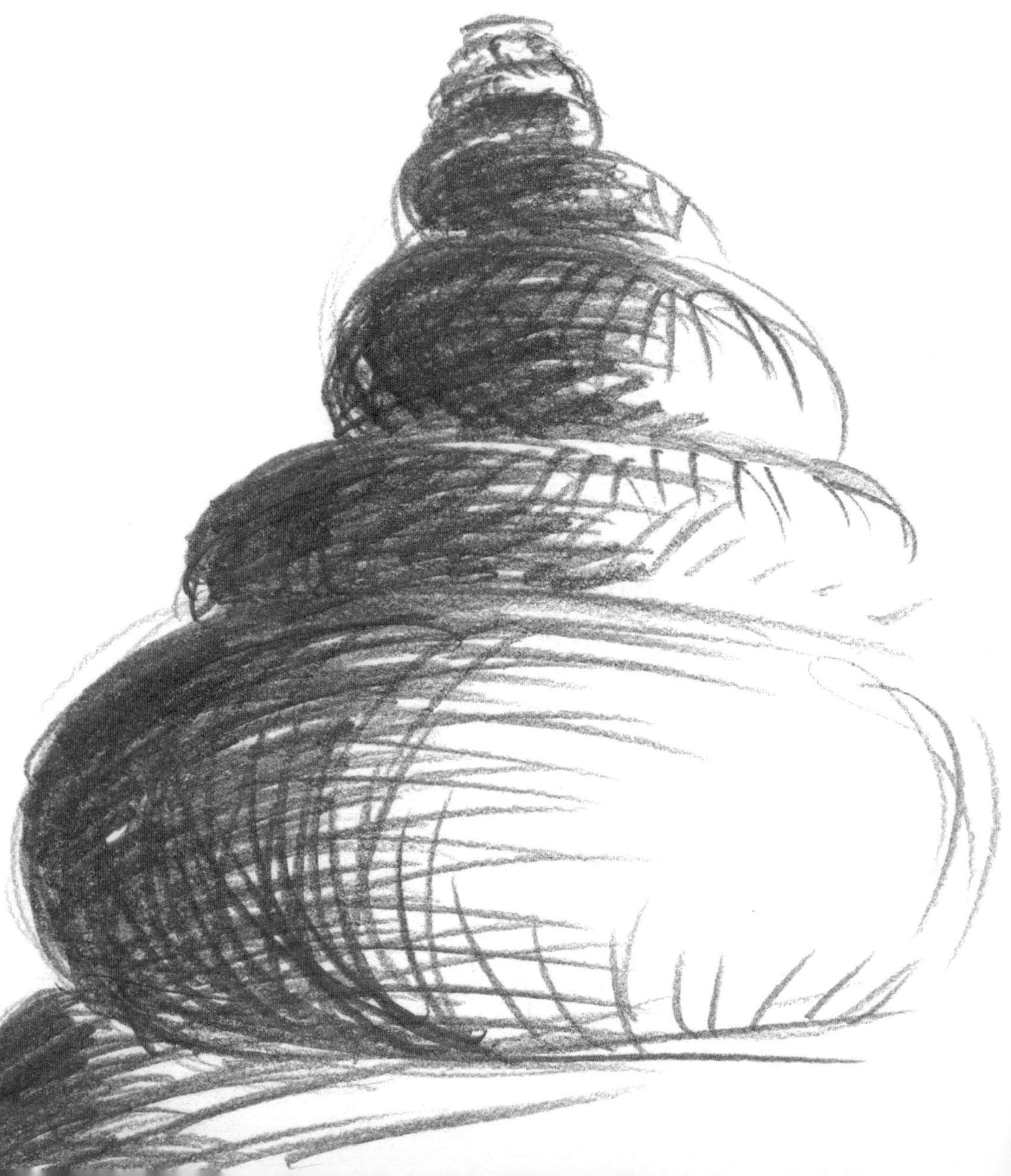

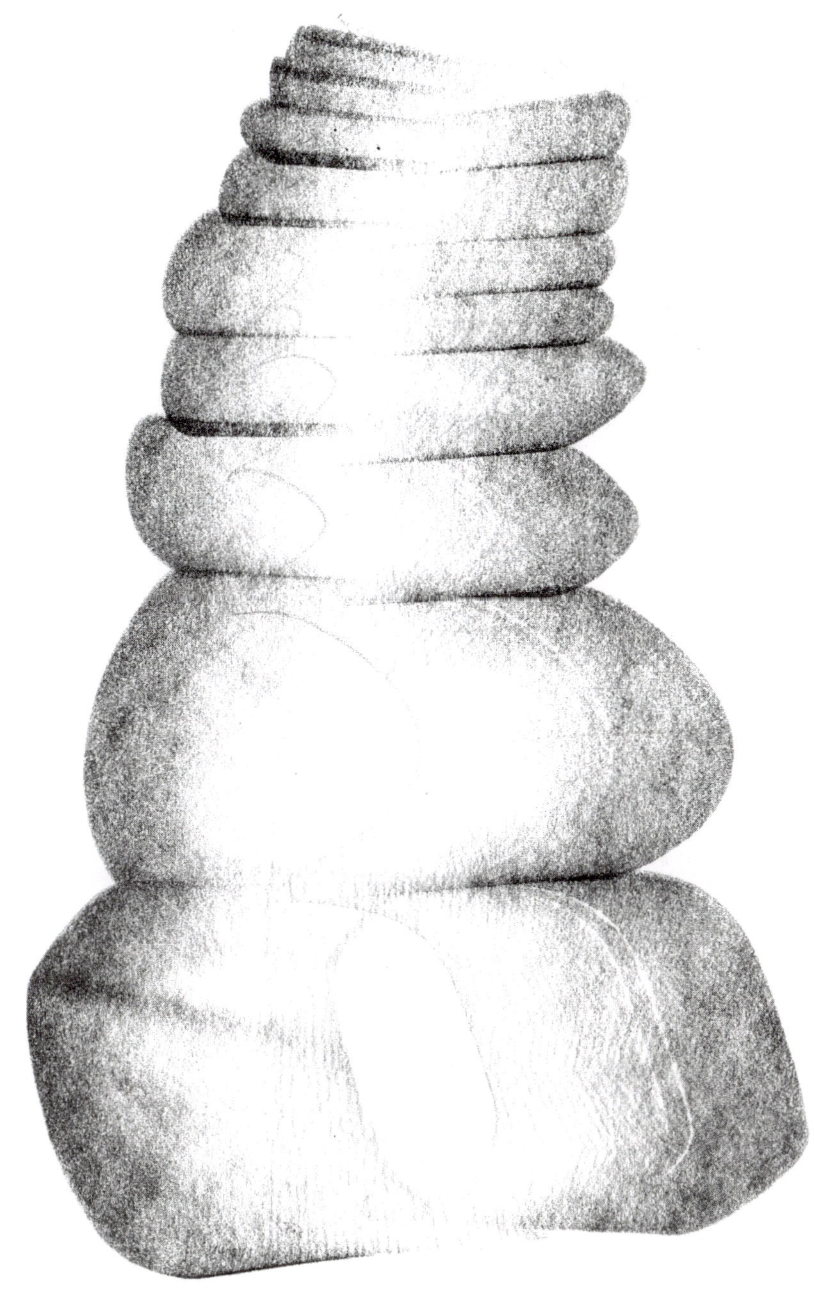

Successful 3-D effects are created almost automatically
with the long side of a soft pencil lead.

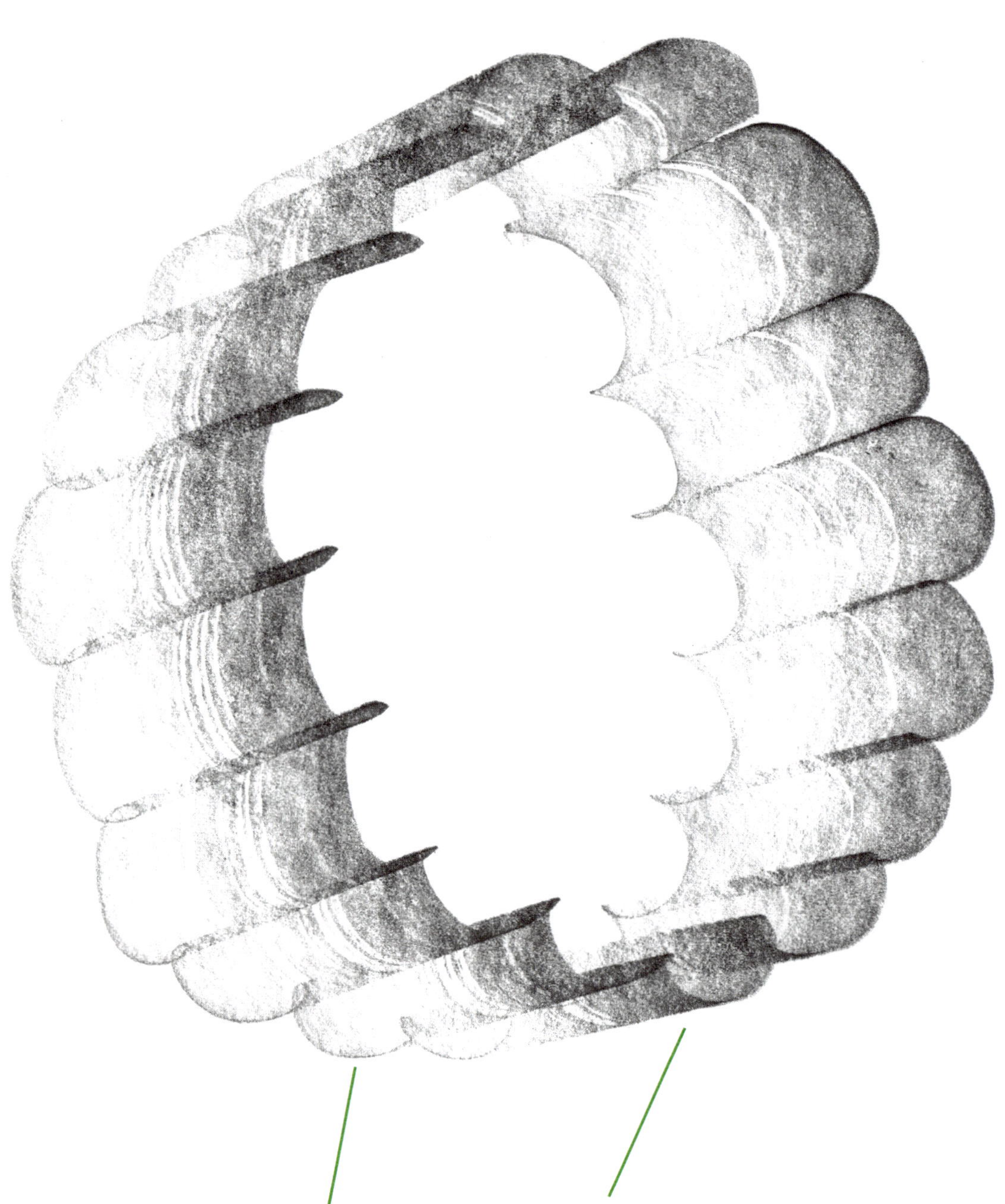

Put either a little pressure or a lot of pressure on the pencil.

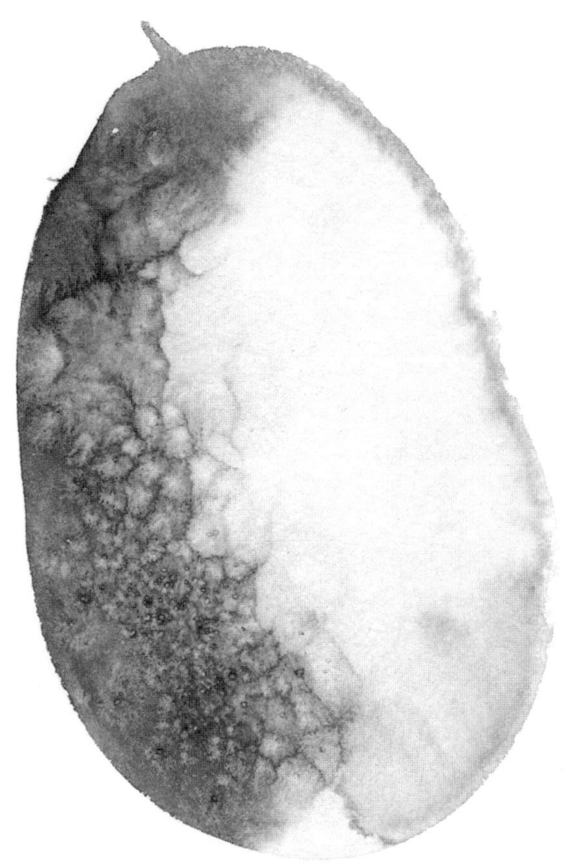

Gray-scale values can emerge by accident or on purpose.

6. Fade

Gray-scale is a series of tones ranging from black to white through intermediate shades of gray. There is less contrast and a smaller range of gray-scale values in the background of a picture. Forms and objects that are closer to the foreground are not only bigger but also much clearer than the ones in the distance.

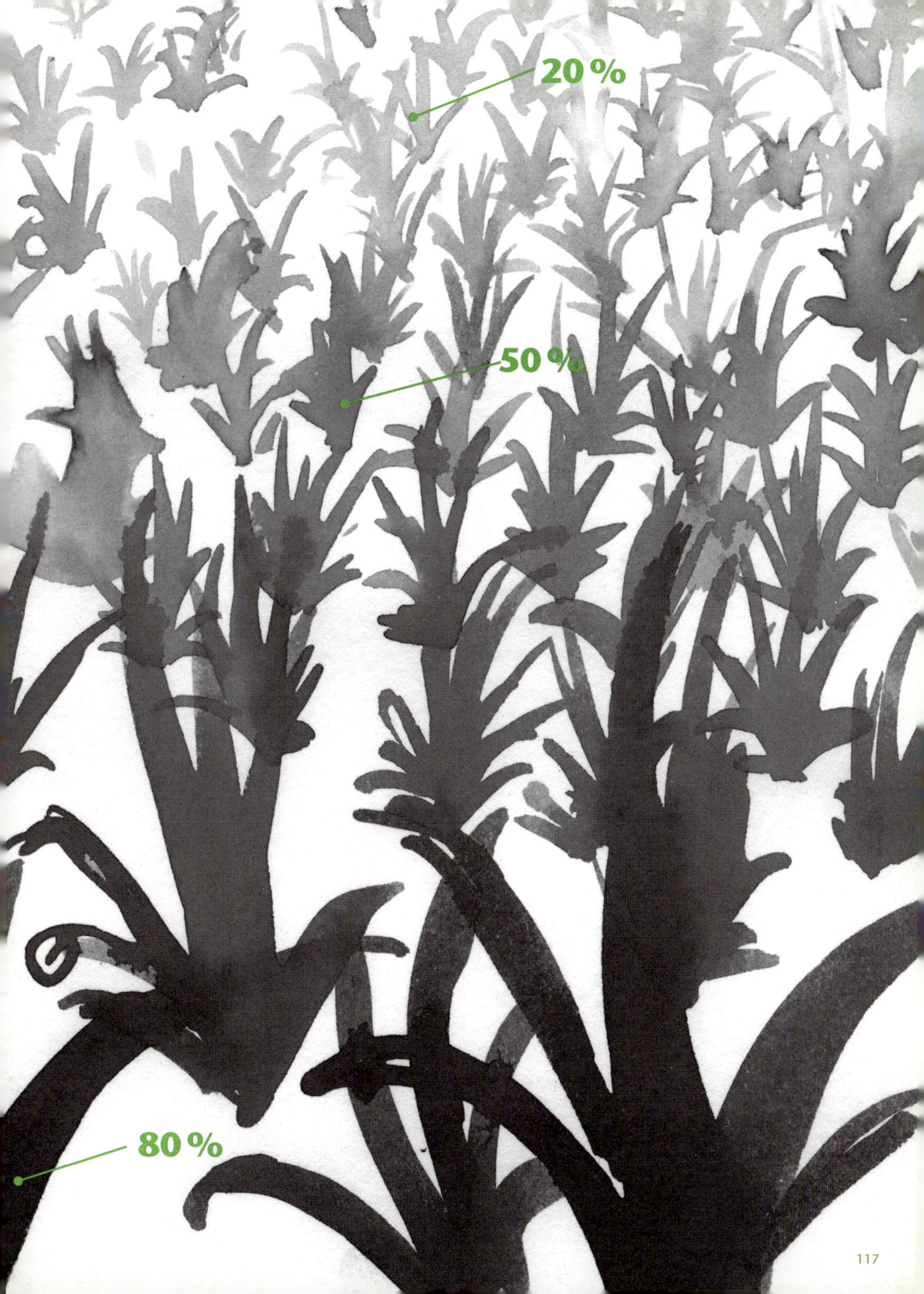

20 %
50 %
80 %

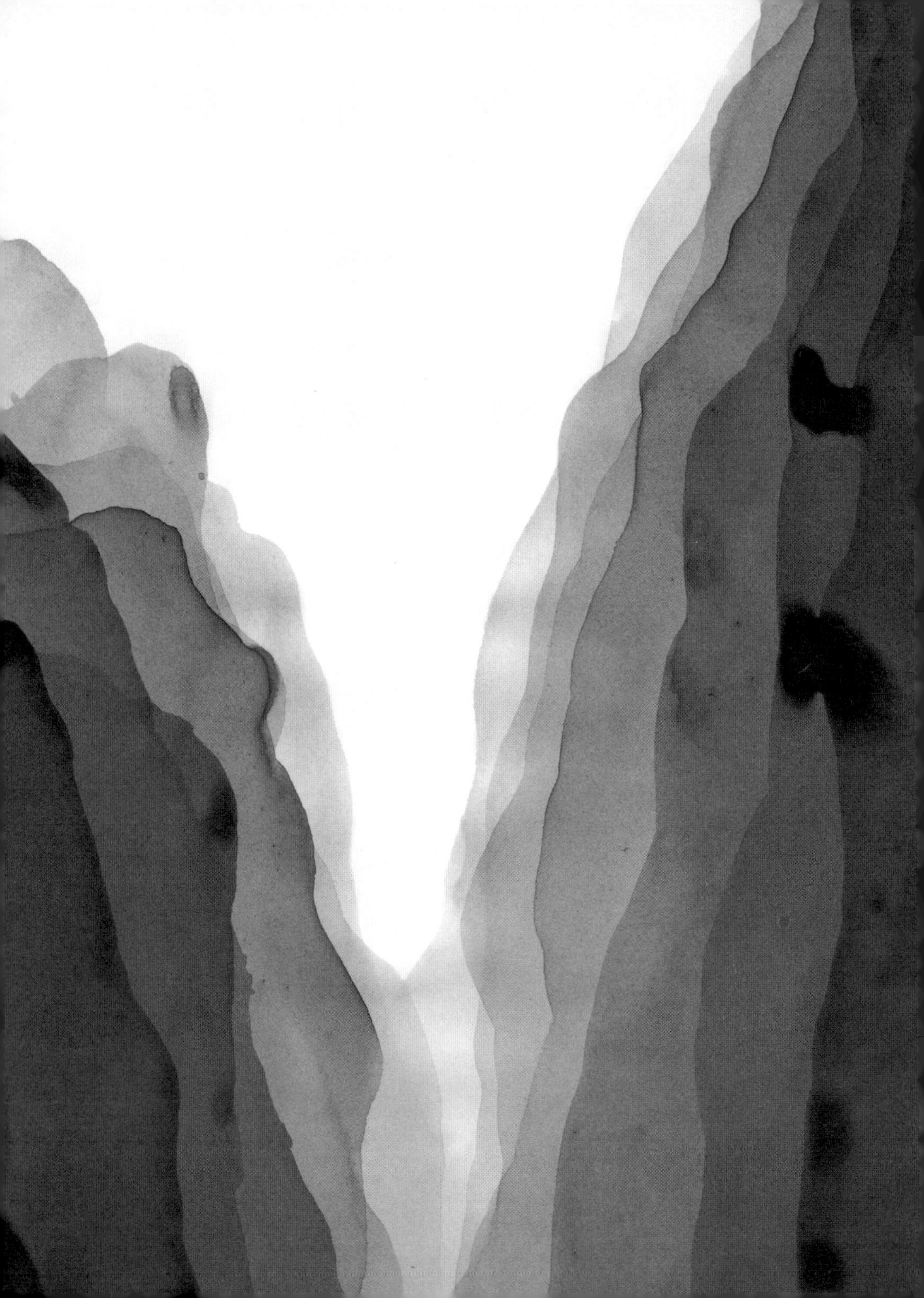

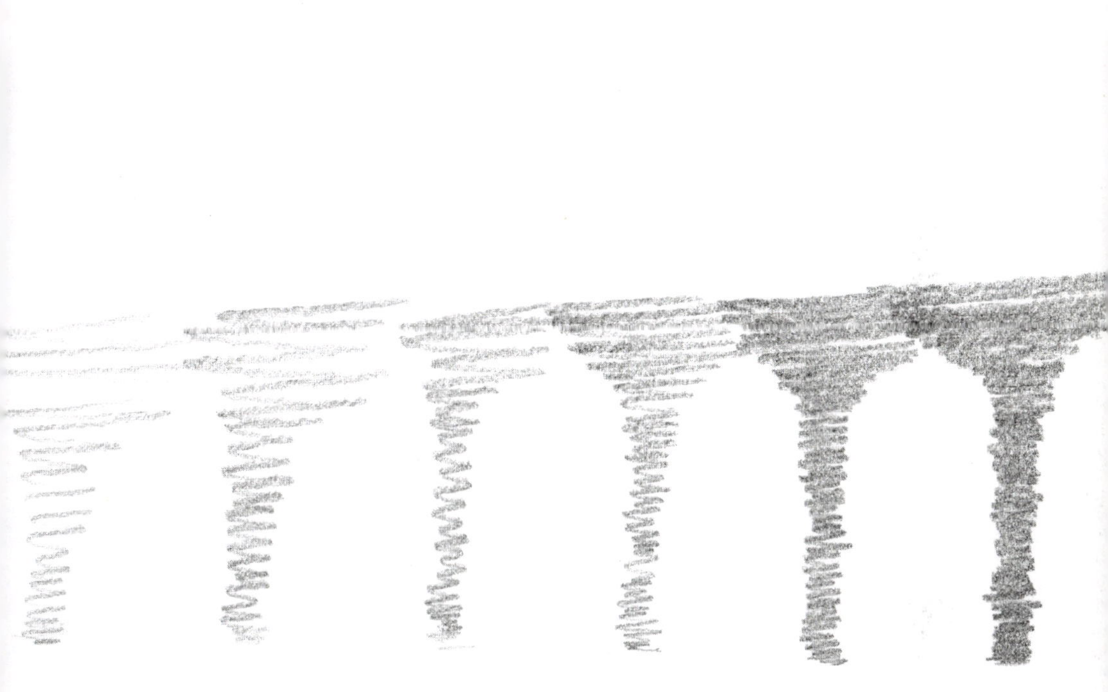

Water droplets and dust in the air
cloud the view into the distance.

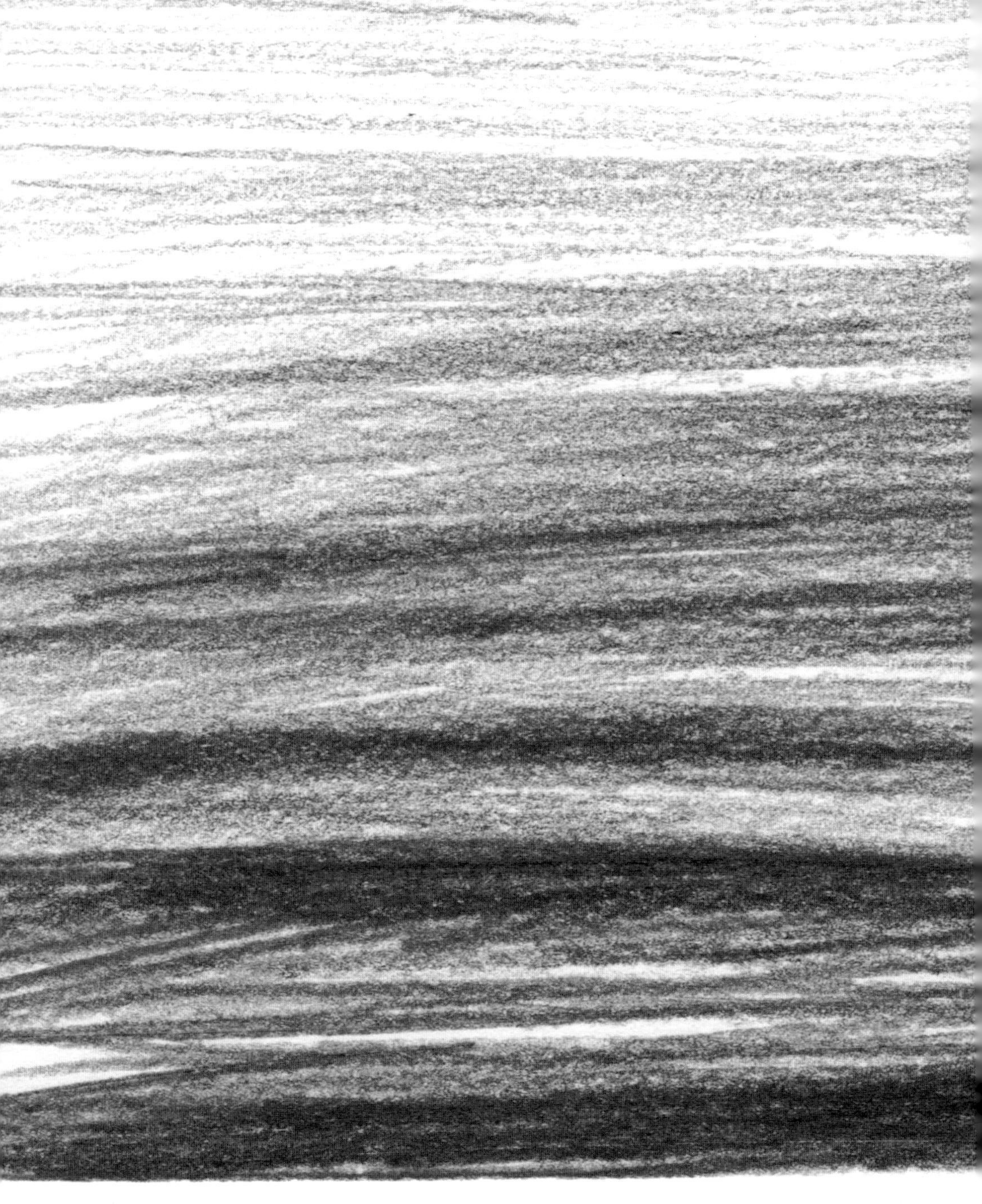

Where shapes are missing, contrast alone
can generate spatiality.

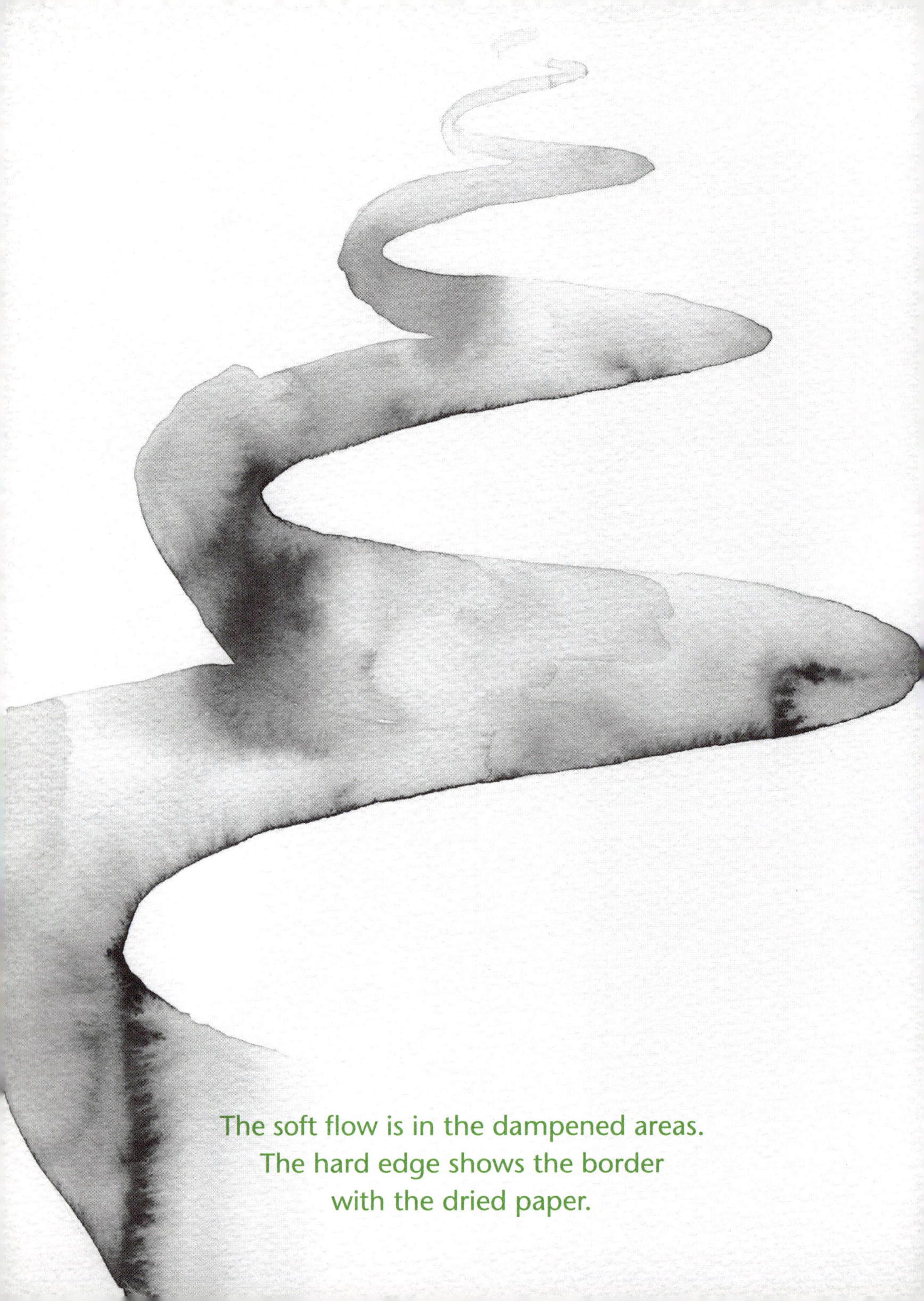

The soft flow is in the dampened areas.
The hard edge shows the border
with the dried paper.

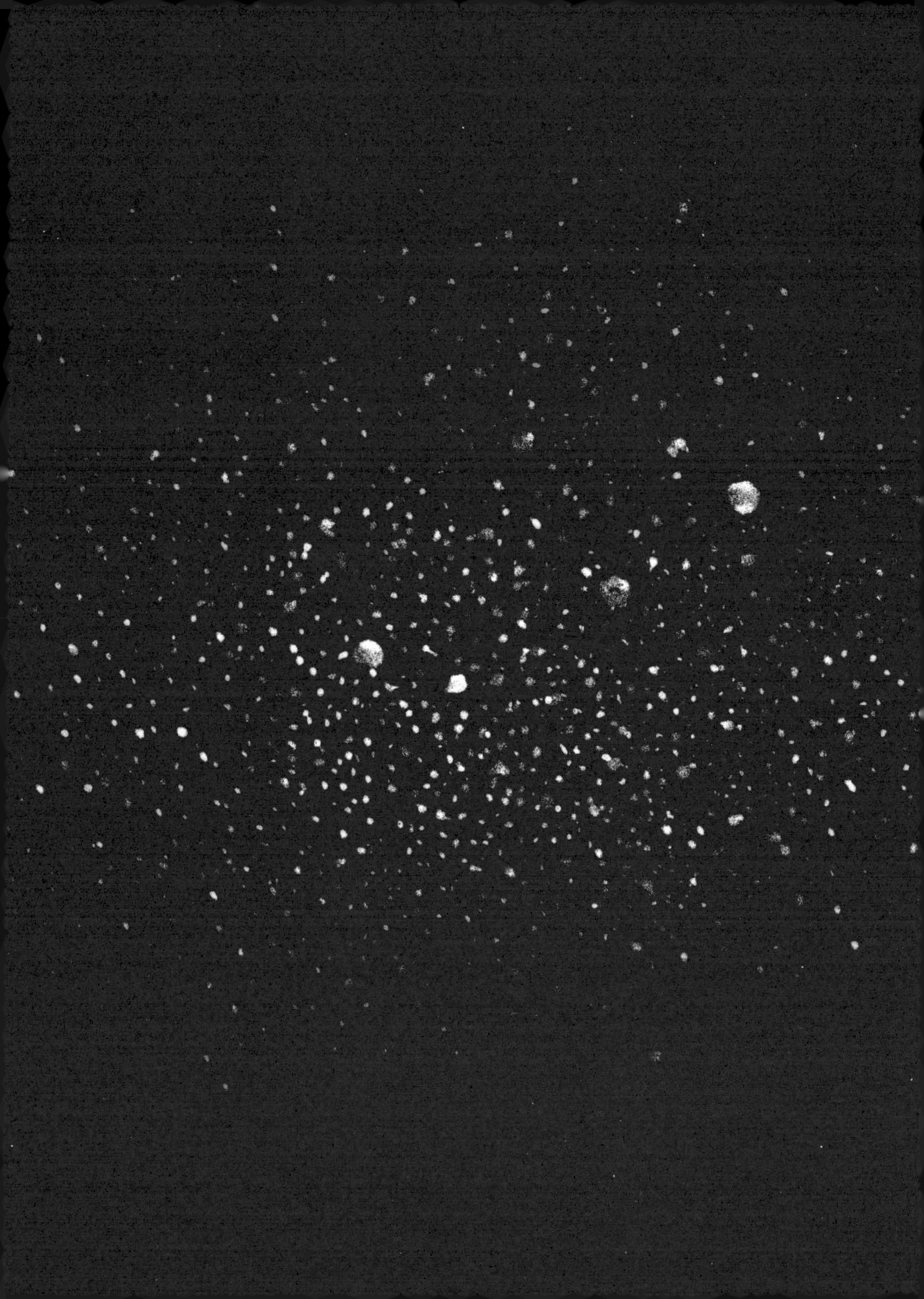

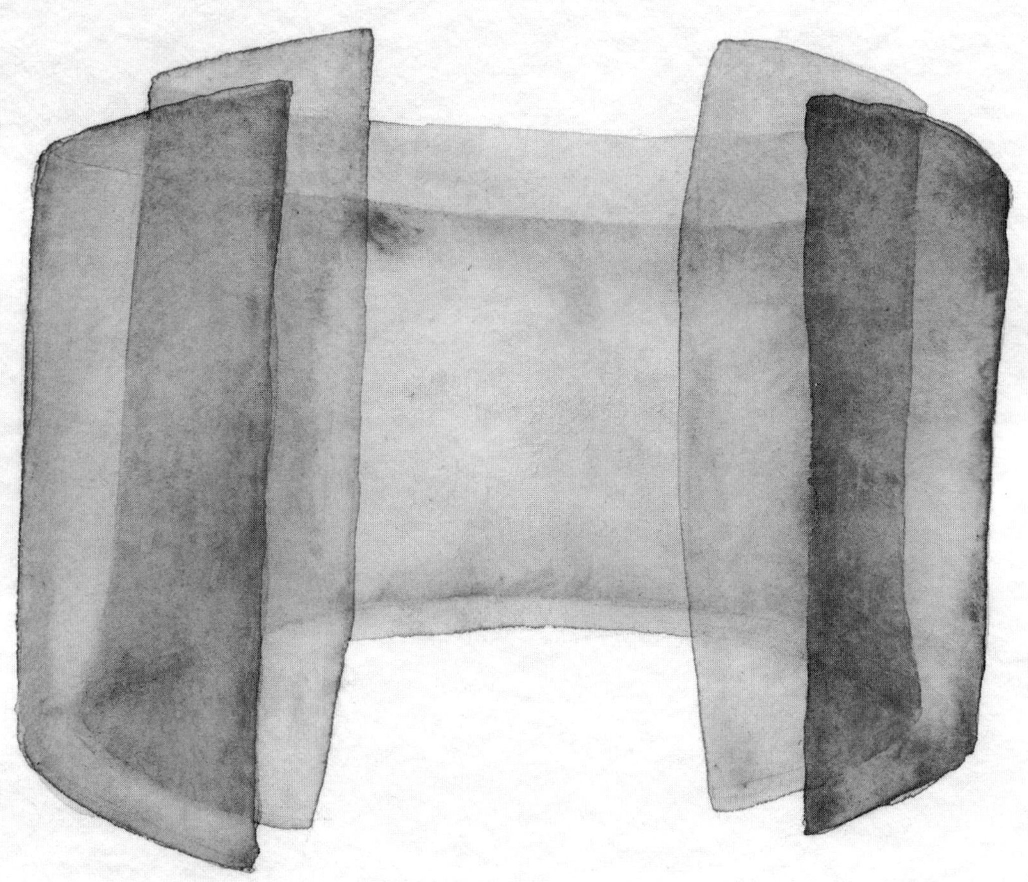

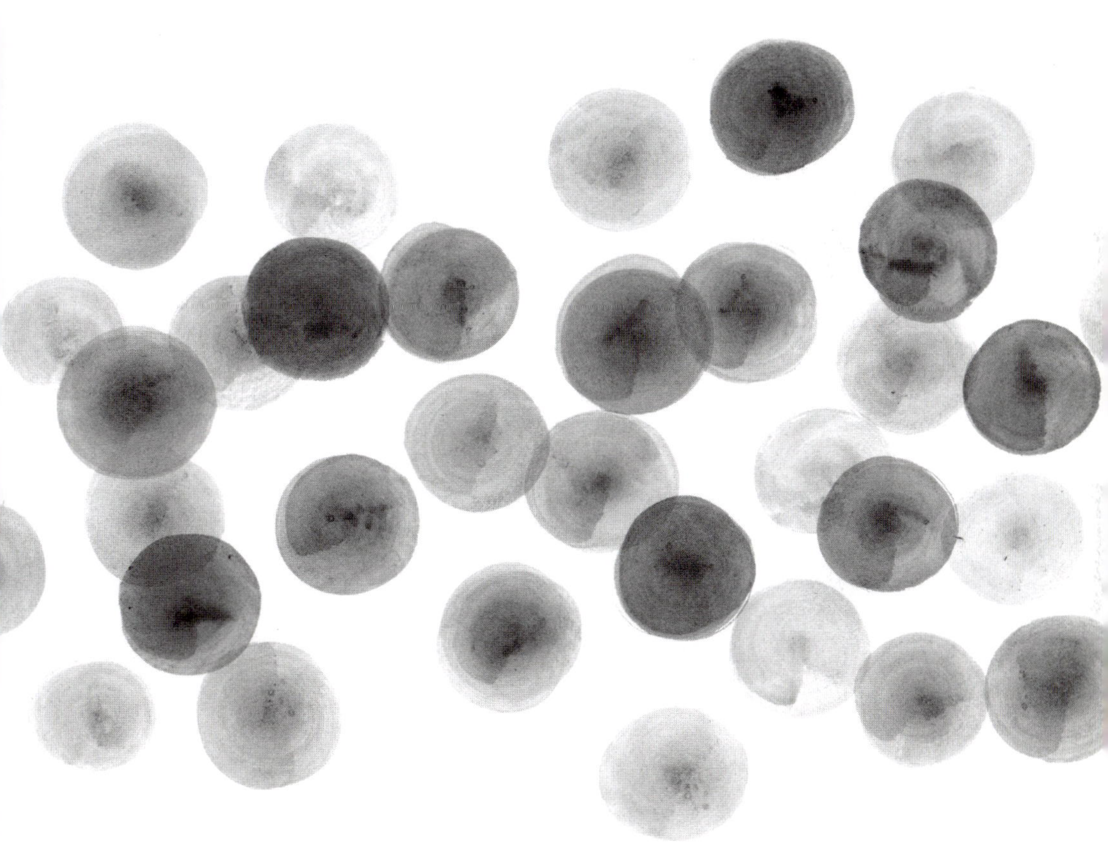

Transparencies emerge from thinned layers of paint.

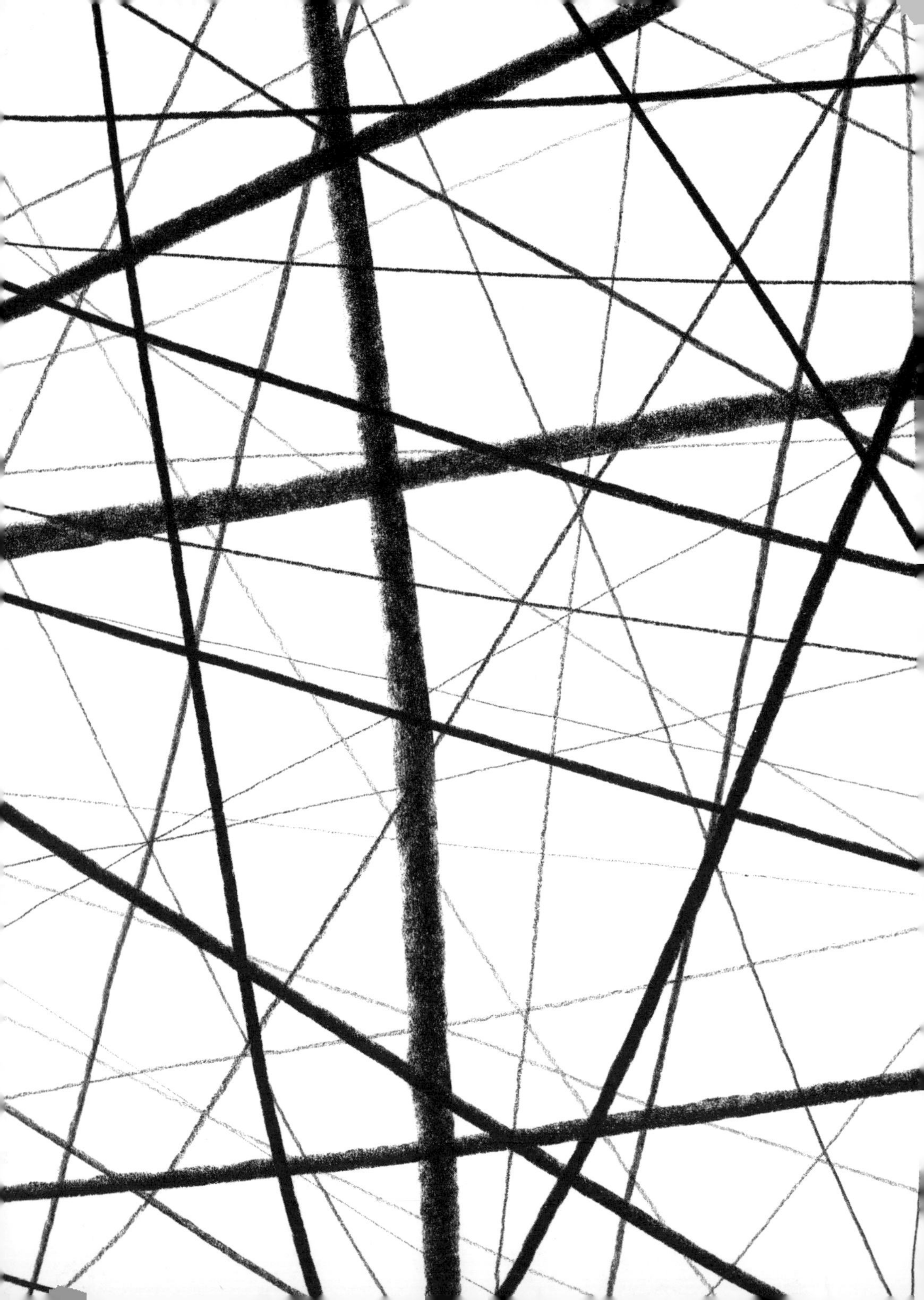

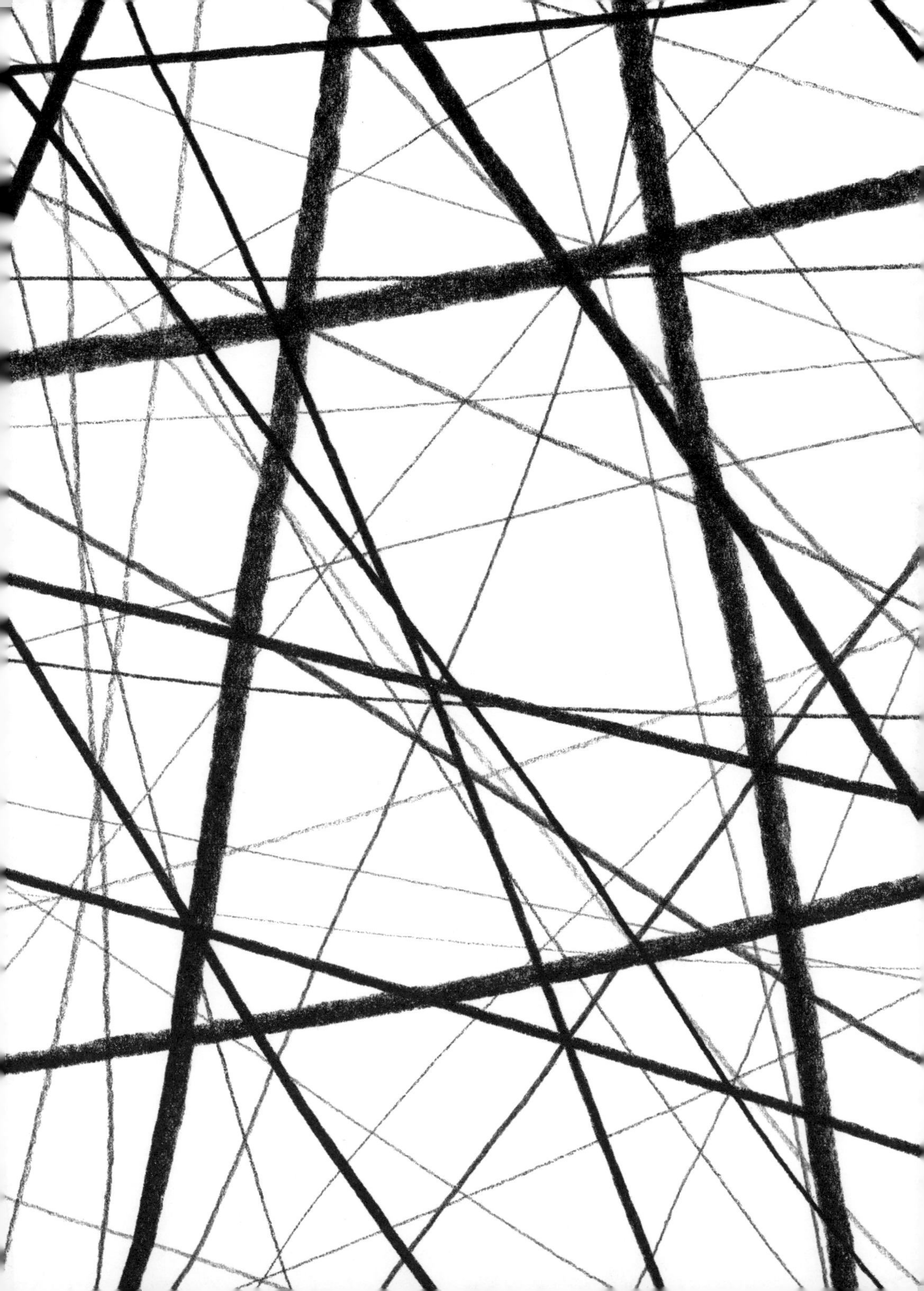

7. Blur

Things get lost in the distance; they seem blurred, inconclusive. There is something secretive and mysterious about this vagueness. It sits at the edge of our field of view and it remains unfocused in our perception.

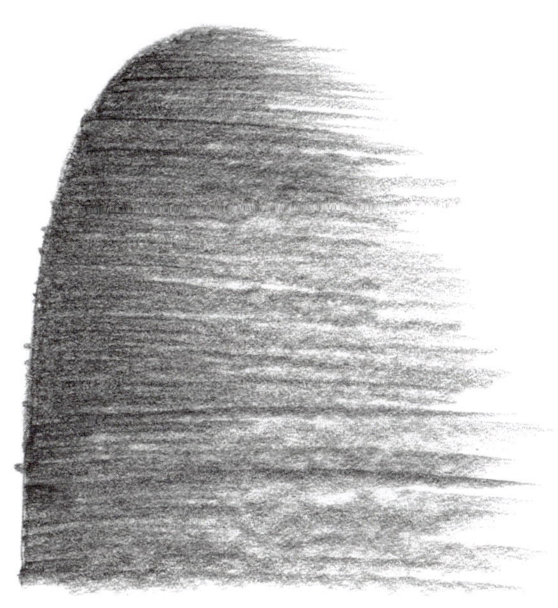

Soft drawing mediums such as graphite, red chalk, and charcoal are best for creating blurred objects.

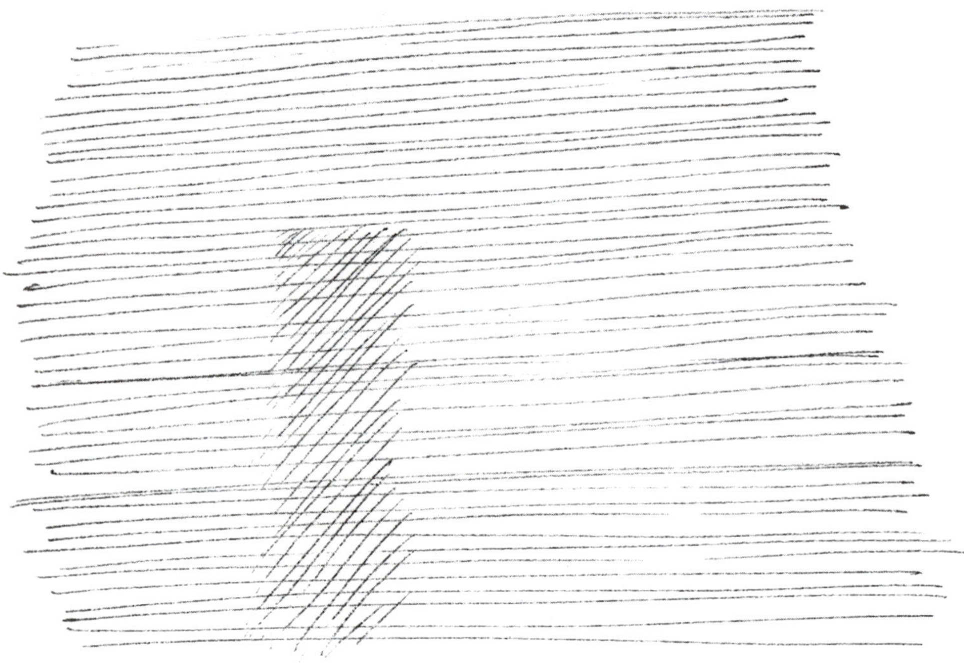

The contourless object stays shadowy
behind the horizontal hatching.

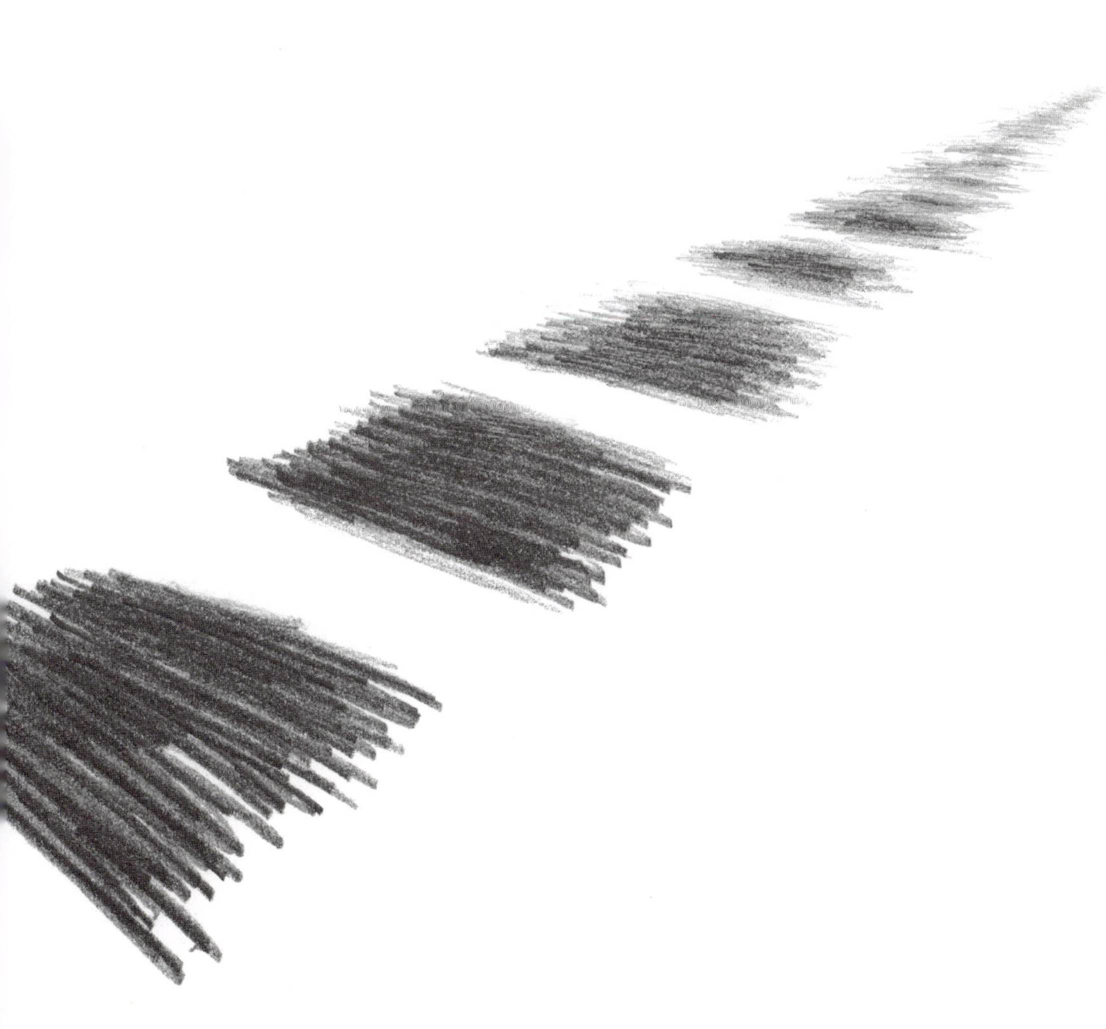

Without the hard, defined shapes in the foreground, the
blurry shapes farther back would be impossible to classify.

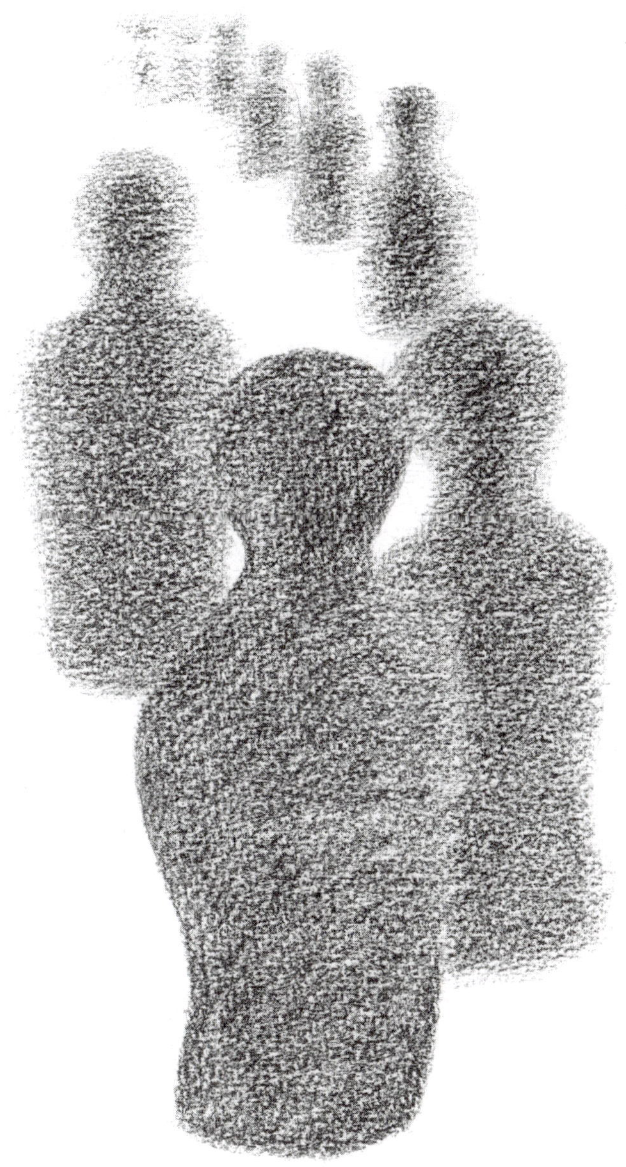

The contours become less and less defined and
start to dissolve the farther back they are.

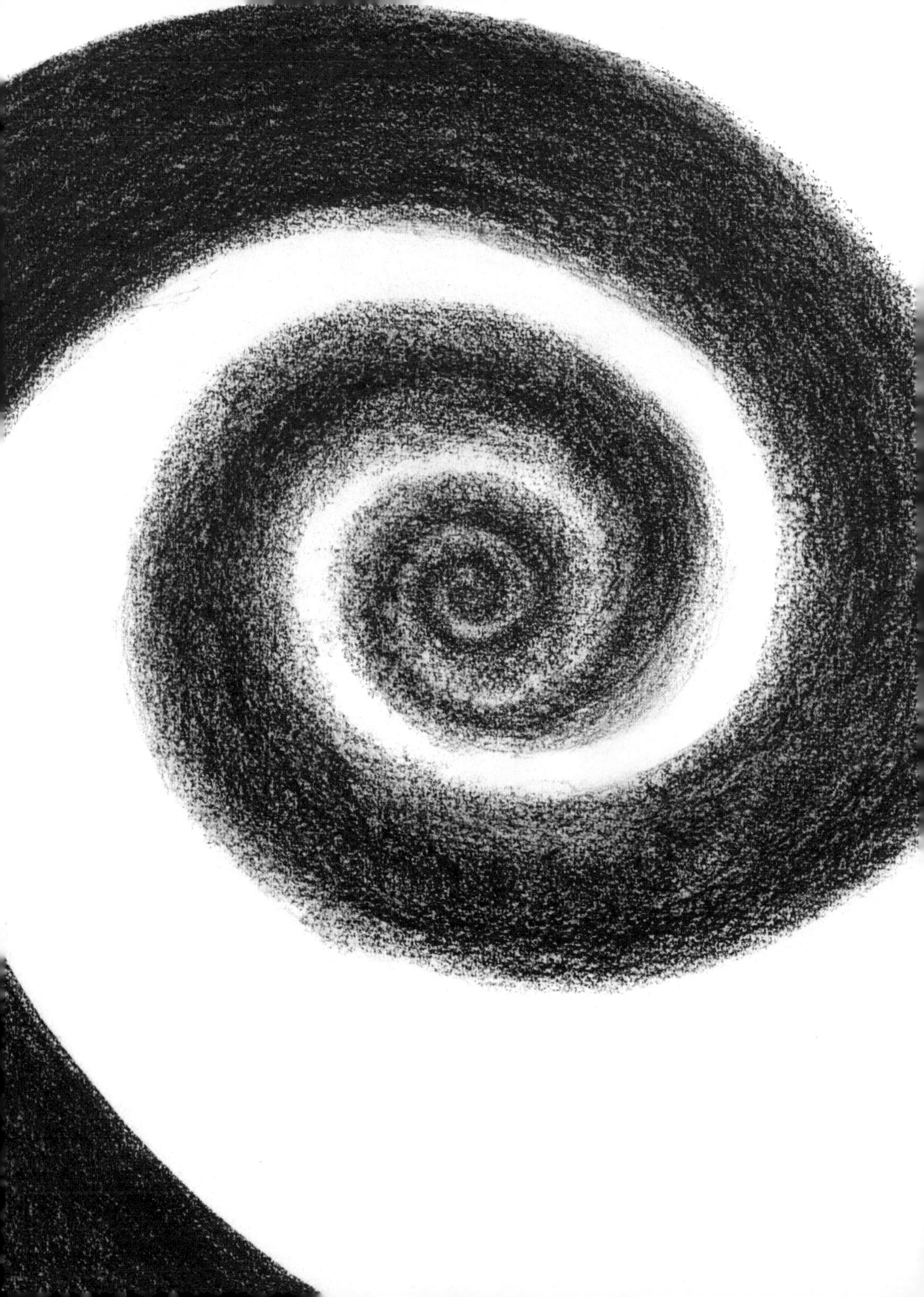

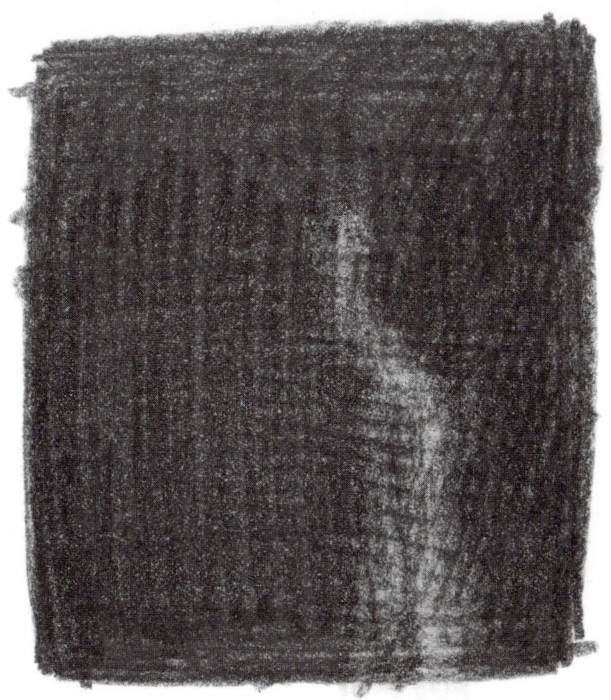

By removing and smudging in the dark areas,
the suggestion of objects emerges.

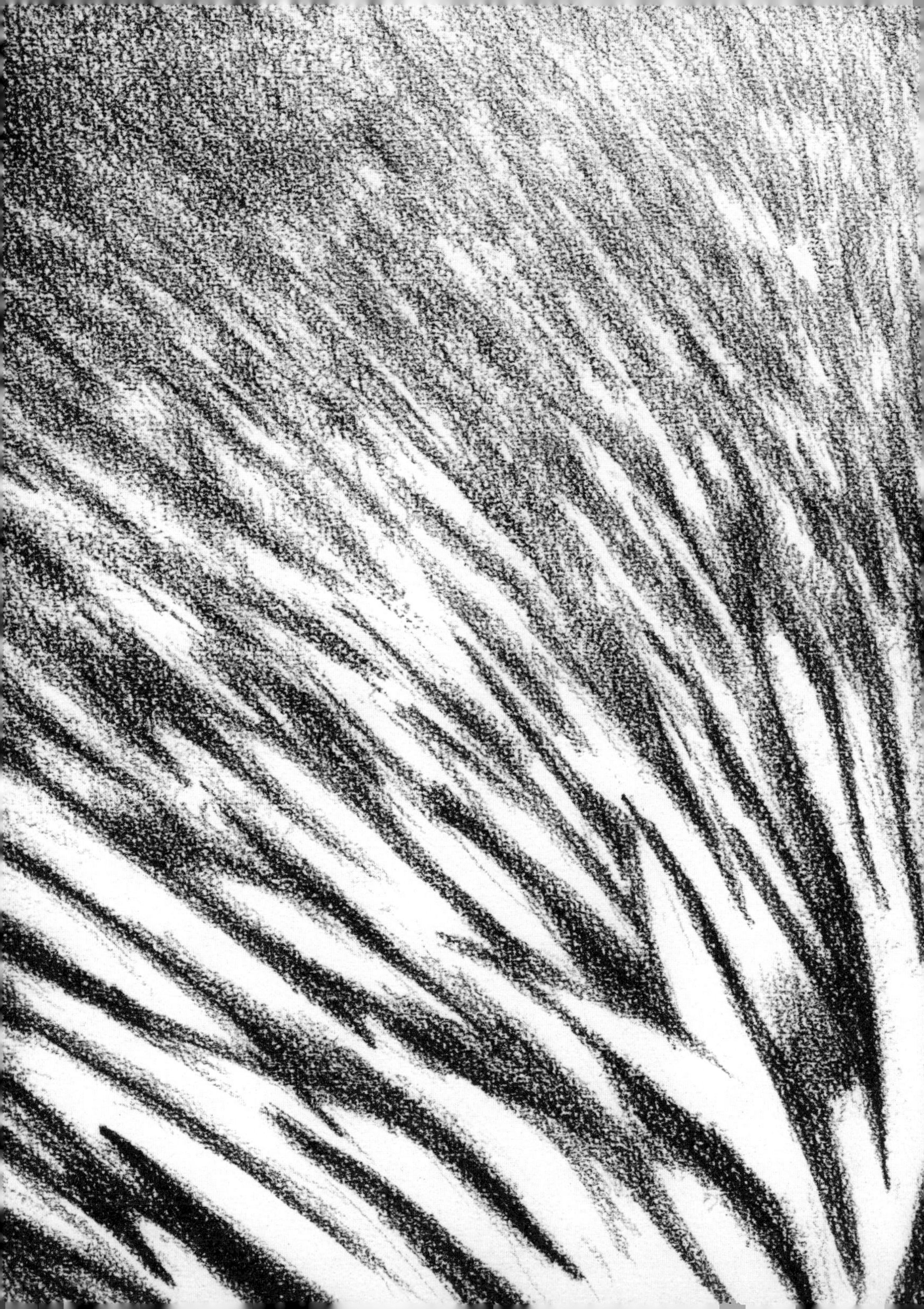

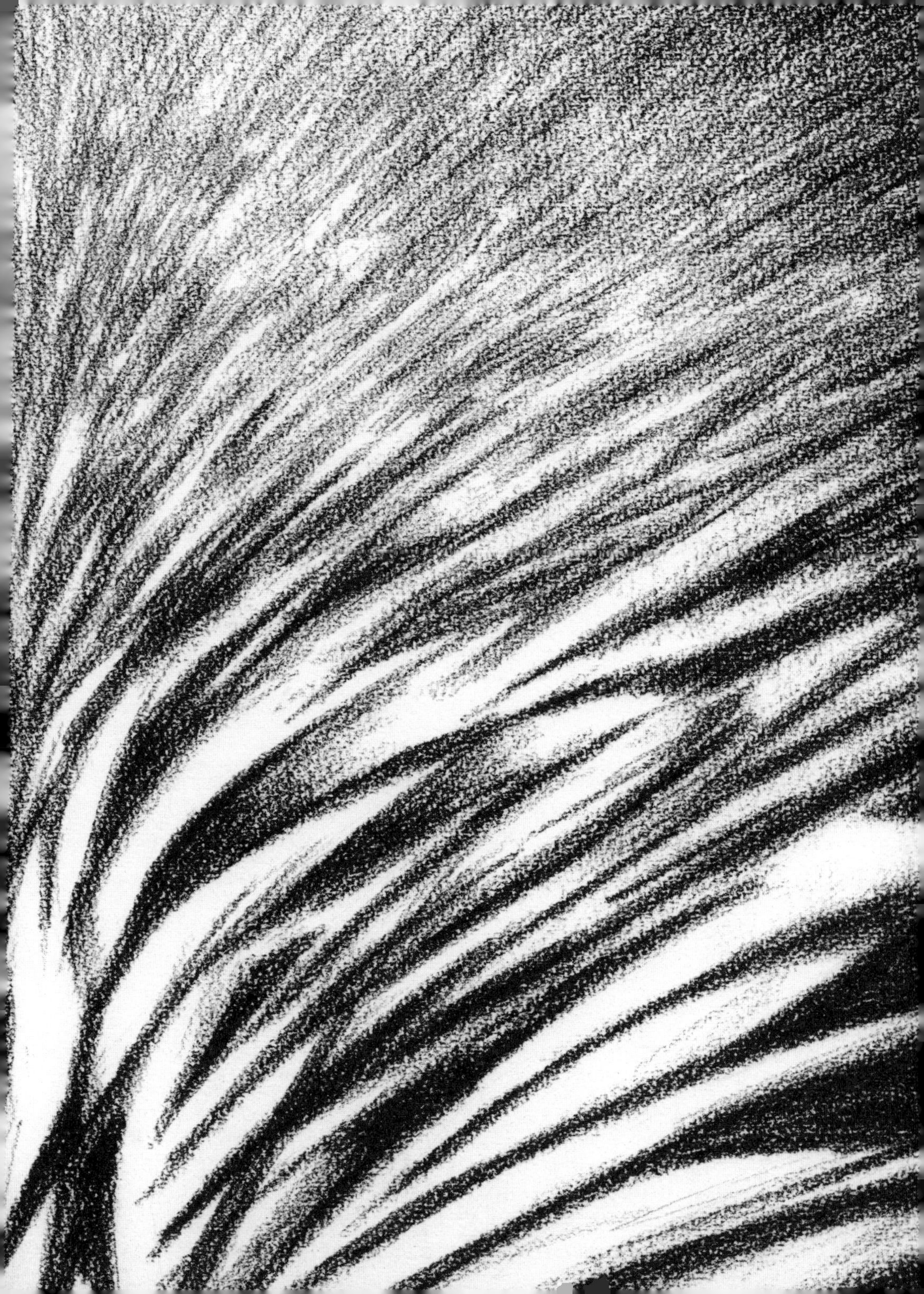

An unexpected sharp shape stirs up excitement, as if
suddenly something tangible is appearing in the fog.

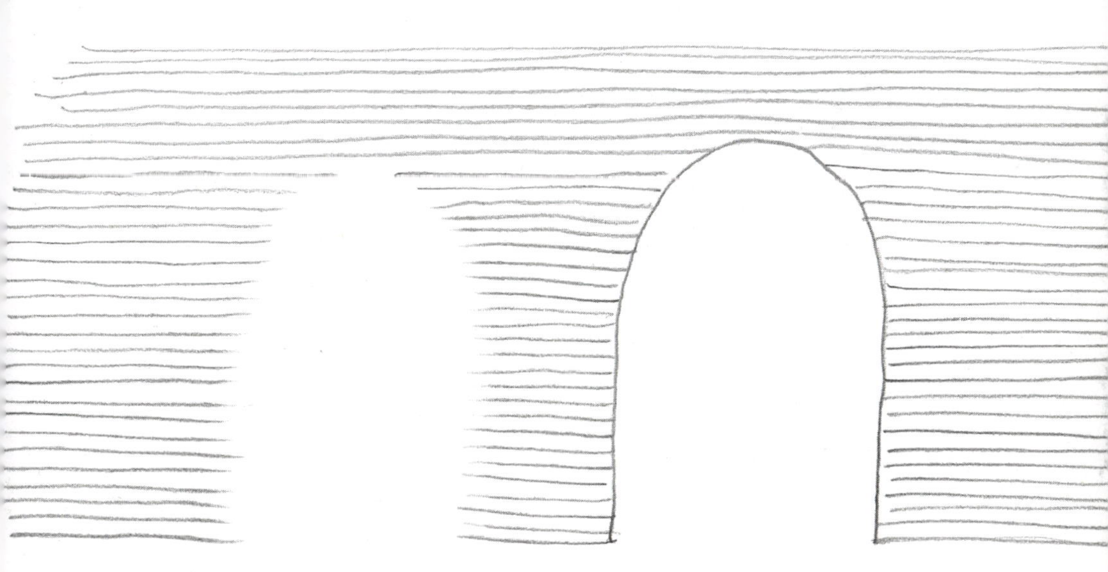

Sharpness and fuzziness are also emotionally and even
symbolically charged. For example, it feels safer to walk
through the gate on the right with the contours;
the other gate seems amorphous.

8. Shadow and Environment

Light is created from shadow—it emerges from the areas that haven't been drawn in. A shadow cast by an object—a cast shadow—becomes softer the farther away it is from the object. Shadows on the object itself are less defined and sit on the side or area facing away from the light. The interaction of light and shadow opens up many possibilities for juxtaposing the foreground and background, making the subject three dimensional.

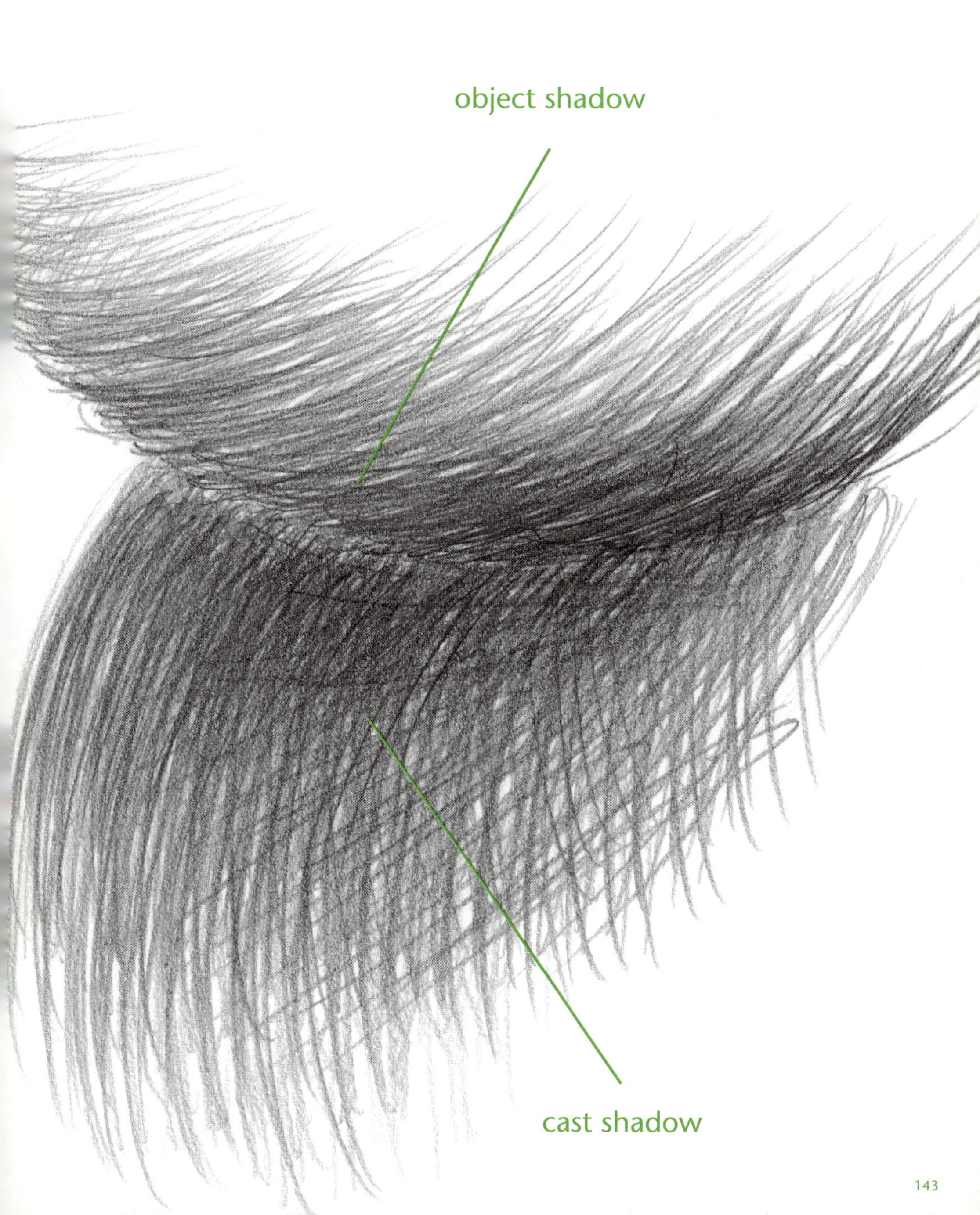

object shadow
cast shadow

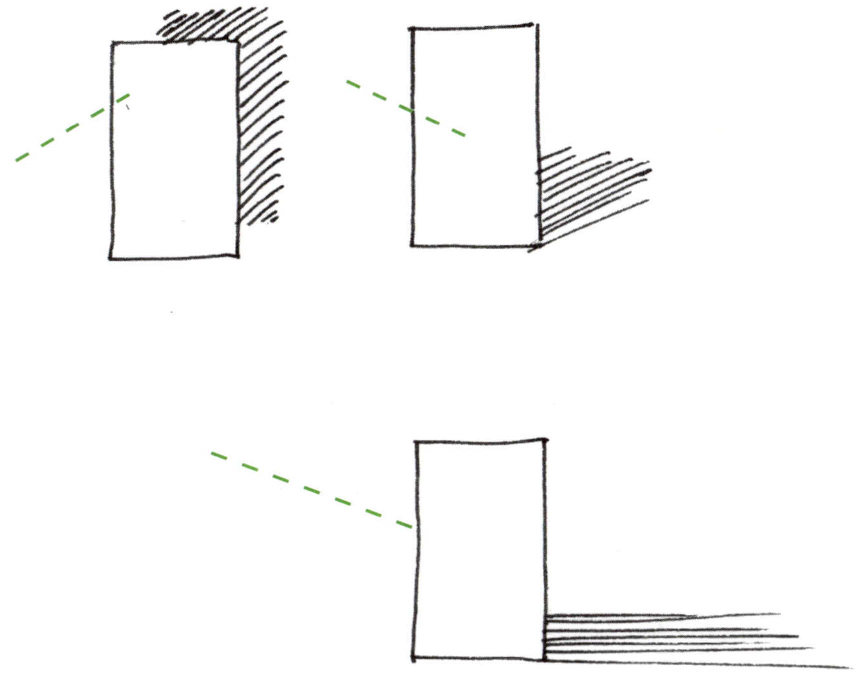

Shadow doesn't just show the direction of light;
it also helps locate objects in an environment.

The shadow turns the image plane into a surface.
It fixes the object and stabilizes it.

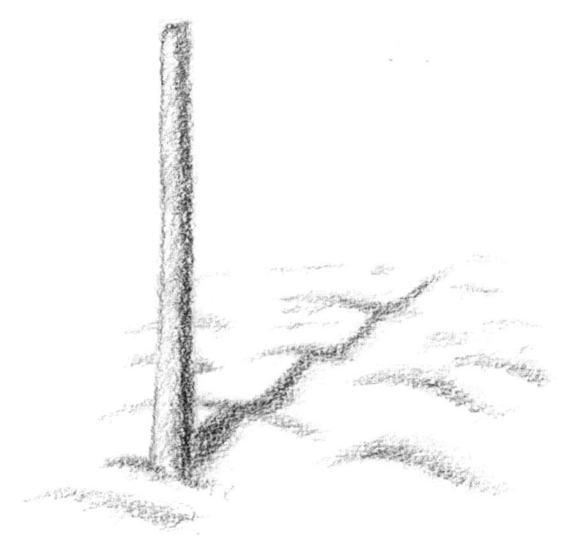

Shadow adds characteristics to the surface.

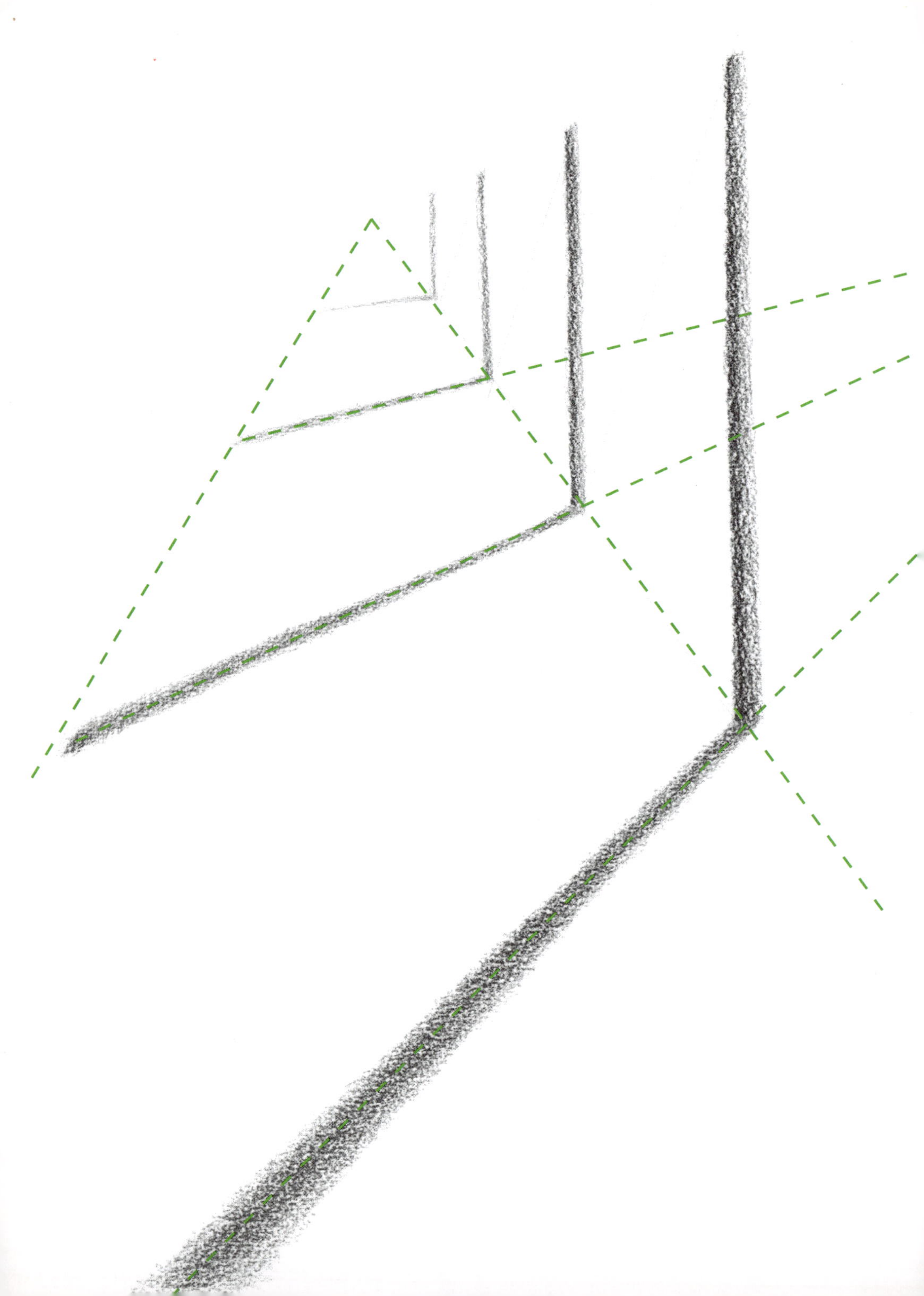

Shadows can have vanishing points, too. The sunlight casts
parallel shadows, which, in a perspective depiction, taper
toward one common vanishing point.

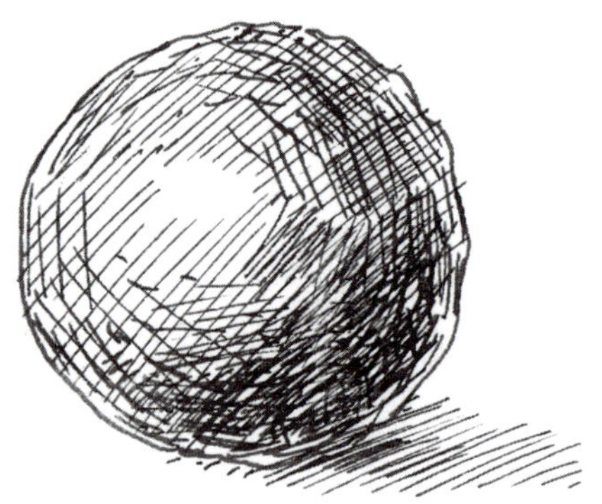

Shadows can be everywhere:
on objects, on the ground, or on walls.

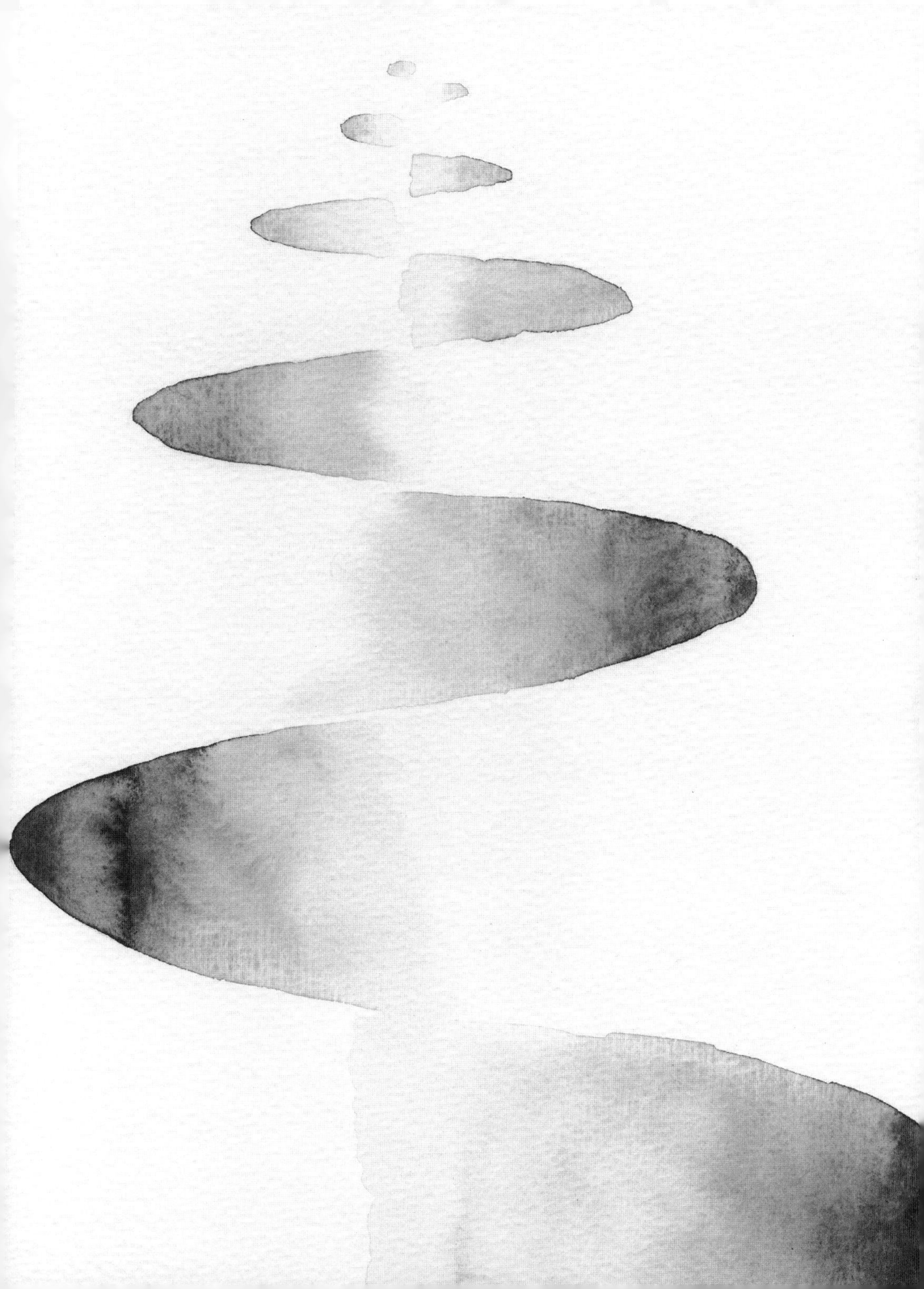

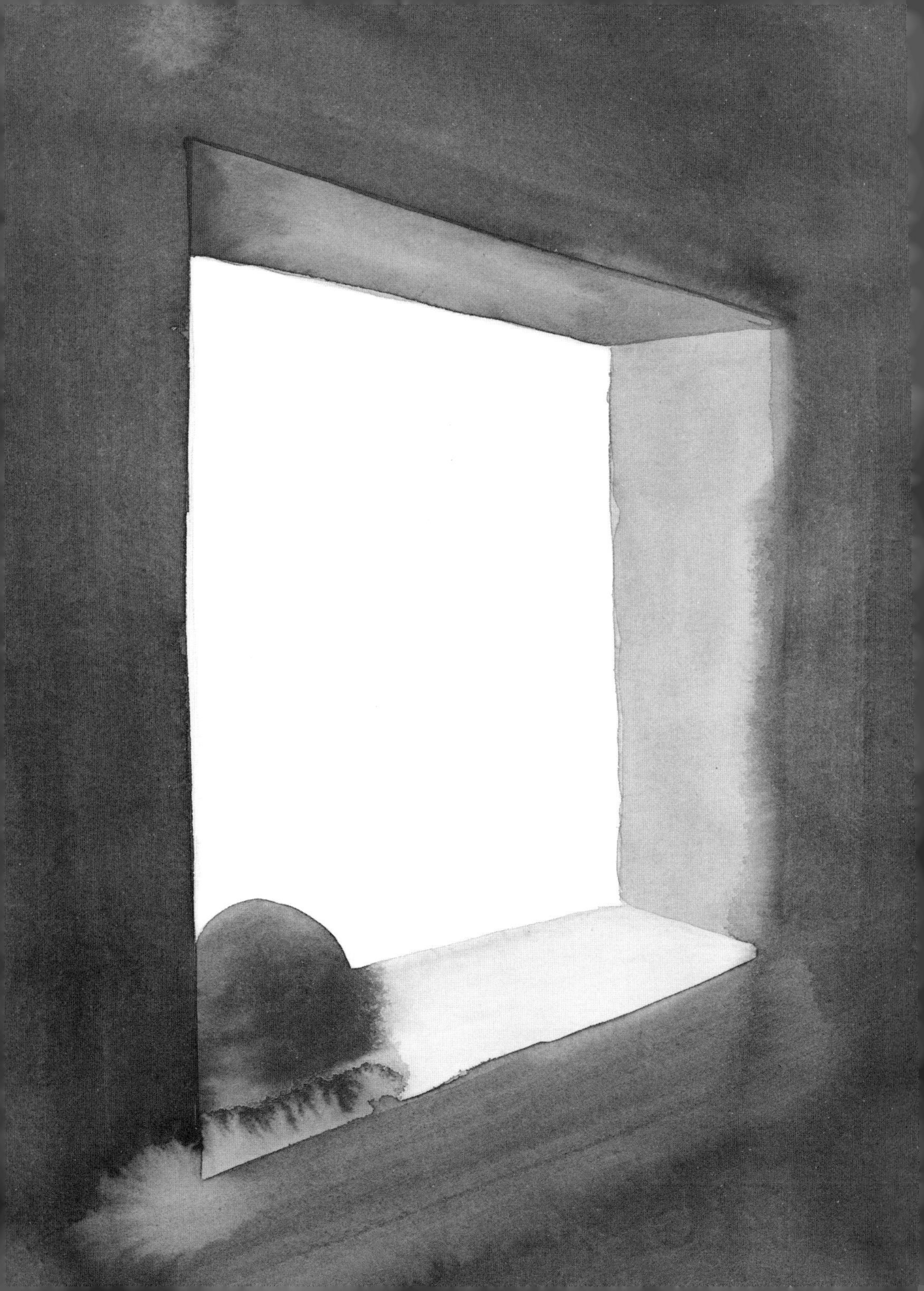

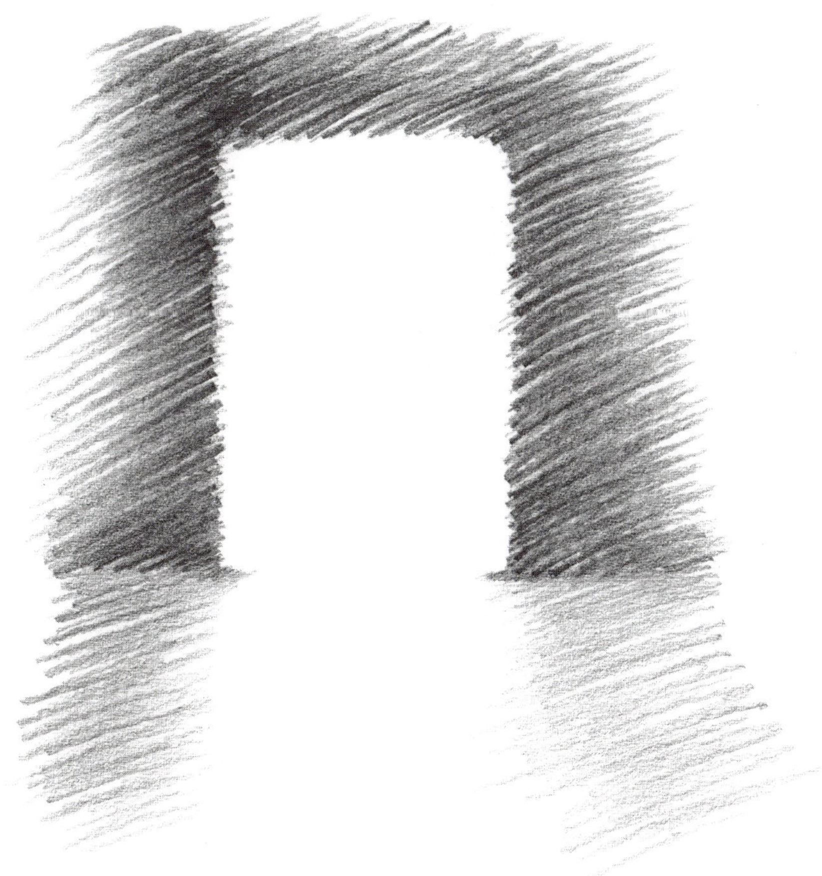

The light coming through the open door
makes the walls on the inside appear dark;
the door frame separates the inside from the outside.

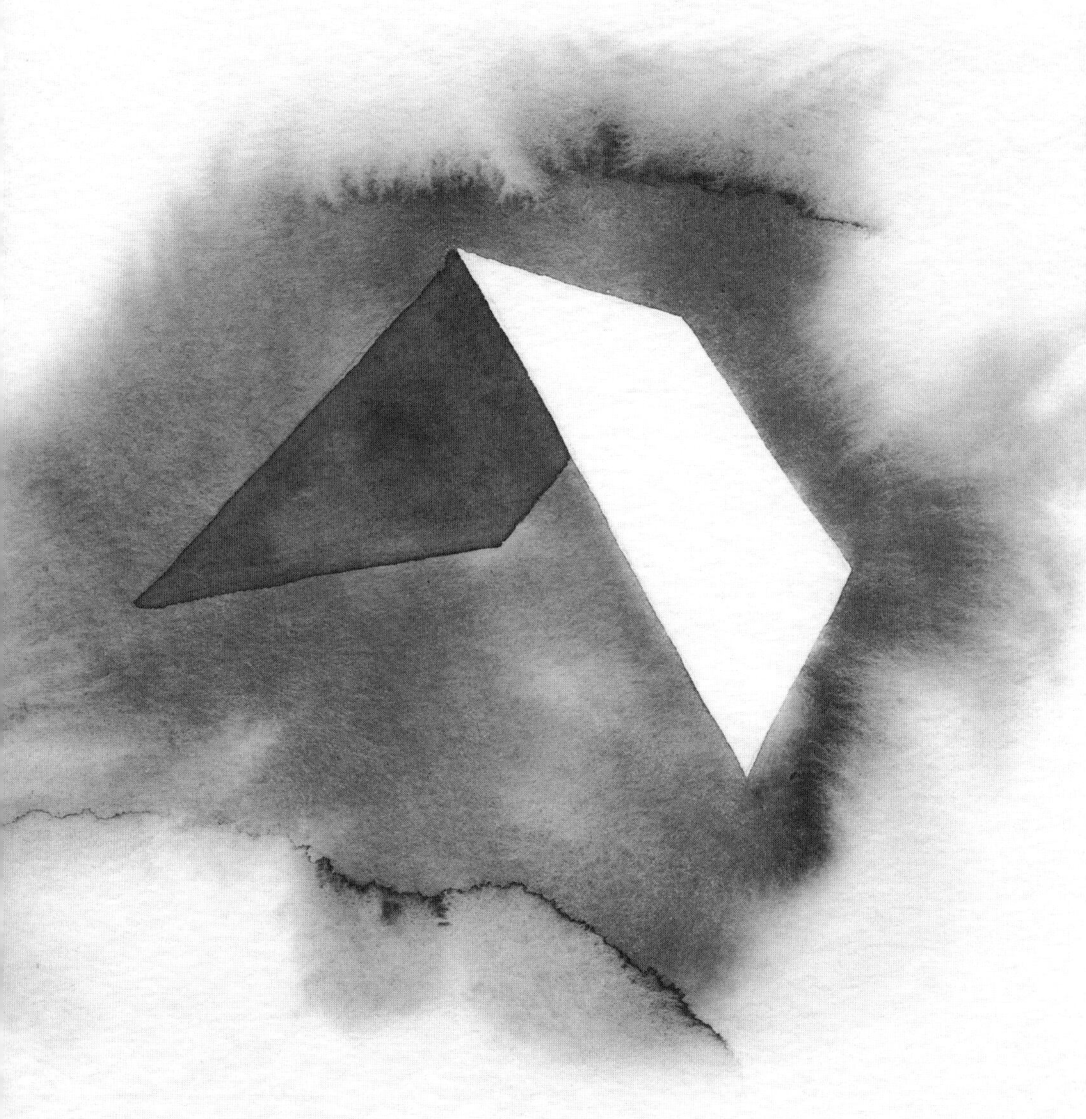

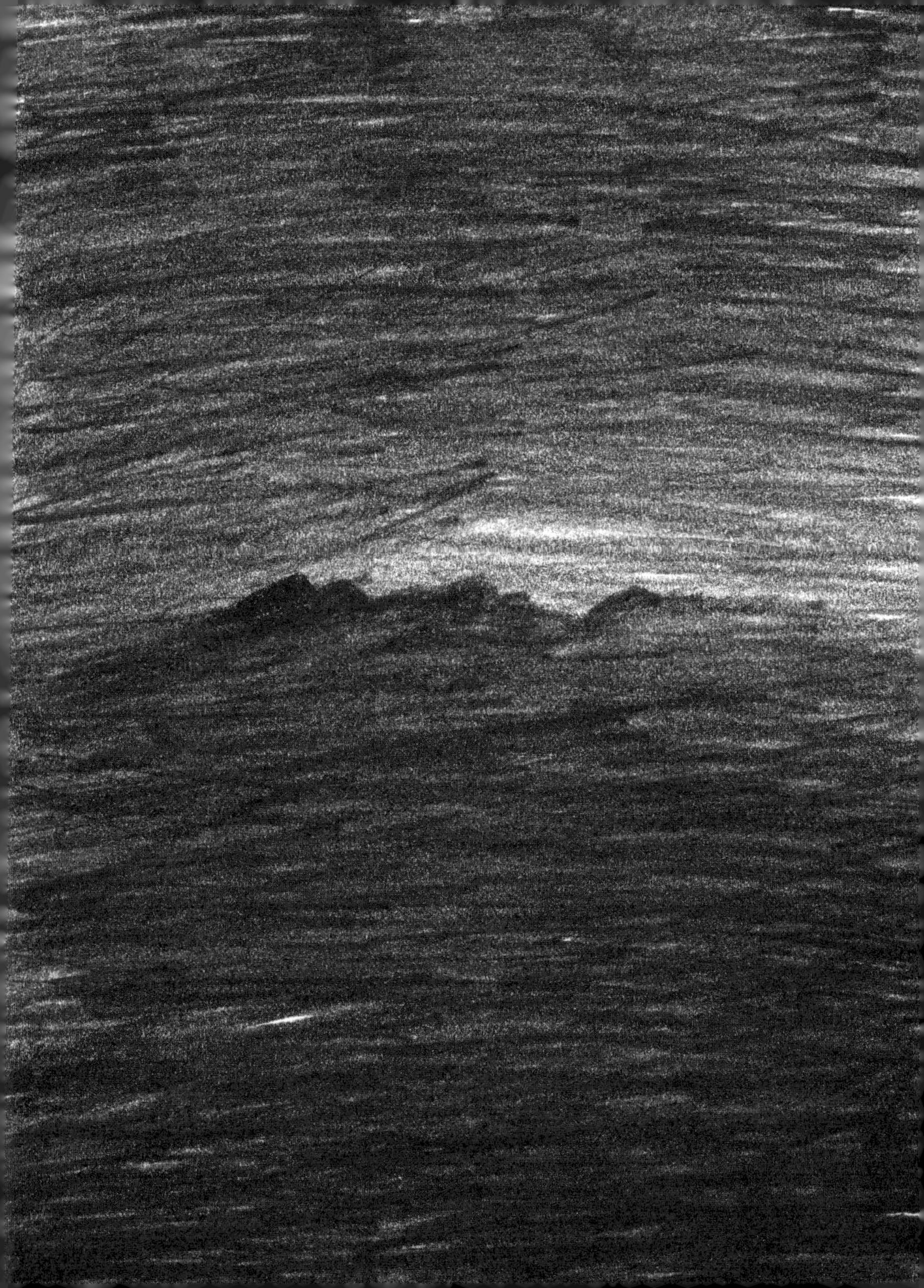

Definitions

Air Perspective

This is the phenomenon when the view through the air becomes clouded. It is especially noticeable in the mountains. Staggered mountain ridges become paler, less contrasting, and bluer the farther away they are. The painter Caspar David Friedrich implemented air perspective and lazure technique artfully in his paintings.

Below and Above

This may be the most traditional spatial structure on a piece of paper. Small children who are starting to draw pictures with multiple objects near one another structure the space this way: people below, house and tree in the middle, and the sky above.

Color Perspective

Some colors are perceived to be farther back than others. As a general rule, warm colors are usually closer, while cool colors step into the background. But a deciding factor for the effect is the composition of color. Red and green next to blue can appear closer while the same hues next to orange move into the background. Classical landscape paintings use these effects by dominating the foreground with warm brown hues, the middle ground with a lot of green, and blue hues in the background.

Contour

Contours are the most memorable optical marks of a form. Though it is easy to start with the outer contour by outlining while drawing, this method runs the risk of leading to schematic, precast depictions. To avoid that, start drawing the middle of a form and let it grow organically or use an unusual point of view; then the contours change with the perspective. In three dimensions, contours do not exist because all visible objects, even a piece of paper, are sculptural. It is only the process of seeing that simplifies the objects, so that from the abundance of optical impressions, objects are made seperate, bordered by contours.

Contrast

Contrasts refer to differences and opposites. They create tension and attract attention. Contrast usually refers to the relationship of light and dark, but also size differences, opposite color values (complementary colors, cold and warm colors), forms, and surfaces. Strong contrasts appear clear and distinct, but also loud, glaring, and even aggressive; a strong contrast comes at the cost of not being able to use mid-hues. The decrease of contrast in the distance is closely related to terms such as *sfumato* and *air perspective.*

Diagonals

The slanted line is the most important one when creating three dimensionality. While horizontal and vertical lines describe a flat plane, the diagonal goes into depth. Diagonals can also make meaningful composition lines, as they move the viewer into the picture. The diagonal is not static; it adds movement and a dynamic quality. This creative feature is part of a common experience—the most stable things are lying flat. To stand up a straw is a possible but shaky experience. To stand it up slanted without support is not possible; it falls over. Slanted areas in a picture also seem unstable as they seem to fall backward.

Eye Level

Eye level depends on where the viewer is and determines where the horizon lies, namely at the eye level of the observer. The point of view high up and the viewer looking downward is called a bird's-eye view. The view upward from a low viewpoint is a worm's-eye perspective. Changing eye levels are of great meaning for a picture's dramaturgy, i.e., dramatic composition, in comics and movies.

Foreshortening

When an arm sticks straight out toward the observer, mostly just the hand is visible. Depending of vantage point, the arm becomes foreshortened, just like bent legs or backs or the sides of cars. To draw foreshortening convincingly takes a lot of practice and exact observing. One of the most surprising pictures with foreshortening is the *Bewitched Stable Groom* by Hans Baldung Grien.

Hatching

This refers to line clusters or line orientations. There are countless variations of hatching, depending on the drawing medium, speed of drawing, and characteristics of the line. Hatchings describe the surface, distribution of light and shadow, or intensity and emotionality of a drawing. The signature of an illustrator becomes the most obvious through the use of hatchings.

Horizon

Even though the horizon is as impossible to touch as a rainbow, it is of elementary importance for our viewing experience. Just a simple horizontal line is enough for basic separations of picture elements; it arranges the picture into top and bottom. A high horizon creates space for numerous depictions on the ground; a low horizon opens up the sky.

Parallel Perspective

This is the spatial depiction of simple and clear shapes in architecture, technical drawing, and geometry. Edges that move into the space are drawn as diagonals. Objects do not get smaller the farther back they are, and room lines do not meet in a vanishing point. Therefore, parallel edges in reality (as in a cube) stay parallel in the drawing too. It is like looking into a drawing from up above.

Pencils

Pencil leads are not made of lead but rather a mix of graphite and clay. Larger amounts of graphite make for a softer pencil; adding more clay makes it harder. Softer pencils are usually better for drawing because they make clear lines and are easier to distinguish by brightness levels, but they also smudge more easily. Hard pencils only produce light gray marks, but they are good for making guidelines and precise marks.

Sfumato

Sfumato refers to the smudging and blurring of distant objects; it is a painting technique developed during the Renaissance and has close connections to the discovery of oil paint. All soft drawing materials, such as charcoal, red chalk, pastels, and graphite, are suited for smudging. This technique is easier than hatching, and can create smooth transitions. (See contrast on page 157.) A smoky or even foggy atmosphere can be created with it.

Shadow

Because light spreads in a linear way, the creation of shadow follows a simple logic. Still, the drawing of shadow is not easy because the three parameters of light source, object, and projection surface (the surface on which the drop shadow falls) have to be set into a spatial relationship. Legend has it that painting originated from the drawing of a dropped shadow to capture a loved one. Nonetheless, shadows were not used in painting until the early Renaissance, as done by Masaccio in the fresco *St. Peter Healing the Sick with His Shadow*. Half shadows, the tones between light and dark, create interest in a drawing and transitional areas between light and dark.

Staggering

This refers to the set up of a picture into fore-, middle-, and background, and if shapes overlap, the impression of three dimensions is reinforced; similar shapes become smaller the farther back they are. Landscape paintings from the seventeenth through the nineteenth centuries show spatial areas were staggered according to clear principles.

About the Authors

Peter Boerboom and **Tim Proetel** both studied at the Academy of Fine Arts in Munich between 1991 and 1998 under renowned painter and teacher Horst Sauerbruch. Their long friendship has repeatedly led to joint work. This book is the latest result of their collaboration, which included many drawings and discussions. Three volumes about perspective, light, and motion are already published; more volumes on new themes are being planned.

Tim Proetel is an advisor for art at the state institution of school quality and educational research and teaches art and theater at an academic high school, both in Munich.

Peter Boerboom also studied communications design at the College for Design in Munich. He is a founding member of the artist group Department for Public Appearance and executes art and photography projects together with Carola Vogt.